CRE TIVE
HOMEOWNER®

Home Plans for

Baby
Boomers

CREATIVE HOMEOWNER®, Upper Saddle River, New Jersey

Home Plans Editor: Kenneth D. Stuts
Home Plans Consultant: James McNair
Home Plans Designer Liaison: Sara Markowitz

Design and Layout: iiCREATiVE (David Kroha, Cindy DiPierdomenico, Judith Kroha); Maureen Mulligan; Michelle Kalinski

Cover Design: Kathy Wityk, David Geer

Vice President and Publisher: Timothy O. Bakke
Production Director: Kimberly H. Vivas

Current Printing (last digit)
10 9 8 7 6 5 4 3 2 1

Home Plans for Baby Boomers
Library of Congress Control Number: 2008921050
ISBN-10: 1-58011-299-4
ISBN-13: 978-1-58011-299-4

CREATIVE HOMEOWNER®
A Division of Federal Marketing Corp.
24 Park Way
Upper Saddle River, NJ 07458
www.creativehomeowner.com

Note: The homes as shown in the photographs and renderings in this book may differ from the actual blueprints. When studying the house of your choice, please check the floor plans carefully.

Contents

Finding the ME in Boomer

Pop Quiz: Were you born between the years of 1946 and 1964?

If your answer was yes, then you are a Baby Boomer, one of nearly 80 million people in the United States that make up 29 percent of the country's population. After American soldiers returned home from World War II in 1946, the United States experienced an explosion of births that continued for the next 18 years.

Because baby boomers make up such a sizable portion of the consuming public, their spending habits and lifestyles have a powerful influence on the economy. Boomers control the largest amount of discretionary income in history because they represent 45 percent of the work force.

Like everything else in life, not all boomers want the same things. Most boomers are not interested in down-sizing, they are interested in "right-sizing." In the not too distant future, you may be looking for that perfect "right-sized" home. Maybe that means building a smaller home designed for easy living. Maybe that means building a home with interior and exterior entertaining areas. In many cases, it means building a home that can accommodate the occasional guest or guests. Maybe it means all of these things.

The homes in this book were specially chosen to fit all of the Baby Boomer generation's varying wants and needs. While the homes in this book have unique elements, all of the homes featured have a master suite on the main level, which ensures that your personal oasis is close by and easily accessible.

We hope that you find your dream home among those on the following pages. To browse further through our collection of over 10,000 home plans, visit our website at www.ultimateplans.com.

"Celebrate my uniqueness."

Boomers are not a cultural or economic monolith. On the contrary, they are very diverse. They may be empty nesters, grandparents, single parents with teens, or even couples with young children who chose to have children in their 40s. They may be retired or embarking on a whole new career path, moving from the suburbs to a downtown loft, or leaving a

Right-sizing your home, above, can mean different things to different people.

One-story homes, such as the opposite, are appealing to those who no longer want stairs in their home.

small house in the city to move out to a country estate where they can garden or even farm.

In the past, the typical "boomer house" was a downsized, one-story patio or villa home with wide doors, a master suite, and one other bedroom that doubled as a

a combination office/guest room. Today, that no longer fits all boomers. An example is the person who always wanted a two-story, Southern colonial. Now in their 50s, they can finally afford their dream home and don't want anything less. Some boomers choose homes with steps-because they need or enjoy the exercise. Others aren't averse to having secondary bedrooms upstairs or on the lower level. They don't mind going up and down steps a few times a year to pre-pare guest rooms when their grown children and grandchildren plan a visit.

There are countless other options boomers are divided on, such as the decision on whether or not to include a dining room in their home. Approximately half of boomers want a formal dining room because it fits their style of entertaining, and they own a beautiful dining set that they would love to use rather than keep hidden away. Others believe that having a dining room that will only be used two or three times a year when their kids come home or company visits is extravagant, preferring to have an office or even his and her offices. There are some boomers who insist on having a jetted tub in the master suite, while others would rather have a deluxe, oversized shower. Boomers are also divided on where the ideal laundry location is: near the kitchen to allow homeowners to do laundry while preparing meals, or near the master bedroom where dirty clothes are stored and clean clothes are stored.

"Age is only a mindset."

Indeed, staying and feeling young has always been a part of the boomer DNA. Their dream houses should reflect their anti-aging attitude. Homes are reflections of who they are-their values and their tastes.

Boomers were born between 1946 and 1964, so they're anywhere from 44 to 62 years old. But they can't be labeled as

"early boomers" or "late boomers," because some 60-year-olds look, think, and act more like 40-year-olds.

"I know where I want to live."

Compared with their predecessors, boomers are less likely to move to a Sun Belt area, often choosing to "age in place"

in their own communities. Those who are less root bound may enjoy a gated community where maintenance is provided, allowing them to enjoy carefree travel during the winter months.

But not everyone wants to live in an age-restricted community. Many people prefer mixed-use developments that are created for the entire family-boomers, their parents, and their grown children and families.

Some boomers seek a quiet, out of the way neighborhood-but not so far that it's inconvenient to get to shopping and restaurants. Others love to live in the middle of the action. The latter may opt for a downtown condominium that allows them to get away from yard work and be able to walk to the places they want to go.

As boomers look ahead to retirement, taxes may be another important factor to consider, because different areas may have markedly higher rates.

"Give me back a little more time."

One of the best ways a boomer can streamline everyday life is by finding a home plan with lots of storage and organization. Point-of-use storage is ideal because it's located where it's needed most. For example, linen closets should be near or inside each full bath to make storage and access of different bathroom items, such as soaps, toothpastes, or towels, easy. Low-maintenance materials, such as brick, cultured stone, fiber-cement siding, and vinyl windows, are particularly popular with boomers, as are windows that tilt out for easy cleaning. Inside, quartz, solid-surface, or granite counters will be appreciated for their ease of cleaning. Appliances in white or brushed stainless steel will show fewer smudges than black or shinier steel.

Numerous home styles are applicable to baby boomers, depending on their own personal and specific needs.

When choosing a home, consider not only what you want today but what you may need in the future.

"Help me accommodate future needs."

Floor plans that can adapt over time are always an asset. For instance, a flexible room with a Murphy bed can double as a home office/guest room for an older parent or boomerang child. Or the right secondary bedroom and bath arrangement can function as a semiprivate in-law suite.

Non-slippery tile or stone on the bathroom floor is an added safety feature for all. Door levers are easier for everyone to use than knobs. Wherever possible, drawers instead of cabinets are universally appreciated for ease of access.

"What would I regret not having considered?"

Boomers like to be shown solutions to problems they have not anticipated. They appreciate thoughtful plans with adequate storage for their grandchildren's toys and games, a convenient spot for the vacuum cleaner, extra space in the laundry room to fold and hang clothes, sufficient room to store their holiday decorations, and outdoor storage for their patio furniture.

Special accommodations for their pets are becoming increasingly popular. They may include a built-in pet Murphy bed, a feeding station under the kitchen cabinets, or a pet shower in the laundry room, garage, or rear entry.

"Help me be environmentally responsible."

Because boomers wonder what kind of world future generations will live in, they are concerned about the impact their choices make on it. In addition to using green and energy-efficient products, design elements with the potential to save energy-such as which direction the house faces and windows that align to produce

produce cross breezes-are important.

Many boomers, learning to stop and smell the roses, are interested in some type of outdoor living space. Outdoor fountains, fireplaces, and kitchens are becoming more and more common.

"Give me my space."

With husbands and wives retiring and boomerang children or older parents sometimes living with them, boomers desire their own personal space. It might be a sunroom, a flexible room for reading or crafts, an exercise room, a relaxing master bath, or a sitting area located in the master bedroom.

"Give me practical pizzazz."

Some boomers are very well off financially, while others are on a fixed income. Both groups tend to be practical. They want style, but nothing over the top or hard to maintain. They may shy away from cathe-

dral ceilings because they view them as inefficient to heat and difficult to paint and dust. Yet they'll appreciate special ceiling details, columns, and arched openings that provide elegance without taking up floor space. Tile and wood flooring are popular choices because they're stylish and easy to clean. A kitchen island adds convenience and glamour, particularly when topped with stunning pendant lights. On the exterior, they often choose to upgrade their garage doors for added style and energy efficiency.

"Finally, it can be about me."

Boomers have devoted their lives to others, so they feel it's their turn to have a home the way they want to live. They no longer need four bedrooms or a three-car garage to accommodate their children. If they want granite countertops in a modestly priced home, they don't want someone to try to dissuade them. They want what they want, the way they want it.

Ten Steps You Should Do Before Submitting Your Plans For a Permit

1.Check Your Plans to Make Sure That You Received What You Ordered

You should immediately check your plans to make sure that you received exactly what you ordered. All plans are checked for content prior to shipping, but mistakes can happen. If you find an error in your plans, call 1-800-523-6789. All plans are drawn on a particular type of foundation and all details of the plan will illustrate that particular foundation. If you ordered an alternate foundation type, it should be included immediately after the original foundation. Tell your builder which foundation you wish to use and disregard the other foundation.

2.Check to Make Sure You Have Purchased the Proper Plan License

If you purchased prints, your plan will have a round red stamp stating, "If this stamp is not red it is an illegal set of plans." This license grants the purchaser the right to build one home using these construction drawings. It is illegal to make copies, doing so is punishable up to $150,000 per offense plus attorney fees. If you need more prints, call 1-800-523-6789. The House Plans Market Association monitors the home building industry for illegal prints.

It is also illegal to modify or redraw the plan if you purchased a print. If you purchased prints and need to modify the plan, you can upgrade to the reproducible master or CAD file — call 1-800-523-6789. If you purchased a reproducible master or CAD file, you have the right to modify the plan and make up to 10 copies. A reproducible master or CAD file comes with a license that you must surrender to the printer or architect making your changes.

3.Complete the "Owner Selection" Portion of the Building Process

The working drawings are very complete, but there are items that you must decide upon. For example, the plans show a toilet in the bathroom, but there are hundreds of models from which to choose. Your individual selection should be made based upon the color, style, and price you wish to pay. This same thing is true for all of the plumbing fixtures, light fixtures, appliances, and interior finishes (for the floors, walls, and ceilings) and the exterior finishes. The selection of these items is required in order to obtain accurate competitive bids for the construction of your home

4.Complete Your Permit Package by Adding Other Documents That May Be Required

Your permit department, lender, and builder will need other drawings or documents that must be obtained locally. These items are explained

5.Obtain a Heating & Cooling Calculation and Layout

The heating and cooling system must be calculated and designed for your exact home and your location. Even the orientation of your home can affect the system size. This service is normally provided free of charge by the mechanical company that is supplying the equipment and installation. However, to get an unbiased calculation and equipment recommendation, we suggest employing the services of a mechanical engineer.

6.Obtain a Site Plan

A site plan is a document that shows the relationship of your home to your property. It may be as simple as the document your surveyor provides, or it can be a complex collection of drawings such as those prepared by a landscape architect. Typically, the document prepared by a surveyor will only show the property boundaries and the footprint of the home. Landscape architects can provide planning and drawings for all site amenities, such as driveways and walkways, outdoor structures such as pools, planting plans, irrigation plans, and outdoor lighting.

7.Obtain Earthquake or Hurricane Engineering if You Are Planning to Build in an Earthquake or Hurricane Zone

If you are building in an earthquake or hurricane zone, your permit department will most likely require you to submit calculations and drawings to illustrate the ability of your home to withstand those forces. This information is never included with pre-drawn plans because it would penalize the vast majority of plan purchasers who do not build in those zones. A structural engineer licensed by the state where you are building usually provides this information.

8.Review Your Plan to See Whether Modifications Are Needed

These plans have been designed to assumed conditions and do not address the individual site where you are building. Conditions can vary greatly, including soil conditions, wind and snow loads, and temperature, and any one of these conditions may require some modifications of your plan. For example, if you live in an area that receives snow, structural changes may be necessary. We suggest:

(i)Have your soil tested by a soil-testing laboratory so that subsurface conditions can be determined at your specific building site. The findings of the soil-testing laboratory should be reviewed by a structural engineer to determine if the existing plan foundation is suitable or if modifications are needed.

(ii)Have your entire plan reviewed by your builder or a structural engineer to determine if other design elements, such as load bearing beams, are sized appropriately for the conditions that exist at your site.

Now that you have the complete plan, you may discover items that you wish to modify to suit your own personal taste or decor. To change the drawings, you must have the reproducible masters or CAD files (see item 2). We can make the changes for you. For complete information regarding modifications, including our fees, go to www.ultimateplans.com and click the "resources" button on the home page; then click on "our custom services."

9.Record Your Blueprint License Number

Record your blueprint license number for easy reference. If you or your builder should need technical support, the license number is required.

10.Keep One Set of Plans as Long as You Own the Home

Be sure to file one copy of your home plan away for safe keeping. You may need a copy in the future if you remodel or sell the home. By filing a copy away for safe keeping, you can avoid the cost of

Plan #131034

Dimensions: 40' W x 32' D
Levels: 2 (upper unfinished)
Heated Square Footage: 1,040
Bedrooms: 5 or 4
Bathrooms: 2½
Foundation: Crawl space, slab, or basement
Materials List Available: Yes
Price Category: C

Images provided by designer/architect.

You'll love the versatility this expandable ranch-style home gives, with its unfinished, second story that you can transform into two bedrooms and a bath if you need the space.

Features:

- **Porch:** Decorate this country-style porch to accentuate the charm of this warm home.

- **Living Room:** This formal room features a wide, dramatic archway that opens to the kitchen and the dining room.

- **Kitchen:** The angled shape of this kitchen gives it character, while the convenient island and well-designed floor plan make cooking and cleaning tasks unusually efficient.

- **Bedrooms:** Use the design option in the blueprints of this home to substitute one of the bedrooms into an expansion of the master bedroom, which features an amenity-laden, private bathroom for total luxury.

Optional Main Level Floor Plan

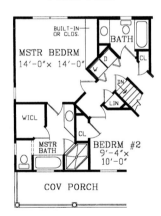

Main Level Floor Plan

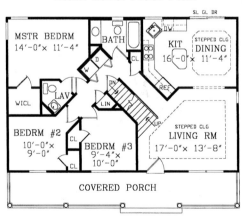

Kitchen

Optional Upper Level Floor Plan

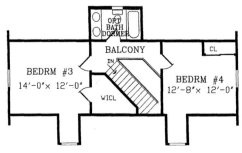

Copyright by designer/architect.

Plan #121414

Dimensions: 49'6" W x 40' D

Levels: 1

Heated Square Footage: 1,142

Bedrooms: 3

Bathrooms: 2

Foundation: Slab; crawl space or basement for fee

Materials List Available: Yes

Price Category: B

Images provided by designer/architect.

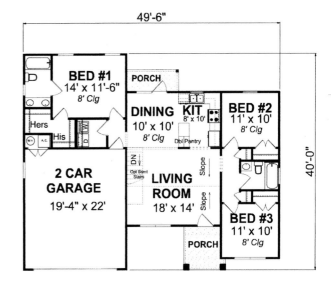

Copyright by designer/architect.

Plan #541051

Dimensions: 30' W x 46' D

Levels: 1

Heated Square Footage: 1,200

Bedrooms: 2

Bathrooms: 2

Foundation: Basement

Materials List Available: No

Price Category: B

Images provided by designer/architect.

Copyright by designer/architect.

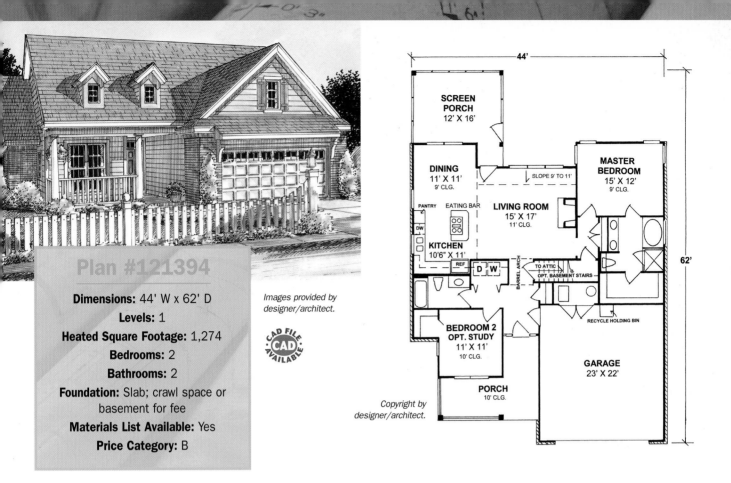

Plan #121394

Dimensions: 44' W x 62' D

Levels: 1

Heated Square Footage: 1,274

Bedrooms: 2

Bathrooms: 2

Foundation: Slab; crawl space or basement for fee

Materials List Available: Yes

Price Category: B

Images provided by designer/architect.

Copyright by designer/architect.

SCREEN PORCH 12' X 16'

DINING 11' X 11' 9' CLG.

SLOPE 9' TO 11'

MASTER BEDROOM 15' X 12' 9' CLG.

PANTRY

EATING BAR

LIVING ROOM 15' X 17' 11' CLG.

DW

KITCHEN 10'6" X 11'

REF

D W

BARREL ARCH

TO ATTIC OPT. BASEMENT STAIRS

RECYCLE HOLDING BIN

BEDROOM 2 OPT. STUDY 11' X 11' 10' CLG.

PORCH 10' CLG.

GARAGE 23' X 22'

44'

62'

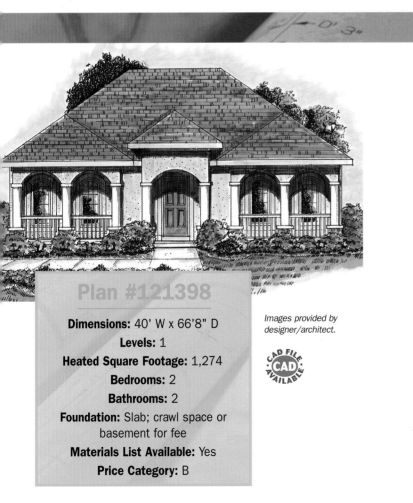

Plan #121398

Dimensions: 40' W x 66'8" D

Levels: 1

Heated Square Footage: 1,274

Bedrooms: 2

Bathrooms: 2

Foundation: Slab; crawl space or basement for fee

Materials List Available: Yes

Price Category: B

Images provided by designer/architect.

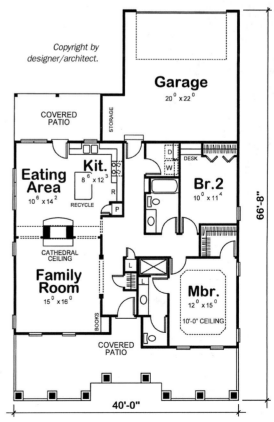

Copyright by designer/architect.

Garage 20'0" x 22'0"

COVERED PATIO

STORAGE

Kit. 8'6" x 12'3"

D W

DESK

Eating Area 10'6" x 14'2"

RECYCLE

R

P

Br.2 10'0" x 11'4"

CATHEDRAL CEILING

Family Room 15'0" x 16'0"

BOOKS

L

L

L

Mbr. 12'0" x 15'0" 10'-0" CEILING

COVERED PATIO

40'-0"

66'-8"

Plan #131014

Dimensions: 48' W x 43'4" D
Levels: 1
Heated Square Footage: 1,380
Bedrooms: 3
Bathrooms: 2
Foundation: Crawl space, slab, or basement
Materials List Available: Yes
Price Category: C

CAD FILE AVAILABLE

Living Room

The exterior of this home looks formal, thanks to its twin dormers, gables, and the bay windows that flank the columned porch, but the inside is contemporary in both design and features.

Features:

- Great Room: Centrally located, this great room has a 10-ft. ceiling. A fireplace, built-in cabinets, and windows that overlook the rear covered porch make it as practical as it is attractive.

- Dining Room: A bay window adds to the charm of this versatile room.

- Kitchen: This U-shaped room is designed to make cooking and cleaning jobs efficient.

- Master Suite: With a bay window, a walk-in closet, and a private bath with an oval tub, the master suite may be your favorite area.

- Additional Bedrooms: Located on the opposite side of the house from the master suite, these rooms share a full bath in the hall.

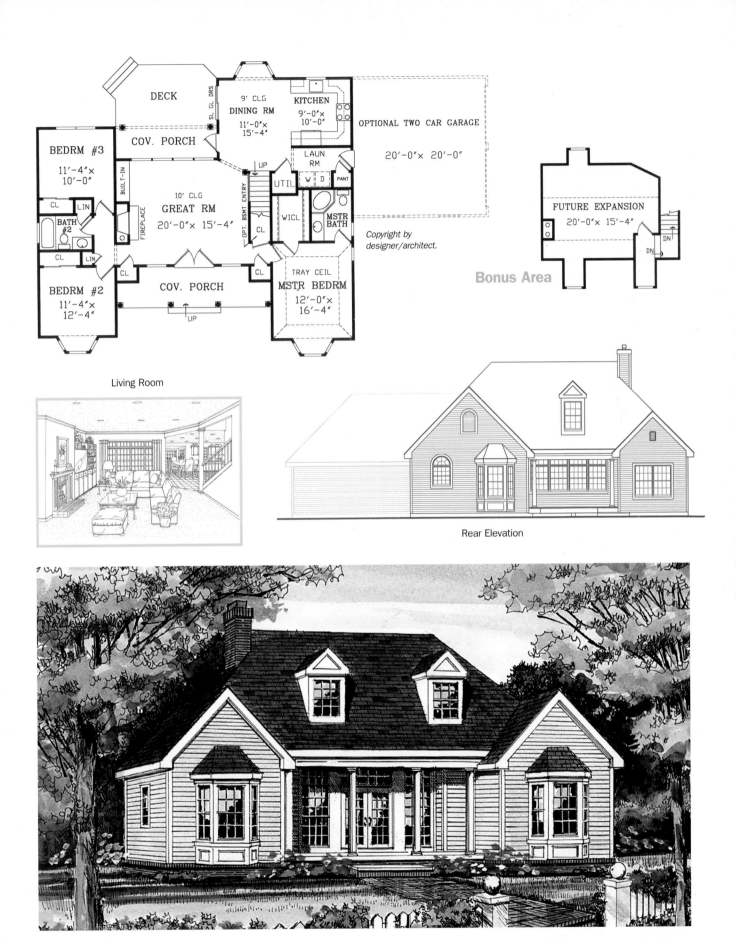

DECK

9' CLG
DINING RM
11'-0"x
15'-4"

KITCHEN
9'-0"x
10'-0"

OPTIONAL TWO CAR GARAGE

20'-0"x 20'-0"

COV. PORCH

BEDRM #3
11'-4"x
10'-0"

CL   LIN

BATH #2

CL   LIN

BUILT-IN

FIREPLACE

10' CLG
GREAT RM
20'-0"x 15'-4"

UP

OPT. BSMT ENTRY

CL

UTIL

WICL

LAUN RM

W D   PANT

MSTR BATH

FUTURE EXPANSION
20'-0"x 15'-4"

DN

DN

Bonus Area

Copyright by
designer/architect.

CL

COV. PORCH

UP

CL

TRAY CEIL
MSTR BEDRM
12'-0"x
16'-4"

BEDRM #2
11'-4"x
12'-4"

Living Room

Rear Elevation

Plan #121396

Dimensions: 40' W x 64' D

Levels: 1

Heated Square Footage: 1,361

Bedrooms: 2

Bathrooms: 2

Foundation: Slab; crawl space or basement for fee

Materials List Available: Yes

Price Category: B

Images provided by designer/architect.

Copyright by designer/architect.

Plan #121397

Dimensions: 40' W x 65' D

Levels: 1

Heated Square Footage: 1,385

Bedrooms: 2

Bathrooms: 2

Foundation: Slab; crawl space or basement for fee

Materials List Available: Yes

Price Category: B

Images provided by designer/architect.

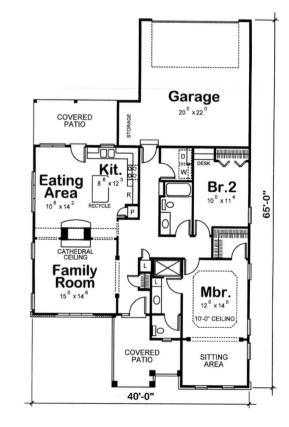

Copyright by designer/architect.

Plan #121424

Dimensions: 52' W x 50' D

Levels: 1

Heated Square Footage: 1,436

Bedrooms: 2

Bathrooms: 2

Foundation: Slab; crawl space or basement for fee

Materials List Available: Yes

Price Category: B

Images provided by designer/architect.

Copyright by designer/architect.

Plan #121436

Dimensions: 52' W x 56' D

Levels: 1

Heated Square Footage: 1,462

Bedrooms: 1

Bathrooms: 2

Foundation: Basement; crawl space for fee

Materials List Available: Yes

Price Category: B

Images provided by designer/architect.

Copyright by designer/architect.

Plan #351009

Dimensions: 54' W x 47' D

Levels: 1

Heated Square Footage: 1,400

Bedrooms: 3

Bathrooms: 2

Foundation: Crawl space, slab, or basement

Materials List Available: Yes

Price Category: B

Images provided by designer/architect.

This design offers a great value in space planning by using the open concept, with split bedrooms, in a layout that is easy to build.

Features:

- Ceilings: All ceilings are a minimum of 9-ft. high.

- Great Room: This large gathering area provides room for family activities as well as being open to the kitchen and dining area.

- Master Suite: This oversized private area provides a great bathroom arrangement for busy couples as well as a large walk-in closet.

- Bedrooms: The split bedroom layout provides zoned privacy and improved noise control.

- Patio: This area is the perfect place to enjoy the afternoons grilling out or relaxing with friends and family.

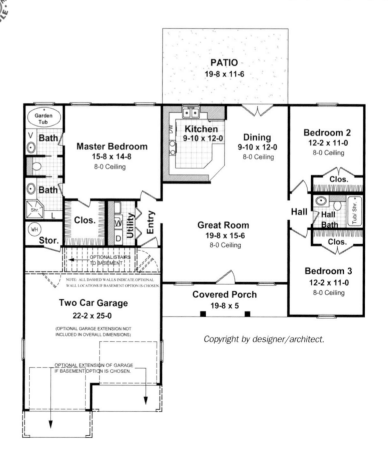

Copyright by designer/architect.

Plan #121199

Dimensions: 49' W x 58' D
Levels: 1
Heated Square Footage: 1,416
Bedrooms: 3
Bathrooms: 2
Foundation: Slab
Materials List Available: Yes
Price Category: B

Multiple porches, a home workshop, and an eating bar set this one-story plan apart from the rest.

Features:

- Porches: At the front of the house, an ample 9-ft.-high ceiling covers this large open porch. At the rear, the screened-in porch connects to the dining room, which is perfect for enjoying a meal outside.

- Kitchen: This functional kitchen is open to the dining and living rooms. A snack bar connects the spaces.

- Shop: Located off of the two-car garage, the shop provides a place to work on a project or just get away and unwind.

- Bedrooms: All three bedrooms in this house feature 9-ft.-high ceilings. The master suite has access to a private bath, while the other two bedrooms share a centrally located bathroom.

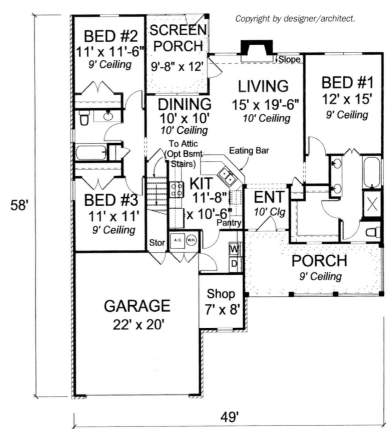

Copyright by designer/architect.

BED #2
11' x 11'-6"
9' Ceiling

SCREEN PORCH
9'-8" x 12'

LIVING
15' x 19'-6"
10' Ceiling

BED #1
12' x 15'
9' Ceiling

DINING
10' x 10'
10' Ceiling

To Attic
(Opt Bsmt Stairs)

Eating Bar

BED #3
11' x 11'
9' Ceiling

KIT
11'-8"
x 10'-6"

Pantry

ENT
10' Clg

Stor

A.C.
W.H.

W
D

PORCH
9' Ceiling

58'

GARAGE
22' x 20'

Shop
7' x 8'

49'

Plan #131003

Dimensions: 60' W x 39'10" D

Levels: 1

Heated Square Footage: 1,466

Bedrooms: 3

Bathrooms: 2

Foundation: Crawl space, slab, or basement

Materials List Available: Yes

Price Category: C

This home, as shown in the photograph, may differ from the actual blueprints. For more detailed information, please check the floor plans carefully.

Images provided by designer/architect.

Victorian styling adds elegance to this compact and easy-to-maintain ranch design.

Features:

• Ceiling Height: 8 ft.

• Foyer: Bridging between the front door and the great room, this foyer is a surprise feature.

• Great Room: A 10-ft. ceiling adds to the spacious feeling of this room, while the corner fireplace gives it an intimate feeling. Sliding glass doors at the rear of the room open to the backyard.

• Dining Room: This formal room adjoins the great room, allowing guests and family to flow between the rooms.

• Breakfast Room: Turrets add a Victorian feeling to this room that's just off the kitchen and overlooks the front porch.

• Master Suite: Privacy is assured in this suite, which is separated from the main part of the house. A separate toilet room and large walk-in closet add convenience to its beauty.

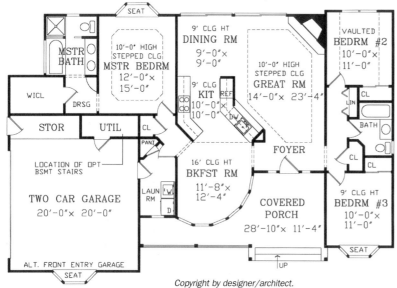

Copyright by designer/architect.

Kitchen

Plan #151169

Dimensions: 51'6" W x 49'10" D
Levels: 1
Heated Square Footage: 1,525
Bedrooms: 3
Bathrooms: 2
Foundation: Crawl space, slab, basement, or daylight basement
CompleteCost List Available: Yes
Price Category: C

This comfortable home is filled with amenities that will thrill both friends and family.

Features:

- Great Room: This spacious room has a gas fireplace in the corner, 9-ft. boxed ceiling, and convenient door to the rear covered porch.

- Dining Room: Bay windows look out to the rear porch and let light flood into this room.

- Kitchen: An angled work and snack bar and large pantry are highlights in this well-planned room.

- Breakfast Room: A door to the rear porch, wide windows, and computer desk are highlights here.

- Master Suite: You'll feel pampered by the 9-ft. boxed ceiling and bath with two huge closets, whirlpool tub, separate shower, and dual vanity.

- Additional Bedrooms: Transform bedroom 3 into a study or home office if you can, and add the optional door to the foyer for total convenience.

Images provided by designer/architect.

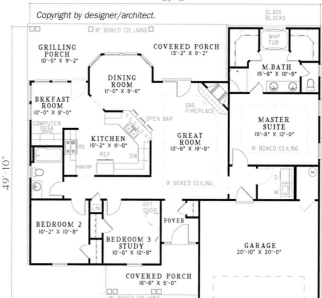

Rear View

Plan #521043

Dimensions: 36' W x 43'8" D
Levels: 2
Heated Square Footage: 1,536
Main Level Sq. Ft.: 1,038
Upper Level Sq. Ft.: 498
Bedrooms: 3
Bathrooms: 2½
Foundation: Crawl space
Materials List Available: No
Price Category: C

You'll love to relax on this adorable country home's large wraparound porch.

Features:

- Kitchen: Located at the heart of the home, this kitchen is at the perfect location for transporting meals to the dining area, living room, or porches.

- Living Room: This large area is wonderful for entertaining or relaxing with your family.

- Master Suite: Some of the features in this master suite include a large walk-in closet, dual sink vanity, and direct access to the rear screened-in porch, great for relaxing on summer evenings.

- Secondary Bedrooms: Upstairs, two bedrooms, each with a closet, are perfect for siblings. A bathroom is located between them.

Images provided by designer/architect.

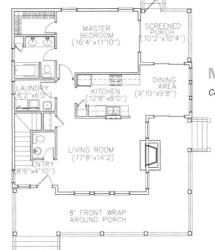

Main Level Floor Plan

Copyright by designer/architect.

Upper Level Floor Plan

Plan #151037

Dimensions: 50' W x 56' D

Levels: 1

Heated Square Footage: 1,538

Bedrooms: 3

Bathrooms: 2

Foundation: Crawl space, slab, or basement

CompleteCost List Available: Yes

Price Category: C

Images provided by designer/architect.

You'll love this traditional-looking home, with its covered porch and interesting front windows.

Features:

- Ceiling Height: 8 ft.

- Great Room: This large room has a boxed window that emphasizes its dimensions and a fireplace where everyone will gather on chilly evenings. A door opens to the backyard.

- Dining Room: A bay window overlooking the front porch makes this room easy to decorate.

- Kitchen: This well-planned kitchen features ample counter space, a full pantry, and an eating bar that it shares with the dining room.

- Master Suite: A pan ceiling in this lovely room gives an elegant touch. The huge private bath includes two walk-in closets, a whirlpool tub, a dual-sink vanity, and a skylight in the ceiling.

- Additional Bedrooms: On the opposite side of the house, these bedrooms share a large bath, and both feature excellent closet space.

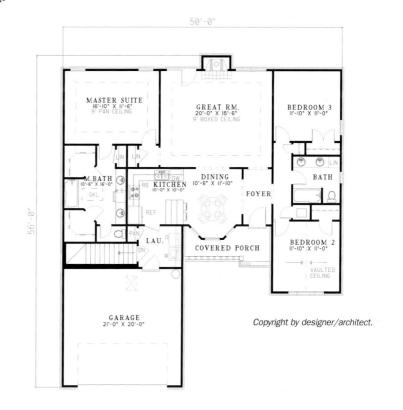

Copyright by designer/architect.

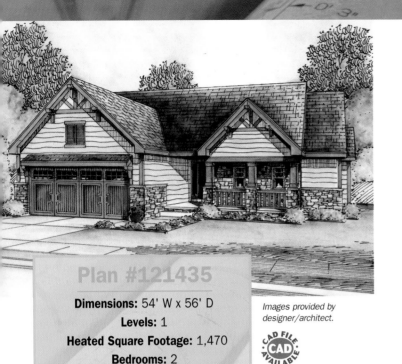

Images provided by
designer/architect.

Plan #121435

Dimensions: 54' W x 56' D

Levels: 1

Heated Square Footage: 1,470

Bedrooms: 2

Bathrooms: 2

Foundation: Slab; crawl space
or basement for fee

Materials List Available: Yes

Price Category: B

Copyright by designer/architect.

Images provided by
designer/architect.

Plan #121431

Dimensions: 44' W x 54' D

Levels: 1

Heated Square Footage: 1,548

Bedrooms: 2

Bathrooms: 2

Foundation: Basement;
crawl space for fee

Materials List Available: Yes

Price Category: C

Copyright by designer/architect.

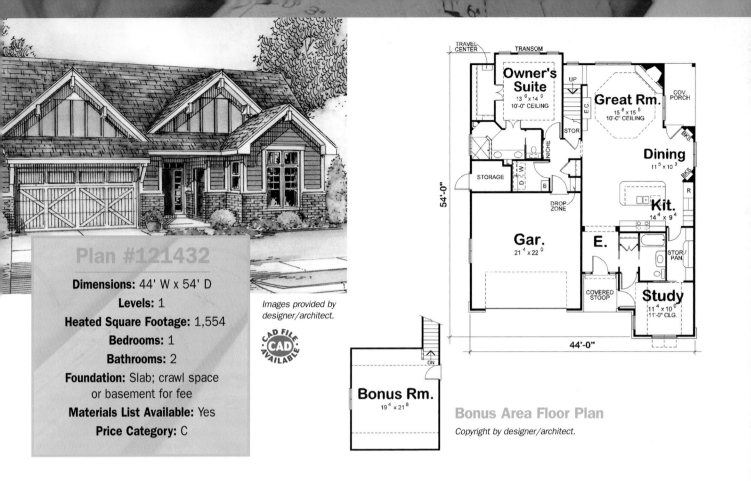

Plan #121432

Dimensions: 44' W x 54' D
Levels: 1
Heated Square Footage: 1,554
Bedrooms: 1
Bathrooms: 2
Foundation: Slab; crawl space or basement for fee
Materials List Available: Yes
Price Category: C

Images provided by designer/architect.

CAD FILE AVAILABLE

Bonus Rm. 19⁴ x 21⁸

Bonus Area Floor Plan
Copyright by designer/architect.

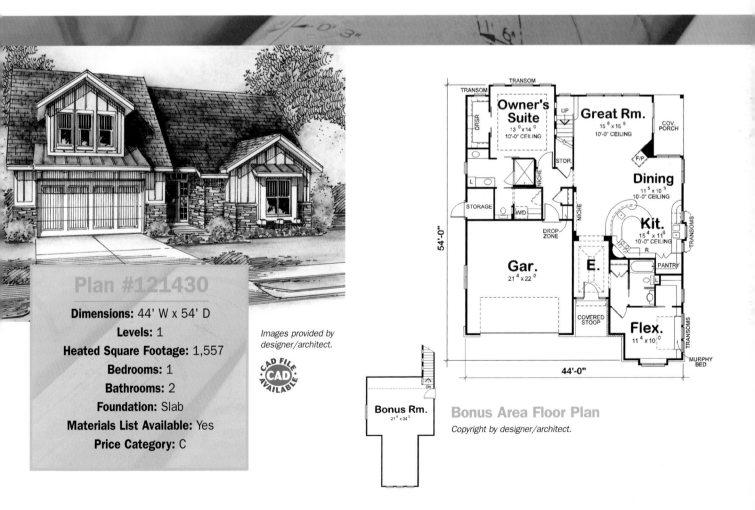

Plan #121430

Dimensions: 44' W x 54' D
Levels: 1
Heated Square Footage: 1,557
Bedrooms: 1
Bathrooms: 2
Foundation: Slab
Materials List Available: Yes
Price Category: C

Images provided by designer/architect.

CAD FILE AVAILABLE

Bonus Rm. 21⁴ x 34⁰

Bonus Area Floor Plan
Copyright by designer/architect.

Plan #611104

Dimensions: 40' W x 54'6" D

Levels: 1

Heated Square Footage: 1,551

Bedrooms: 3

Bathrooms: 2

Foundation: Slab

Materials List Available: No

Price Category: C

Tucked away from the busier areas of the home, the master suite in this house was designed with privacy in mind.

Features:

- Living Room: This open and inviting area is wonderful for relaxing with a book or playing a game with the kids.

- Kitchen: This angled kitchen is great for preparing meals while entertaining guests on any day of the week. Connections to the dining room, family room, and living room make transporting food a breeze.

- Master Suite: You'll love to relax and unwind in this large master suite area with its walk-in closet, tub, and dual vanity.

- Secondary Bedrooms: Two additional bedrooms share a bathroom. They are perfect for siblings or can be used as a home office or guest room.

Images provided by designer/architect.

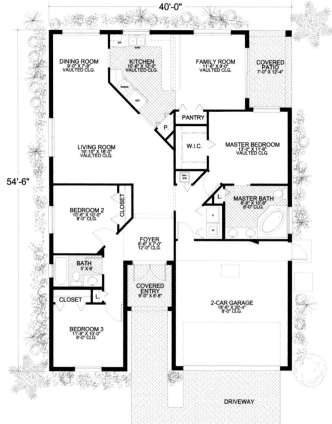

Copyright by designer/architect.

Plan #121235

Dimensions: 50' W x 50' D
Levels: 1
Heated Square Footage: 1,561
Bedrooms: 2
Bathrooms: 2
Foundation: Basement
Materials List Available: Yes
Price Category: C

Images provided by designer/architect.

Beauty, comfort, and convenience are all yours in this wonderful traditional home.

Features:

- **Great Room:** Your home will be a popular place for parties and get-togethers thanks to the open design and the 10-ft.-high ceilings.

- **Living Room:** This room solves many family space problems. Use it as a living room or convert it to an extra bedroom.

- **Breakfast Room:** The children will never again lose papers or assignments around the house with this room's convenient desk. Open shelves also provide space for book bags and other necessities.

- **Master Suite:** You'll have enough closet space for all of the seasons in this room's large walk-in closet. After a long day, relax in the whirlpool tub under the skylight.

Copyright by designer/architect.

Plan #121391

Dimensions: 50' W x 65' D
Levels: 1
Heated Square Footage: 1,574
Bedrooms: 2
Bathrooms: 2
Foundation: Slab
Materials List Available: Yes
Price Category: C

This home's beautiful exterior and interesting architecture will make it a standout in your neighborhood.

Features:

- **Family Room:** This octagonal family room with its 12-ft.-high coffered ceiling is perfect for entertaining guests or just relaxing in the space. Windows line part of the room, making for beautiful and interesting views.

- **Kitchen:** The U-shape of this kitchen makes it easy for the chefs in the family to find what they need.

- **Eating Area:** Opening out into the kitchen, the eating area connects to the screened-in porch in the rear of the home, making it perfect for outdoor dining on the porch or patio.

- **Master Suite:** Feel luxurious and pampered every day with the master suite's 11-ft.-high trayed and his and her sinks.

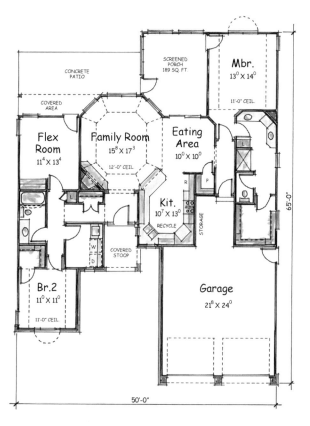

Copyright by designer/architect.

Plan #441003

Dimensions: 50' W x 48' D
Levels: 1
Heated Square Footage: 1,580
Bedrooms: 3
Bathrooms: 2½
Foundation: Crawl space;
slab or basement available for fee
Materials List Available: No
Price Category: C

Craftsman styling with modern floor planning—that's the advantage of this cozy design. Covered porches at front and back enhance both the look and the livability of the plan.

Features:

- Great Room: This vaulted entertaining area boasts a corner fireplace and a built-in media center. The area is open to the kitchen and the dining area.

- Kitchen: This large, open island kitchen will please the chef in the family. The raised bar is open to the dining area and the great room.

- Master Suite: Look for luxurious amenities such as double sinks and a separate tub and shower in the master bath. The master bedroom has a vaulted ceiling and a walk-in closet with built-in shelves.

- Bedrooms: Two secondary bedrooms are located away from the master suite. Each has a large closet and access to a common bathroom.

Images provided by designer/architect.

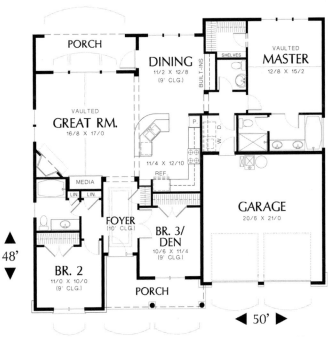

Copyright by designer/architect.

Rear Elevation

Plan #121419

Dimensions: 54' W x 55' D

Levels: 1

Heated Square Footage: 1,568

Bedrooms: 3

Bathrooms: 2

Foundation: Slab; crawl space for fee

Materials List Available: Yes

Price Category: C

Images provided by designer/architect.

CAD FILE AVAILABLE

Copyright by designer/architect.

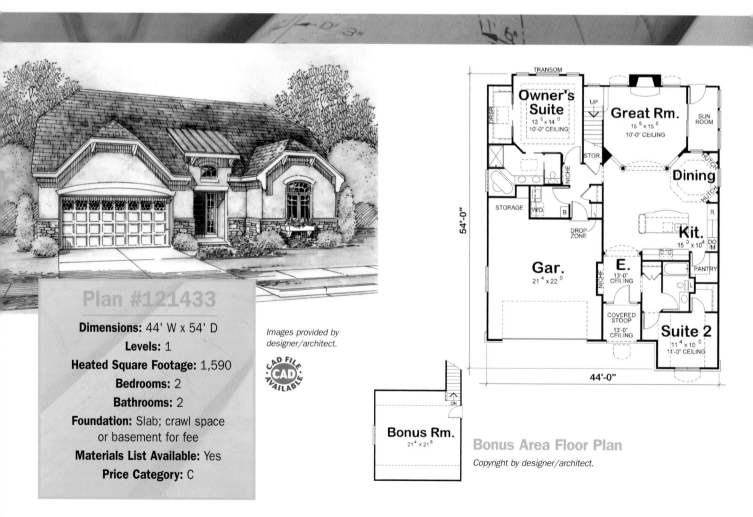

Plan #121433

Dimensions: 44' W x 54' D

Levels: 1

Heated Square Footage: 1,590

Bedrooms: 2

Bathrooms: 2

Foundation: Slab; crawl space or basement for fee

Materials List Available: Yes

Price Category: C

Images provided by designer/architect.

CAD FILE AVAILABLE

Bonus Area Floor Plan

Copyright by designer/architect.

Plan #121262

Dimensions: 52' W x 56' D

Levels: 1

Heated Square Footage: 1,595

Bedrooms: 1

Bathrooms: 1½

Foundation: Basement

Materials List Available: Yes

Price Category: C

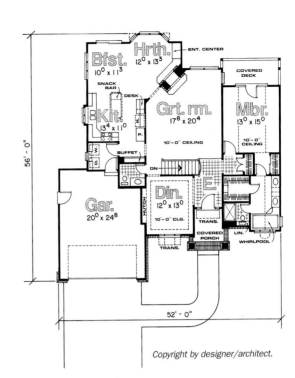

Images provided by designer/architect.

CAD FILE AVAILABLE

Copyright by designer/architect.

Plan #121383

Dimensions: 45' W x 60' D

Levels: 1

Heated Square Footage: 1,596

Bedrooms: 2

Bathrooms: 2

Foundation: Slab

Materials List Available: Yes

Price Category: C

Images provided by designer/architect.

CAD FILE AVAILABLE

Copyright by designer/architect.

Plan #131005

Dimensions: 70' W x 37'4" D
Levels: 1
Heated Square Footage: 1,595
Bedrooms: 3
Bathrooms: 2
Foundation: Crawl space, slab, or basement
Materials List Available: Yes
Price Category: D

SMARTtip

Create a Courtyard

Create a private walled-garden retreat with fences covered by climbing vines. Add height with trellises, and divide spaces with clipped boxwood hedges. Include an (almost) instant patio by digging away an area of sod and then covering it with a layer of sand and landscaping mesh to discourage weeds. Then cover it with pea gravel, and add a garden bench, statuary, and perhaps an antique or two. The result? European ambiance for even the most nondescript suburban yard.

Images provided by designer/architect.

With the finest features of an open design in the main living areas, this home gives privacy where you need it. Best of all, it's wheelchair accessible.

Features:

- Foyer: A high ceiling gives this area real presence and serves to blend it seamlessly with the great room and the dining room.

- Great Room: The open design allows you to use this room as an extension of the dining room or, if you wish, furnish it to create a private reading nook or visually separate media center.

- Breakfast Room: Both this room and the adjacent well-appointed kitchen flow into the rest of the living area. However, access to the rear porch, where you can sit out and enjoy the weather while you eat, distinguishes this room.

- Master Suite: Located in the same wing as the other bedrooms, this suite has a separate entrance and features a vaulted ceiling, three closets, and a compartmented bath.

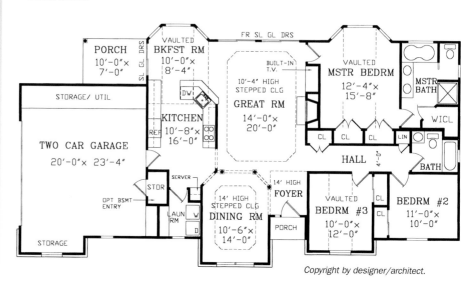

Copyright by designer/architect.

Foyer

Dining Room

Great Room

Living Room

SMARTtip

Natural Trellis

Create a natural rustic trellis that might even, if growing conditions are right, produce its own pretty blooms. Cut and place saplings in the ground as uprights. Then weave old grapevines with smaller saplings for the lattice.

Plan #161005

Dimensions: 60' W x 48'10" D
Levels: 1
Heated Square Footage: 1,593
Bedrooms: 3
Bathrooms: 2
Foundation: Basement
Materials List Available: Yes
Price Category: C

Images provided by designer/architect.

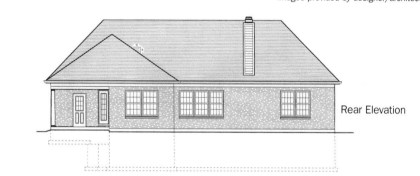

Rear Elevation

This delightful ranch home includes many thoughtful conveniences and a full basement to expand your living enjoyment.

Features:

- Great Room: Take pleasure in welcoming guests through a spacious foyer into the warm and friendly confines of this great room with corner fireplace, sloped ceiling, and view to the rear yard.

- Kitchen: Experience the convenience of enjoying meals while seated at the large island that separates the dining area from this well-designed kitchen. Also included is an over-sized pantry with an abundance of storage.

- Master Suite: This master suite features a compartmented bath, large walk-in closet, and master bedroom that has a tray ceiling with 9-ft. center height.

- Porch: Retreat to this delightful rear porch to enjoy a relaxing evening.

Copyright by designer/architect.

Plan #161007

Dimensions: 66'4" W x 43'10" D
Levels: 1
Heated Square Footage: 1,611
Bedrooms: 3
Bathrooms: 2
Foundation: Basement; crawl space option for fee
Materials List Available: Yes
Price Category: C

A lovely front porch and an entry with sidelights invite you to experience the impressive amenities offered in this exceptional ranch home.

Features:

- **Great Room:** Grand openings, featuring columns from the foyer to this great room and continuing to the bayed dining area, convey an open, spacious feel. The fireplace and matching windows on the rear wall of the great room enhance this effect.

- **Kitchen:** This well-designed kitchen offers convenient access to the laundry and garage. It also features an angled counter with ample space and an abundance of cabinets.

- **Master Suite:** This deluxe master suite contains many exciting amenities, including a lavishly appointed dressing room and a large walk-in closet.

- **Porch:** Sliding doors lead to this delightful screened porch for relaxing summer interludes.

Images provided by designer/architect.

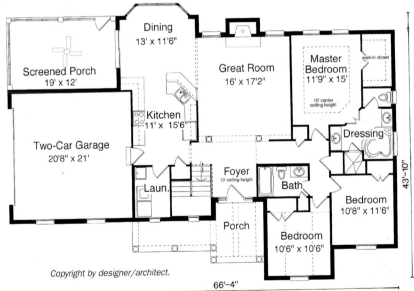

Copyright by designer/architect.

Rear Elevation

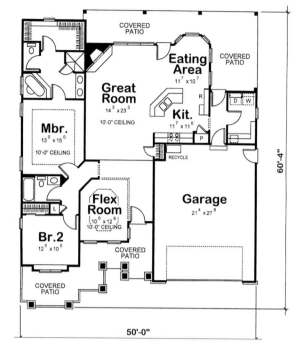

Images provided by designer/architect.

CAD FILE AVAILABLE

Plan #121400

Dimensions: 50' W x 60'4" D

Levels: 1

Heated Square Footage: 1,615

Bedrooms: 2

Bathrooms: 2

Foundation: Slab; crawl space or basement for fee

Materials List Available: Yes

Price Category: C

Copyright by designer/architect.

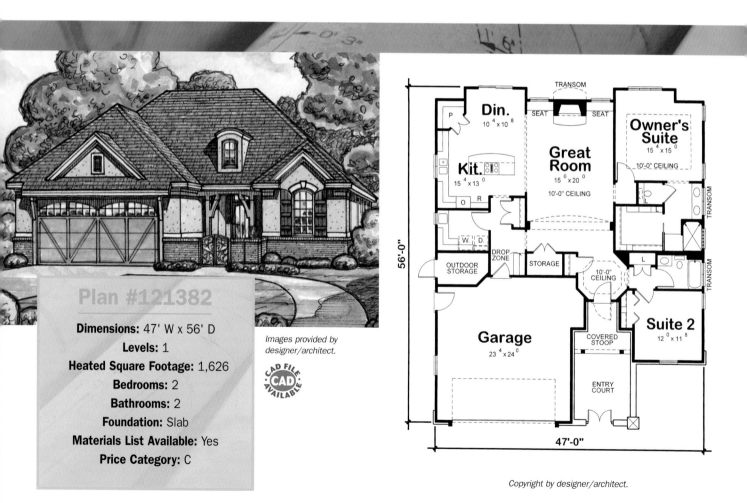

Plan #121382

Dimensions: 47' W x 56' D

Levels: 1

Heated Square Footage: 1,626

Bedrooms: 2

Bathrooms: 2

Foundation: Slab

Materials List Available: Yes

Price Category: C

Images provided by designer/architect.

CAD FILE AVAILABLE

Copyright by designer/architect.

Plan #351006

Dimensions: 64' W x 39' D

Levels: 1

Heated Square Footage: 1,638

Bedrooms: 3

Bathrooms: 2

Foundation: Crawl space, slab, or basement

Materials List Available: Yes

Price Category: D

CAD FILE AVAILABLE

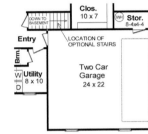

Stair Location for Basement Option

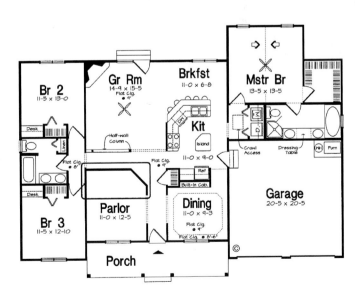

Plan #391038

Dimensions: 59' W x 44' D

Levels: 1

Heated Square Footage: 1,642

Bedrooms: 3

Bathrooms: 2

Foundation: Crawl space, slab, and basement

Materials List Available: Yes

Price Category: C

Plan #121008

Dimensions: 62' W x 56' D
Levels: 1
Heated Square Footage: 1,651
Bedrooms: 2
Bathrooms: 2
Foundation: Basement; crawl space or slab for fee
Materials List Available: Yes
Price Category: C

This elegant home is packed with amenities that belie its compact size.

Features:

• Ceiling Height: 8 ft.

• Dining Room: The foyer opens into a view of the dining room, with its distinctive boxed ceiling.

• Great Room: The whole family will want to gather around the fireplace and enjoy the views and sunlight streaming through the transom-topped window.

• Breakfast Area: Next to the great room and sharing the transom-topped windows, this cozy area invites you to linger over morning coffee.

• Covered Porch: When the weather is nice, take your coffee through the door in the breakfast area and enjoy this large covered porch.

• Master Suite: French doors lead to this comfortable suite featuring a walk-in closet. Enjoy long, luxurious soaks in the corner whirlpool accented with boxed windows.

Images provided by designer/architect.

CAD FILE AVAILABLE

Optional Bedroom

Br.3
10² x 10⁰

WHIRLPOOL

Mbr.
14⁰ x 13⁰
9'-0" CEILING

Den
10² x 10⁰
OPTIONAL BEDROOM
WET BAR

Br. 2
11⁰ x 10⁰
10'-0" CLG.

Grt. rm.
17⁰ x 17⁰
10'-0" CEILING

TRANSOMS

SERVERY

Din.
12⁰ x 11⁰
9'-0" CEILING

COVERED PORCH

Bfst.
11⁰ x 11⁰
10'-0" CEILING

SNACK BAR

Kit.
13⁰ x 11⁸

COVERED PORCH

Gar.
30⁰ x 20⁸

56' - 0"

62' - 0"

Copyright by designer/architect.

SMARTtip

Finishing Your Fireplace with Tile

An excellent finishing material for a fireplace is tile. Luckily, there are reproductions of art tiles today. Most showrooms carry examples of Arts and Crafts, Art Nouveau, California, Delft, and other European tiles. Granite, limestone, and marble tiles are affordable alternatives to custom stone slabs.

Plan #351033

Dimensions: 62'2" W x 45'8" D

Levels: 1

Heated Square Footage: 1,654

Bedrooms: 3

Bathrooms: 2

Foundation: Crawl space, slab, or basement

Materials List Available: Yes

Price Category: C

Images provided by designer/architect.

This gorgeous three-bedroom brick home would be the perfect place to raise your family.

Features:

- Great Room: This terrific room has a gas fireplace with built-in cabinets on either side.

- Kitchen: This island kitchen with breakfast area is open to the great room.

- Master Suite: This private room features a vaulted ceiling and a large walk-in closet. The bath area has a walk-in closet, jetted tub, and double vanities.

- Bedrooms: The two additional bedrooms share a bathroom located in the hall.

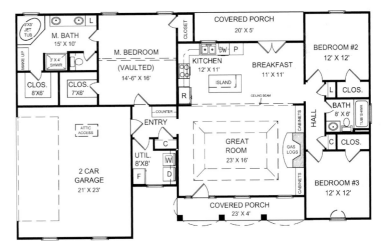

Copyright by designer/architect.

Plan #121027

Dimensions: 46' W x 48' D

Levels: 2

Heated Square Footage: 1,660

Main Level Sq. Ft.: 1,265

Upper Level Sq. Ft.: 395

Bedrooms: 3

Bathrooms: 2½

Foundation: Basement

Materials List Available: Yes

Price Category: C

Images provided by designer/architect.

This elegant home is designed for architectural interest and gracious living.

Features:

• Ceiling Height: 8 ft. unless otherwise noted.

• Great Room: Family and guests will be drawn to this inviting, sun-filled room with its 13-ft. ceiling and raised-hearth fireplace.

• Formal Dining Room: An angled ceiling lends architectural interest to this elegant room. Alternately, this room can be used as a parlor.

• Master Suite: Corner windows are designed to ease furniture placement. The sunlit whirlpool bath invites you to take time to luxuriate and rejuvenate. There's a double vanity, separate shower, and a walk-in closet.

• Garage: This two bay garage offers plenty of space for storage in addition to parking.

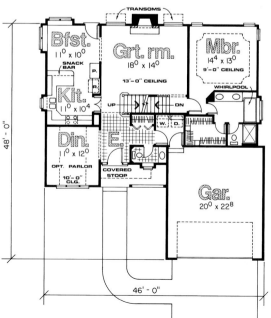

Main Level Floor Plan

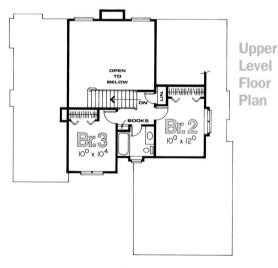

Upper Level Floor Plan

Copyright by designer/architect.

Plan #121004

Dimensions: 55'4" W x 48' D
Levels: 1
Heated Square Footage: 1,666
Bedrooms: 3
Bathrooms: 2
Foundation: Basement;
crawl space or slab for fee
Materials List Available: Yes
Price Category: C

An efficient floor plan and plenty of amenities create a luxurious lifestyle.

Features:

- Ceiling Height: 8 ft. except as noted.

- Entry: Enjoy summer breezes on the porch; then step inside the entry where sidelights and an arched transom create a bright, cheery welcome.

- Great Room: The 10-ft. ceiling and the transom-topped windows flooding the room with light provide a sense of spaciousness. The fireplace adds warmth and style.

- Dining Room: You'll usher your guests into this room located just off the great room.

- Breakfast Area: Also located off the great room, the breakfast area offers another dining option.

- Master Suite: The master bedroom is highlighted by a tray ceiling and a large walk-in closet. Luxuriate in the private bath with its sunlit whirlpool, separate shower, and double vanity.

Images provided by designer/architect.

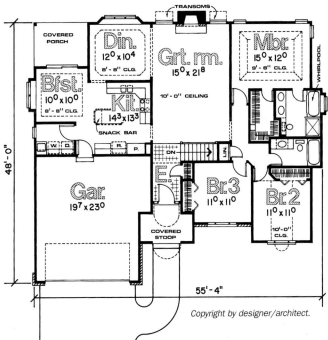

Copyright by designer/architect.

SMARTtip

Carpeting

Install the best underlayment padding available, as well as the highest grade of carpeting you can afford. This will guarantee a feeling of softness beneath your feet and protect your investment for years to come by reducing wear and tear on the carpet.

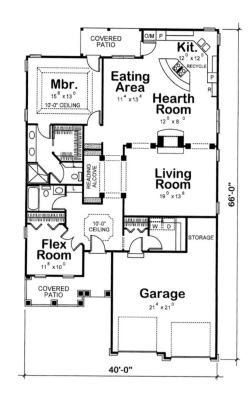

Plan #121405

Dimensions: 40' W x 66' D

Levels: 1

Heated Square Footage: 1,668

Bedrooms: 2

Bathrooms: 2

Foundation: Slab; crawl space or basement for fee

Materials List Available: Yes

Price Category: C

Images provided by designer/architect.

Copyright by designer/architect.

Plan #121315

Dimensions: 56' W x 48' D

Levels: 1

Heated Square Footage: 1,672

Bedrooms: 3

Bathrooms: 2

Foundation: Basement

Materials List Available: Yes

Price Category: C

Images provided by designer/architect.

This home, as shown in the photograph, may differ from the actual blueprints. For more detailed information, please check the floor plans carefully.

Copyright by designer/architect.

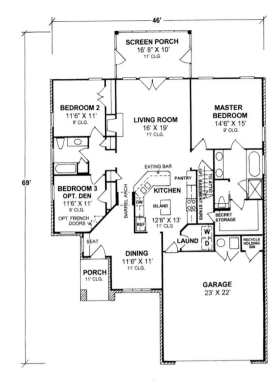

Plan #121409

Dimensions: 46' W x 69' D

Levels: 1

Heated Square Footage: 1,692

Bedrooms: 3

Bathrooms: 2

Foundation: Slab; crawl space or basement for fee

Materials List Available: Yes

Price Category: C

Images provided by designer/architect.

Copyright by designer/architect.

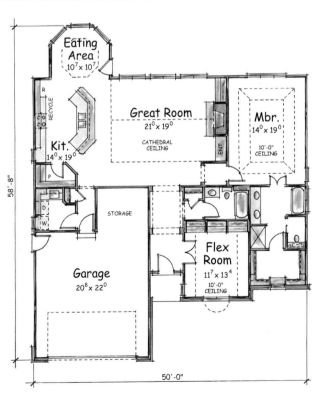

Plan #121296

Dimensions: 50' W x 58'8" D

Levels: 1

Heated Square Footage: 1,692

Bedrooms: 2

Bathrooms: 2

Foundation: Basement

Materials List Available: Yes

Price Category: C

Images provided by designer/architect.

This home, as shown in the photograph, may differ from actual blueprints. For more detailed information, please check the floor plans carefully.

Copyright by designer/architect.

Plan #121274

Dimensions: 54' W x 45'4" D
Levels: 1.5
Heated Square Footage: 1,694
Main Level Sq. Ft.: 1,298
Upper Level Sq. Ft.: 396
Bedrooms: 3
Bathrooms: 2½
Foundation: Basement
Materials List Available: Yes
Price Category: C

Images provided by designer/architect.

CAD FILE AVAILABLE

Upper Level Floor Plan

Copyright by designer/architect.

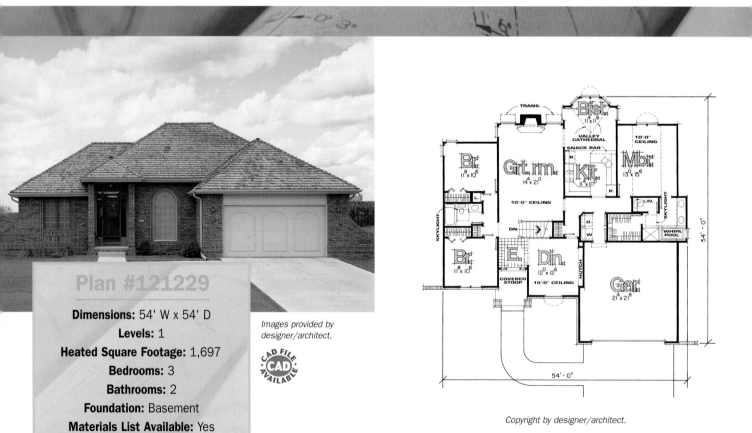

Plan #121229

Dimensions: 54' W x 54' D
Levels: 1
Heated Square Footage: 1,697
Bedrooms: 3
Bathrooms: 2
Foundation: Basement
Materials List Available: Yes
Price Category: C

Images provided by designer/architect.

CAD FILE AVAILABLE

Copyright by designer/architect.

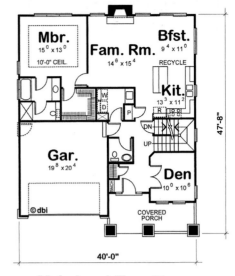

Plan #121221

Dimensions: 40' W x 47'8" D

Levels: 2

Heated Square Footage: 1,699

Main Level Sq. Ft.: 1,268

Upper Level Sq. Ft.: 431

Bedrooms: 3

Bathrooms: 2½

Foundation: Basement; crawl space or slab for fee

Materials List Available: Yes

Price Category: C

Images provided by designer/architect.

This home, as shown in the photograph, may differ from actual blueprints. For more detailed information, please check the floor plans carefully.

CAD FILE AVAILABLE

Main Level Floor Plan

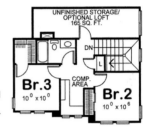

Upper Level Floor Plan

Copyright by designer/architect.

Plan #121242

Dimensions: 53'4" W x 54'10" D

Levels: 1

Heated Square Footage: 1,710

Bedrooms: 3

Bathrooms: 2

Foundation: Basement

Materials List Available: Yes

Price Category: C

Images provided by designer/architect.

CAD FILE AVAILABLE

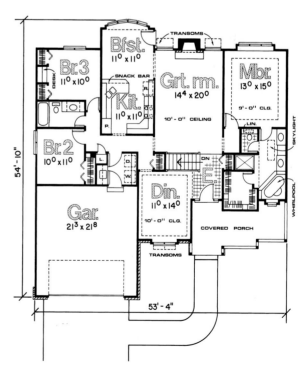

Copyright by designer/architect.

Plan #131041

Dimensions: 42' W x 45' D
Levels: 2
Heated Square Footage: 1,679
Main Level Sq. Ft.: 1,134
Upper Level Sq. Ft.: 545
Bedrooms: 3
Bathrooms: 2½
Foundation: Crawl space, slab, or basement
Materials List Available: Yes
Price Category: D

This rustic-looking two-story cottage includes contemporary amenities for your total comfort.

Features:

- Great Room: With a 9-ft.-4-in.-high ceiling, this large room makes everyone feel at home. A fireplace with raised hearth and built-in niche for a TV will encourage the whole family to gather here on cool evenings, and sliding glass doors leading to

the rear covered porch make it an ideal entertaining area in mild weather.

- Kitchen: When people aren't in the great room, you're likely to find them here, because the convenient serving bar welcomes casual dining, and this room also opens to the p porch.

- Master Suite: Relax at the end of the day in this room, with its 9-ft.-4-in.-high ceiling and walk-in closet, or luxuriate in the private bath with whirlpool tub and dual-sink vanity.

- Optional Basement: This area can include a tuck-under two-car garage if you desire it.

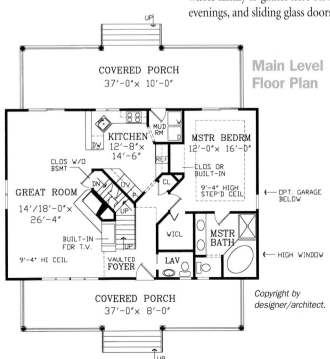

Main Level Floor Plan

COVERED PORCH
37'-0" x 10'-0"

KITCHEN
12'-8" x 14'-6"

MUD RM

DW

CLOS W/D BSMT

MSTR BEDRM
12'-0" x 16'-0"

CLOS OR BUILT-IN

REF

CL

9'-4" HIGH STEP'D CEIL

GREAT ROOM
14'/18'-0" x 26'-4"

DN

UP

OPT. GARAGE BELOW

BUILT-IN FOR T.V.

UP

WICL

MSTR BATH

9'-4" HI CEIL

VAULTED FOYER

LAV

HIGH WINDOW

COVERED PORCH
37'-0" x 8'-0"

UP

Upper Level Floor Plan

BATH

LIN

DN

BALC.

BEDRM #3
12'-0" x 11'-0"

CL

BEDRM #2
16'-4" x 11'-0"

CL

Great Room

Plan #131002

Dimensions: 70'1" W x 60'7" D
Levels: 1
Heated Square Footage: 1,709
Bedrooms: 3
Bathrooms: 2½
Foundation: Crawl space, slab, or basement
Materials List Available: Yes
Price Category: D

Images provided by designer/architect.

Rear View

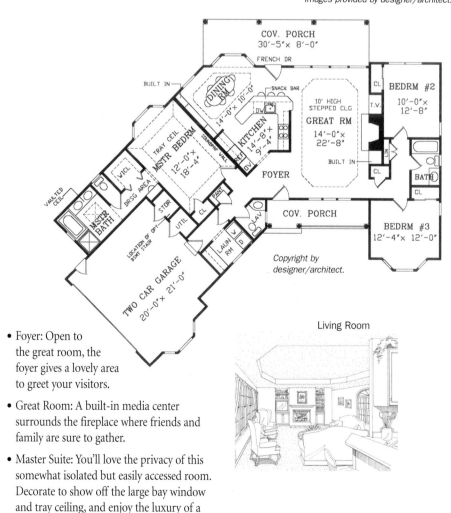

Copyright by designer/architect.

Living Room

You'll love the way this angled ranch brings out the best in a corner lot or on a slope.

Features:

• Ceiling Height: 8 ft.

• Front Porch: Hang baskets of plants from the roof of this porch, which is just the right size for a couple of rockers and a side table.

• Dining Room: Well-placed windows flood this room with sunlight during the day and a built-in cabinet gives ample storage space for all your china, linens, and collectables.

• Foyer: Open to the great room, the foyer gives a lovely area to greet your visitors.

• Great Room: A built-in media center surrounds the fireplace where friends and family are sure to gather.

• Master Suite: You'll love the privacy of this somewhat isolated but easily accessed room. Decorate to show off the large bay window and tray ceiling, and enjoy the luxury of a separate toilet room.

Plan #321001

Dimensions: 83' W x 42' D

Levels: 1

Heated Square Footage: 1,721

Bedrooms: 3

Bathrooms: 2

Foundation: Crawl space, slab, or walkout

Materials List Available: Yes

Price Category: C

Images provided by designer/architect.

You'll love the atrium, which creates a warm, naturally lit space inside this gracious home, as well as the roof dormers that give the house wonderful curb appeal from the outside.

CAD FILE AVAILABLE — CAD

Rear View

Front View

Features:

- **Great Room:** Bathed in light from the atrium window wall, this room, with its vaulted ceiling, will be the hub of your family life.

- **Dining Room:** This room also has a vaulted ceiling and is lit by the atrium, but you can draw drapes at night to create a cozy, warm feeling.

- **Kitchen:** Designed for functionality, this step-saving kitchen is easy to organize and makes cooking a pleasure.

- **Breakfast Room:** For convenience, this room is located between the kitchen and the rear covered porch.

- **Master Suite:** Retire with pleasure to this lovely retreat, with its luxurious bath.

Copyright by designer/architect.

Plan #151173

Dimensions: 58' W x 53'6" D

Levels: 1

Heated Square Footage: 1,739

Bedrooms: 3

Bathrooms: 2

Foundation: Crawl space, slab, basement, or walkout

CompleteCost List Available: Yes

Price Category: C

You'll love the charming architectural features and practical contemporary design of this ranch-style home.

Features:

- **Great Room:** Perfect for entertaining guests or just cozying up to the glowing fireplace with loved-ones, this great room is conveniently located in the center of everything.

- **Kitchen:** This highly efficient design, complete with island and plenty of workspace and storage, is just steps away from the sunlit breakfast room and the formal dining room, simplifying meal transitions.

- **Master Suite:** A romantic getaway in itself, this spacious master bedroom adjoins his and her walk-in closets, and a large compartmentalized master bath with a whirlpool tub,

dual vanities, and a standing shower. The room also includes a private entrance to the back porch.

- **Secondary Bedrooms:** In a remote space of their own, these two nicely sized bedrooms share access to a full bathroom.

Images provided by designer/architect.

Copyright by designer/architect.

Plan #351002

Dimensions: 64' W x 45'10" D

Levels: 1

Heated Square Footage: 1,751

Bedrooms: 3

Bathrooms: 2

Foundation: Crawl space, slab, or basement

Materials List Available: Yes

Price Category: E

This is a beautiful classic traditional home with a European touch.

Features:

- **Great Room:** This gathering area has a gas log fireplace that is flanked by two built-in cabinets. The area has a 10-ft.-tall tray ceiling.

- **Kitchen:** This L-shaped island kitchen has a raised bar and is open to the eating area and great room. The three open spaces work together as one large room.

- **Master Suite:** Located on the opposite side of the home from the secondary bedrooms, this suite has a vaulted ceiling. The master bath has dual vanities and a garden tub.

- **Bedrooms:** The two secondary bedrooms share a hall bathroom and have ample closet space.

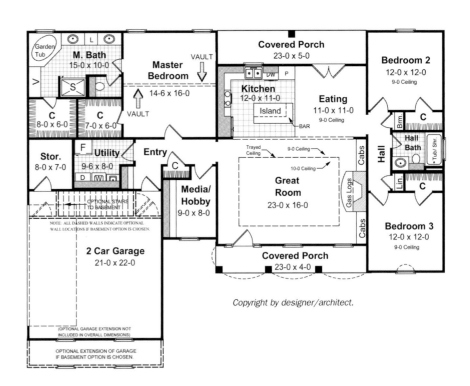

Plan #121006

Dimensions: 46' W x 58' D

Levels: 1

Heated Square Footage: 1,762

Bedrooms: 3

Bathrooms: 2

Foundation: Slab;
crawl space or basement for fee

Materials List Available: Yes

Price Category: C

Images provided by designer/architect.

The entry has a trio of arched openings that leads you to other areas of this amenity-packed home.

Features:

- Ceiling Height: 8 ft. except as noted.

- Eating Bar: Conveniently located between the kitchen and family room, this is sure to be a favorite spot for informal entertaining and family gatherings.

- Family room: A wall of windows, a fireplace, and a vaulted ceiling stretching to 11 ft. work together to make this a bright and warm room.

- Kitchen: There's no shortage of counter space in this well-planned kitchen that features a center island in addition to the eating bar.

- Master Suite: Luxuriate at the end of the day in this large bedroom with its decorative tray ceiling and walk-in closet. Enjoy the pampering bath with its sunlit corner whirlpool flanked by vanities.

- Garage: Two bays provide room for cars and plenty of storage as well.

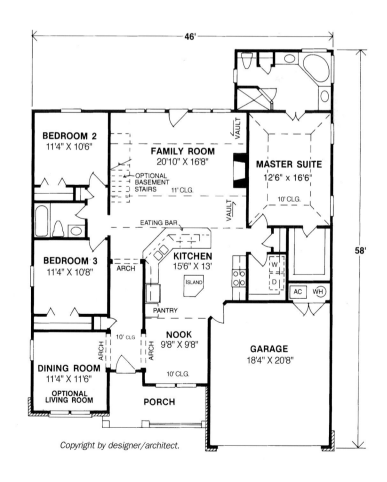

Copyright by designer/architect.

Plan #121385

Dimensions: 56'8" W x 53' D

Levels: 1

Heated Square Footage: 1,732

Bedrooms: 1

Bathrooms: 2

Foundation: Slab

Materials List Available: Yes

Price Category: C

Images provided by designer/architect.

Copyright by designer/architect.

Plan #121434

Dimensions: 54' W x 56' D

Levels: 1.5

Heated Square Footage: 1,733

Main Level Sq. Ft.: 1,412

Upper Level Sq. Ft.: 321

Bedrooms: 1

Bathrooms: 2½

Foundation: Slab; crawl space or basement for fee

Materials List Available: Yes

Price Category: C

Images provided by designer/architect.

Main Level Floor Plan

Upper Level Floor Plan

Copyright by designer/architect.

Plan #121384

Dimensions: 54' W x 60' D
Levels: 1
Heated Square Footage: 1,765
Bedrooms: 1
Bathrooms: 2
Foundation: Slab
Materials List Available: Yes
Price Category: C

Images provided by designer/architect.

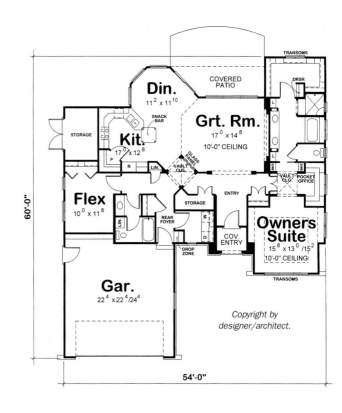

Copyright by designer/architect.

Plan #121437

Dimensions: 52' W x 56' D
Levels: 1.5
Heated Square Footage: 1,765
Main Level Sq. Ft.: 1,436
Upper Level Sq. Ft.: 329
Bedrooms: 1
Bathrooms: 2½
Foundation: Slab; crawl space or fee
Materials List Available: Yes
Price Category: C

Images provided by designer/architect.

Main Level Floor Plan

Upper Level Floor Plan

Copyright by designer/architect.

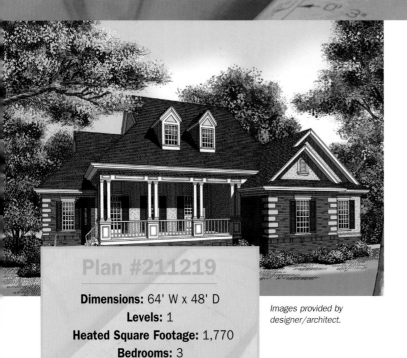

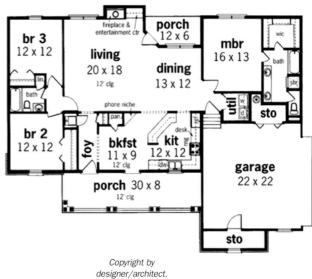

Images provided by designer/architect.

Plan #211219

Dimensions: 64' W x 48' D

Levels: 1

Heated Square Footage: 1,770

Bedrooms: 3

Bathrooms: 2

Foundation: Crawl space; slab for fee

Materials List Available: Yes

Price Category: C

Copyright by designer/architect.

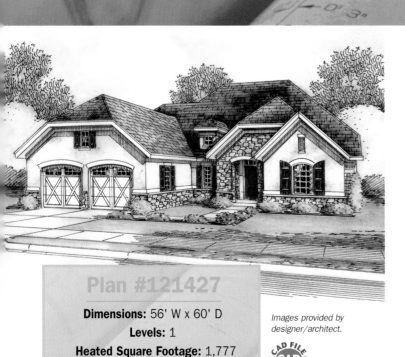

Images provided by designer/architect.

CAD FILE AVAILABLE

Plan #121427

Dimensions: 56' W x 60' D

Levels: 1

Heated Square Footage: 1,777

Bedrooms: 1

Bathrooms: 2

Foundation: Slab; crawl space or basement for fee

Materials List Available: Yes

Price Category: C

Copyright by designer/architect.

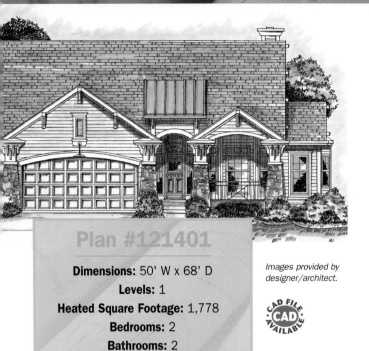

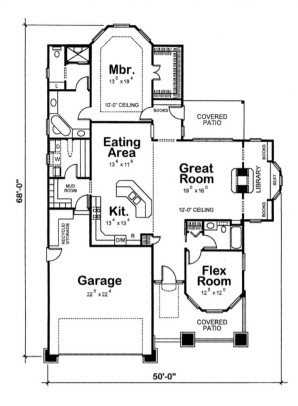

Plan #121401

Dimensions: 50' W x 68' D

Levels: 1

Heated Square Footage: 1,778

Bedrooms: 2

Bathrooms: 2

Foundation: Slab; crawl space or basement for fee

Materials List Available: Yes

Price Category: C

Images provided by designer/architect.

CAD FILE AVAILABLE — CAD

Copyright by designer/architect.

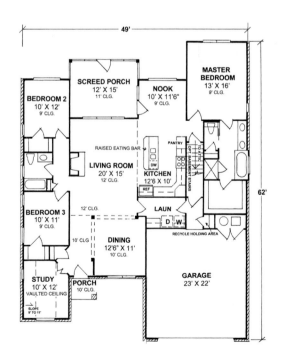

Plan #121395

Dimensions: 49' W x 62' D

Levels: 1

Heated Square Footage: 1,780

Bedrooms: 3

Bathrooms: 2

Foundation: Slab; crawl space or basement for fee

Materials List Available: Yes

Price Category: C

Images provided by designer/architect.

CAD FILE AVAILABLE — CAD

Copyright by designer/architect.

Plan #121031

Dimensions: 52' W x 51'4" D
Levels: 2
Heated Square Footage: 1,772
Main Level Sq. Ft.: 1,314
Upper Level Sq. Ft.: 458
Bedrooms: 3
Bathrooms: 2½
Foundation: Basement
Materials List Available: Yes
Price Category: C

CAD FILE • AVAILABLE • CAD

This home features architectural details reminiscence of earlier fine homes.

Features:

- **Ceiling Height:** 8 ft. unless otherwise noted.

- **Foyer:** This grand entry soars two-stories high. The U-shaped staircase with window leads to a second-story balcony.

- **Great Room:** You'll be drawn to the impressive views through the triple-arch windows at the front and rear of this room.

- **Kitchen:** Designed for maximum efficiency, this kitchen is a pleasure to be in. It features a center island, a full pantry, and a desk for added convenience.

- **Breakfast Area:** This area adjoins the kitchen. Both rooms are flooded with sunlight streaming from a shared bay window.

- **Master Suite:** The stylish bedroom includes a walk-in closet. Luxuriate in the whirlpool tub at the end of a long day .

Main Level Floor Plan

Copyright by designer/architect.

Upper Level Floor Plan

Plan #121059

Dimensions: 52' W x 59'4" D

Levels: 1

Heated Square Footage: 1,782

Bedrooms: 3

Bathrooms: 2

Foundation: Basement

Materials List Available: Yes

Price Category: C

Images provided by designer/architect.

This home is ideal for families looking for luxury and style mixed with convenience.

Features:

- Great Room: This large room is enhanced by the three-sided fireplace it shares with adjacent living areas.

- Hearth Room: Enjoy the fireplace here, too, and decorate to emphasize the bayed windows.

- Kitchen: This kitchen was designed for efficiency and is flooded with natural light.

- Breakfast Area: Picture-awing windows are the highlight in this area.

- Master Suite: A boxed ceiling and walk-in closet as well as a bath with a double-vanity, whirlpool tub, shower, and window with a plant ledge make this suite a true retreat.

- Bedrooms: These lovely bedrooms are served by a luxurious full bath.

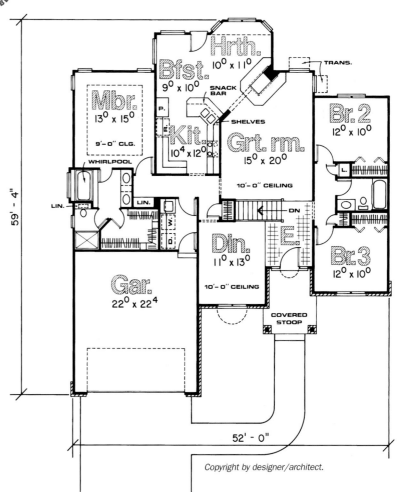

Copyright by designer/architect.

Plan #101004

Dimensions: 55'8" W x 56'6" D

Levels: 1

Heated Square Footage: 1,787

Bedrooms: 3

Bathrooms: 2

Foundation: Crawl space, slab, or basement

Materials List Available: Yes

Price Category: D

Images provided by designer/architect.

This carefully designed ranch provides the feel and features of a much larger home.

Features:

• Ceiling Height: 9 ft. unless otherwise noted.

• Entry: Guests will step up onto the inviting front porch and into this entry, with its impressive 11-ft. ceiling.

• Dining Room: Open to the entry and to its left is this elegant dining room, perfect for entertaining or informal family gatherings.

• Family Room: This family gathering place features an 11-ft. ceiling to enhance its sense of spaciousness.

• Kitchen: This intelligently designed kitchen has an open plan. A breakfast bar and a serving bar are features that add to its convenience.

• Master Suite: This suite is loaded with amenities, including a double-step tray ceiling, direct access to the screened porch, a sitting room, deluxe bath, and his and her walk-in closets.

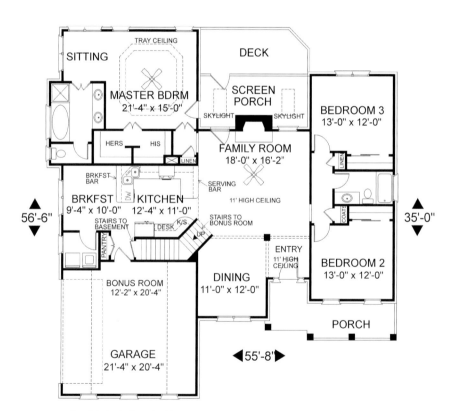

Copyright by designer/architect.

Kitchen

Family Room

Dining Room

Master Bath

Bedroom

Master Bedroom

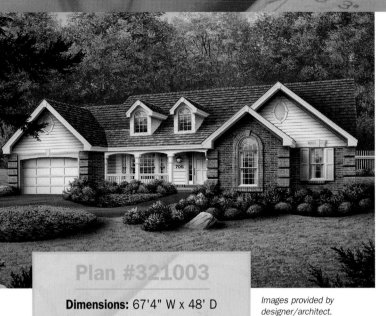

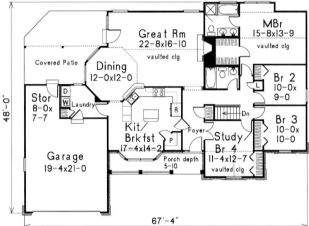

Plan #321003

Dimensions: 67'4" W x 48' D

Levels: 1

Heated Square Footage: 1,791

Bedrooms: 4

Bathrooms: 2

Foundation: Basement

Materials List Available: Yes

Price Category: C

Images provided by designer/architect.

CAD FILE AVAILABLE

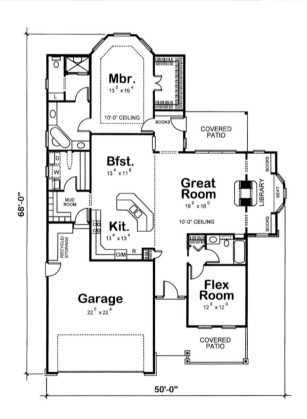

Plan #121402

Dimensions: 50' W x 68' D

Levels: 1

Heated Square Footage: 1,792

Bedrooms: 1

Bathrooms: 2

Foundation: Slab; crawl space or basement for fee

Materials List Available: Yes

Price Category: C

Images provided by designer/architect.

CAD FILE AVAILABLE

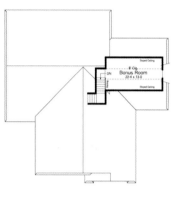

Images provided by designer/architect.

Plan #481150

Dimensions: 60' W x 61' D
Levels: 1.5
Heated Square Footage: 1,792
Bonus Level Sq. Ft.: 296
Bedrooms: 3
Bathrooms: 2
Foundation: Crawl space, basement
Materials List Available: No
Price Category: C

CAD FILE AVAILABLE

Bonus Area Floor Plan

Copyright by designer/architect.

Plan #101153

Dimensions: 50' W x 86'4" D
Levels: 1
Heated Square Footage: 1,800
Bedrooms: 3
Bathrooms: 3
Foundation: Crawl space
Materials List Available: No
Price Category: D

CAD FILE AVAILABLE

Images provided by designer/architect.

Copyright by designer/architect.

Plan #351043

Dimensions: 65' W x 50'10" D

Levels: 1

Heated Square Footage: 1,802

Bedrooms: 3

Bathrooms: 2

Foundation: Crawl space, slab, or basement

Materials List Available: Yes

Price Category: D

This three-bedroom brick home has a wonderful split bedroom plan with open living spaces.

Features:

- **Great Room:** This large room with vaulted ceiling has a gas fireplace that has built-in cabinets on each side.

- **Kitchen:** This kitchen has an optional pocket door to the great room and a raised bar that's open to the dining room.

- **Dining Room:** This dining room has a view of the backyard and access to the rear covered porch.

- **Master Suite:** This area boasts a vaulted ceiling and his and her closets. There is also a private master bath.

- **Bedrooms:** The two additional bedrooms share a bathroom located in the hall.

Optional Floor Plan

Plan #121404

Dimensions: 50' W x 59' D
Levels: 1
Heated Square Footage: 1,806
Bedrooms: 1
Bathrooms: 2
Foundation: Slab; crawl space or basement for fee
Materials List Available: Yes
Price Category: D

Images provided by designer/architect.

You'll love the amount of features and amenities in this home.

Features:

• Great Room: This large and inviting great room features an entertainment center and a see-through fireplace that connects with the hearth room.

• Dining Room: Located at the front of the home, this dining room is wonderful for entertaining guests and family.

• Kitchen: Open to the eating area and hearth room, this kitchen is wonderful for all of your cooking and baking needs, with its center island and recycling area.

• Master Suite: You'll never have to fight about closet space again in this master suite. Two closets have enough space for all of your items, located near the dual sink vanity, separate toilet room, and luxurious tub.

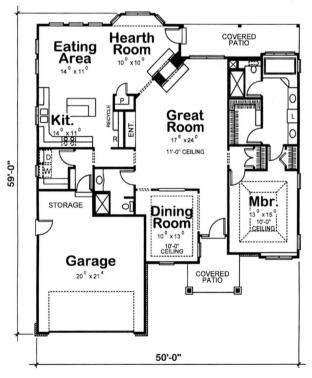

Copyright by designer/architect.

Plan #121124

Dimensions: 55'4" W x 56' D
Levels: 1
Heated Square Footage: 1,806
Bedrooms: 3
Bathrooms: 2
Foundation: Basement;
crawl space for fee
Material List Available: Yes
Price Category: D

This brick ranch will be the best-looking home in the neighborhood.

Features:

- Great Room: This area is a great place to gather with family and friends. The 10-ft.-high ceiling and arched windows make this room bright and airy. On cold nights, gather by the warmth of the fireplace.

- Dining Room: A column off the entry defines this formal dining area. Arched windows and a 10-ft.-high ceiling add to the elegance of the space.

- Kitchen: This island kitchen will inspire the chef in the family to create a symphony at every meal. The triple window in the adjoining breakfast area floods this area with natural light.

Images provided by designer/architect.

- Master Suite: Located on the opposite side of the home from the secondary bedrooms, this private area features a 10-ft.-high ceiling in the sleeping area. The master bath boasts a compartmentalized lavatory and shower area in addition to dual vanities and a walk-in closet.

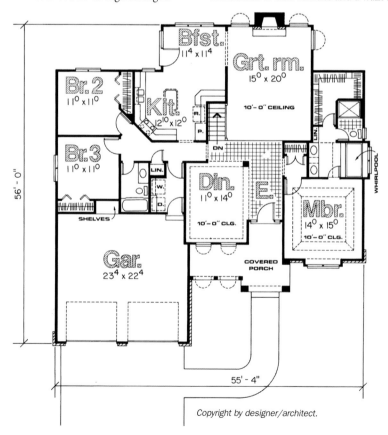

Copyright by designer/architect.

Plan #121040

Dimensions: 50' W x 48' D

Levels: 2

Heated Square Footage: 1,818

Main Level Sq. Ft.: 1,302

Upper Level Sq. Ft.: 516

Bedrooms: 3

Bathrooms: 2½

Foundation: Basement

Materials List Available: Yes

Price Category: D

Offering plenty of architectural style, this home is designed with the busy modern lifestyle in mind.

Features:

- Ceiling Height: 8 ft. unless otherwise noted.
- Great Room: This is sure to be the central gathering place of the home with its volume ceiling, abundance of windows, and its handsome fireplace.
- Kitchen: This convenient and attractive kitchen includes a snack bar that will get lots of use for impromptu family meals.
- Breakfast Area: Joined to the kitchen by the snack bar, this breakfast area will invite you to linger over morning coffee. It includes a pantry and access to the backyard.

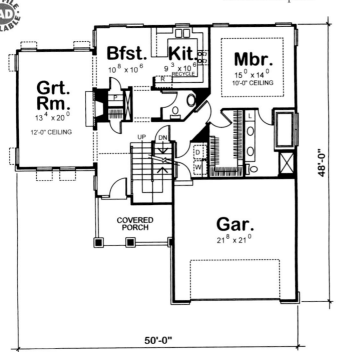

Main Level Floor Plan

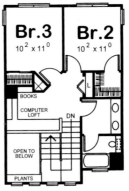

Upper Level Floor Plan

- Master Bedroom: This private retreat offers the convenience of a walk-in closet and the luxury of its own whirlpool bath and shower.
- Computer Loft: Designed with the family computer in mind, this loft overlooks a two-story entry.

Plan #121205

Dimensions: 53' W x 62' D

Levels: 1

Heated Square Footage: 1,820

Bedrooms: 3

Bathrooms: 2

Foundation: Basement; crawl space or slab for fee

Materials List Available: Yes

Price Category: D

Images provided by designer/architect.

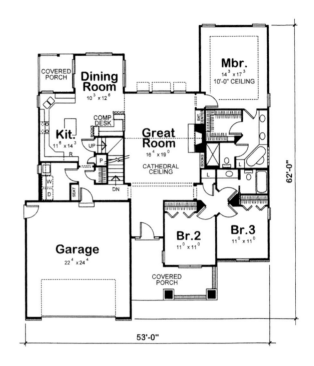

Copyright by designer/architect.

Plan #121410

Dimensions: 49'4" W x 70' D

Levels: 1

Heated Square Footage: 1,821

Bedrooms: 2

Bathrooms: 2

Foundation: Slab

Materials List Available: Yes

Price Category: D

Images provided by designer/architect.

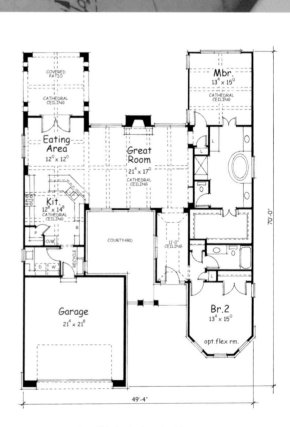

Copyright by designer/architect.

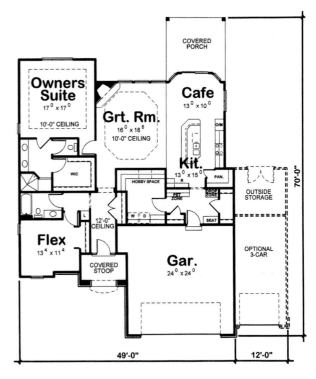

Plan #121420

Dimensions: 49' W x 70' D

Levels: 1

Heated Square Footage: 1,827

Bedrooms: 1

Bathrooms: 2

Foundation: Slab; crawl space or basement for fee

Materials List Available: Yes

Price Category: D

Images provided by designer/architect.

CAD FILE AVAILABLE · CAD ·

Copyright by designer/architect.

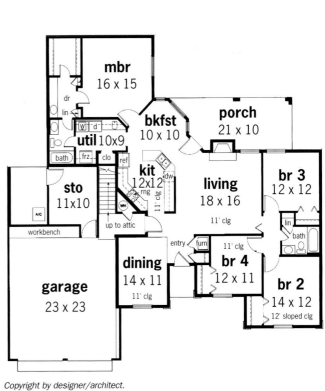

Plan #211004

Dimensions: 64' W x 62' D

Levels: 1

Heated Square Footage: 1,828

Bedrooms: 4

Bathrooms: 2

Foundation: Crawl space, slab, or basement

Materials List Available: Yes

Price Category: D

Images provided by designer/architect.

Copyright by designer/architect.

Main Level Floor Plan

Copyright by designer/architect.

Upper Level Floor Plan

Plan #181133

Dimensions: 38' W x 40' D
Levels: 2
Heated Square Footage: 1,832
Main Level Sq. Ft.: 1,212
Second Level Sq. Ft. 620
Bedrooms: 3
Bathrooms: 2
Foundation: Walkout; crawl space, slab, or basement for fee
Materials List Available: Yes
Price Category: D

Images provided by designer/architect.

CAD FILE AVAILABLE

Plan #121403

Dimensions: 50' W x 59' D
Levels: 1
Heated Square Footage: 1,840
Bedrooms: 1
Bathrooms: 2
Foundation: Slab; crawl space or basement for fee
Materials List Available: Yes
Price Category: D

Images provided by designer/architect.

CAD FILE AVAILABLE

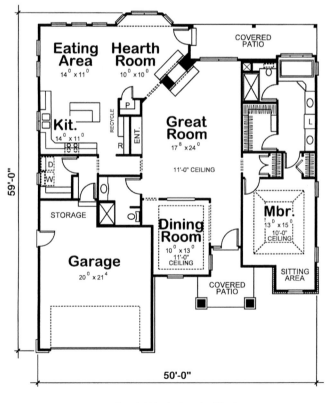

Copyright by designer/architect.

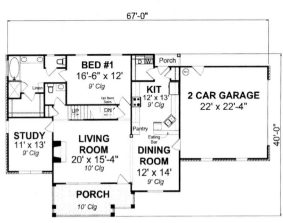

Main Level Floor Plan

BED #1
16'-6" x 12'
9' Clg

KIT
12' x 13'
9' Clg

2 CAR GARAGE
22' x 22'-4"

Porch

67'-0"

40'-0"

STUDY
11' x 13'
9' Clg

LIVING
ROOM
20' x 15'-4"
10' Clg

DINING
ROOM
12' x 14'
9' Clg

Eating Bar

Pantry

PORCH
10' Clg

Linen

UP

DN

Opt Bsmt Stairs

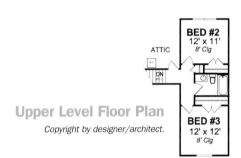

Plan #121413

Dimensions: 67' W x 40' D
Levels: 2
Heated Square Footage: 1,841
Main Level Sq. Ft.: 1,395
Upper Level Sq. Ft.: 446
Bedrooms: 3
Bathrooms: 2½
Foundation: Slab; crawl space or basement for fee
Materials List Available: Yes
Price Category: D

Images provided by designer/architect.

CAD FILE AVAILABLE

Upper Level Floor Plan

Copyright by designer/architect.

ATTIC

BED #2
12' x 11'
8' Clg

BED #3
12' x 12'
8' Clg

DN

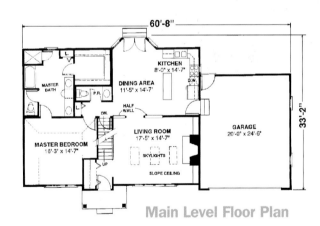

Main Level Floor Plan

60'-8"

33'-2"

MASTER BATH

KITCHEN
8'-0" x 14'-7"

D.W.

DINING AREA
11'-5" x 14'-7"

P.R.

HALF WALL

MASTER BEDROOM
16'-3" x 14'-7"

LIVING ROOM
17'-5" x 14'-7"

GARAGE
20'-0" x 24'-6"

SKYLIGHTS

SLOPE CEILING

DN.

UP

Plan #321308

Dimensions: 60'8" W x 33'2" D
Levels: 2
Heated Square Footage: 1,850
Main Level Sq. Ft.: 1,220
Upper Level Sq. Ft.: 630
Bedrooms: 3
Bathrooms: 2½
Foundation: Basement
Materials List Available: Yes
Price Category: D

Images provided by designer/architect.

CAD FILE AVAILABLE

BEDROOM #2
10'-0" x 14'-7"

BATH 2
SKYLIGHT

BEDROOM #3
12'-0" x 14'-7"

DN.

OPEN TO LIVING ROOM BELOW

Upper Level Floor Plan

Copyright by designer/architect.

Universal Design: Practical, Convenient Features for All

While the average American home is over 30 years old, family life has changed dramatically in the last few decades. Seventy-two percent of females are active in the work force—many of them juggling multiple responsibilities. There is less time to accomplish more and increased distractions demand our attention—for example, Internet searches. Every day we face more "opportunities" than we are able to physically and mentally achieve.

What if your home could make life easier? Wouldn't wider doorways that allow you to carry in twice the amount of groceries in one swoop (instead of having to make two trips through a narrow door) save time and energy? What if you didn't have to get out the step ladder to retrieve the baking pan in the top cabinet, but could simply reach for it at eye level? Not only easier, but safer, too.

Imagine not having to worry about your sauce burning while you run to retrieve a rarely used spice from storage down the hall. A simple pullout drawer beneath your stove could bring all your spices to one, convenient location. And rather than having to make your way

Lever door handles are easy to open—whether your hands are full of groceries or your grip is weakened by arthritis.

Universal Design Home Features

General
- An open floor plan, including wide halls for easy passage with furniture, strollers, or equipment
- Simple access into the home with step-free entries (a ½" or lower threshold)
- Lever handles (doors, plumbing fixtures)
- More cabinet drawers than doors
- C-shaped hardware handles
- Multiheight counter surfaces
- Windows placed low for all to reach, with appropriate locking mechanisms

Circulation
- Even surface routes into and through the home
- Same level floor surfaces
- 34 in. or wider doorways
- A garage entry with convenient access to the kitchen and laundry/utility room

Entrance
- A minimum of one step-free entry
- A 5 x 5 ft. open, clear space in front and behind entry/exit doors
- Overhead protection from the elements outside the door
- Adequate lighting, preferably pointed at the keyhole opening
- An unobscured view to see arriving visitors
- A shelf to set down packages

Bathrooms
- One full, main-level bath adjoining a bedroom with maneuverable space clearance (30 x 48 in.) in front of vanity, toilet, and tub/shower
- A clear space beneath vanities for seating options
- Offset plumbing controls in the tub/shower with available seat
- Textured grab bars mounted on a fully supported maximum wall area
- Nonslip floor surfaces

Kitchens
- Continuous stretches of countertops for easy sliding of heavy objects, especially between the refrigerator, stove, sink, and stove top
- Multiple-task lighting
- Under-counter, drawer-type appliances
- Full-extension, pullout drawers, shelves, and racks for easy reach storage
- A clear space under the sink and cooktop and next to the range for seating options
- Adjustable height work surfaces

Laundry/Utility Areas
- A front loading, raised washer and dryer, with 36 x 48 in. clearance, front and side
- Counter space adjoining or across from appliances with 42 in. clearance
- A sink with clear space underneath for seating option
- Cabinet storage and shelving within a limited reach range

down a dark basement staircase the next time the circuit breaker trips, wouldn't it be nice to be able to reset it a few steps away on your main level?

Sensible Design

These helpful features are components of universal design—an approach that makes spaces safer and more functional. A universally designed home is planned with elements that slide, swing and glide, eliminating the need to bend, stoop, climb, or overreach.

Other examples include step-free entries—a real boon to mothers with strollers, anyone moving furniture or large appliances, or travelers pulling wheeled luggage in and out of the home.

Visiting older parents or friends with mobility limitations will appreciate the convenience of having a full bathroom on the main floor—with enough space for easy access to the toilet, lavatory, and tub/shower. These features can also ease the load of a caregiver helping a family member recoup from surgery.

When it comes time for holiday meals, a universally designed kitchen can add camaraderie and reduce your preparation time and effort, with multi-level work areas, that allow the whole family to pitch in and help.

Whether summer, winter, spring, or fall, universal design can bring new-found comfort, control, and convenience into your life and the lives of those you love. Because universal design or "design for all" as it is often called can benefit the young and old, short and tall, as well as those with varying abilities, new ways to incorporate it are emerging every day.

It is important to note, however, that the best time to include universal design features is before building a new home or while planning a remodeling project. It may be difficult or costly to add them later.

Rebecca Stahr, ASID, CAPS, of LifeSpring Environs, Inc., is a Registered Interior Designer, professional member of the American Society of Interior Designers, and a Certified Aging-in-Place Specialist.

Organized Rear Foyers for Hassle-Free Living

We recently asked home owners what contributes stress to their daily lives at home. One of the most frequent replies was: "Getting my family out the door on time in the morning, with everything they need." Another common response was simply "Clutter."

Thankfully, an organized rear foyer can de-stress takeoffs and provide pleasant landings by eliminating clutter that may otherwise accumulate in the kitchen or family room. Because efficient, practical service entries are emphasized in all of new home plans, we asked two of the designers, Carl Cuozzo and Marshall Wallman, to share their thoughts on these important areas.

"In smaller homes with limited space available, a simple bench with some cubbies above and a few coat hooks between is very popular," Cuozzo begins. "We also include a drop zone somewhere near the garage entrance. Typically, a base cabinet that's 36 inches wide, a drop zone provides a convenient spot to drop your car keys, sort mail, park your briefcase, and recharge cell phones and digital cameras. It may include one or more locking cabinet doors or drawers for expensive items, such as a camcorder or notebook PC."

"It's a great place for emergency items, too—candles, flashlights, batteries, and a battery-operated radio," adds Wallman.

Extra space provides added options, such as including pet amenities. "I've designed several homes with dog centers in the rear entries," notes Wallman. "They included a special space for a kennel under the cabinetry. In another home, I designed a built-in bench with an open space underneath for a kennel for a small Pekinese. It's also nice to provide a hook for leashes, a drawer or tub for toys, and a pullout in a cabinet for dog food."

Marshall prefers not to include a pet shower in the rear foyer area. "If the shower is strictly for the pet, I like to put it in the garage where it doesn't matter if the dog shakes off water, and a messy floor can be hosed down. A garage shower can be used as a boot wash as well. They now make sillcocks (outside water spigots) that mix hot and cold water. Of course, in colder climates, you may need to shut the water off in the winter.

"The rear foyer is also a good place for a message center of some kind," Cuozzo adds. "Since everyone in the family will probably use this entry, it's the best place to leave notes so they aren't missed. Families with young children enjoy blackboards. They're easier to wipe clean than dry-erase boards and chalk doesn't stain clothes. Bulletin boards with pushpins work well with older kids, allowing parents to post soccer schedules or appointment reminder cards."

"Including recycling bins in the rear foyer frees up space in the kitchen and saves steps when it's time to put the recyclables out," remarks Wallman.

"Where extra space is available, a closet for the broom and vacuum, or even a central vacuum's hoses, is a nice addition," continues Wallman. "Some families request a shoe tower; others leave shoes in individual member's cubbies or lockers. Another possibility is to leave an open space under a bench with a metal tray so the family can sit down to remove their shoes and then leave them under the bench.

A drop zone provides a convenient spot for keys, mail, cell phones, and laptops.

advises. "For instance, some people include spice drawers in their cabinets to keep smaller items sorted. But it may be more practical in the long run to choose regular drawers and then add dividers that can be removed or switched later. And, of course, it's important to remember that children grow—so allow space to raise coat hooks, or make sure cubbies are tall enough to accommodate longer coats."

For those who want to maximize the efficiency of an existing space without built-in cabinetry, Chris Kroll, an interior designer in Omaha, Nebraska, says, "ContainerStore.com has an amazing array of organizational products, including message boards, recycling bins, and mail sorting wall units. HoldEverything.com offers a bench with a built-in shoe cabinet, a message center with coat hooks, and countless attractive baskets and boxes. Pottery Barn also has some very attractive benches and cubbies, which are available in black or white finishes."

"Spending some extra time and money planning an efficient, well-organized rear foyer will save the entire family considerable stress for years to come," concludes Cuozzo.

The Wall Message Center from Diamond Cabinets provides a message board, hooks for keys, and slots for mail or note paper—all neatly hidden behind a door on the side of the cabinet.

"When the sky's the limit, a pantry in the rear entry is a convenient spot for homeowners who like to stock up on paper goods, greeting cards, and wrapping paper."

Storage Types

Size restrictions aren't the only things to consider while planning a rear entry. One important consideration is whether to make the storage closed or open. If the foyer is visible from the rest of the home or if guests will be using the entry, homeowners may prefer the formal look provided by a conventional closet or cabinet doors.

"I designed a home for a lady who wanted a dressy rear entry," Wallman recalls. "She chose to have a coat closet and, rather than a built-in drop zone and bench, she asked for enough open space for an antique bench and a chest of drawers with a mirror above it."

"Families with children usually like to leave storage open because that's more convenient," Cuozzo observes. "A row of open lockers or a bench and coat hooks are more popular with these folks than a single coat closet. Anything to make it easier for children to put their backpack where it belongs and hang up their coat. Opening a door and putting something on a hanger can seem like too much effort to a child. I've done several plans where I've designed a bench with a chalkboard above the bench and several lockers on each side."

Whenever possible, it's wise to keep the design flexible so that the area can change with the family and appeal to future homebuyers. "It's probably a good idea not to customize cabinetry too much," Cuozzo

Oak lockers provide a clean, finished look in this Craftsman-style home.

Fitness Rooms: Exercise Your Options

Dimensions

"I've designed fitness rooms as large as 12 × 24 feet," Cuozzo continues. "But a 10 × 12-foot or 12 × 12-foot room is more common. That usually provides enough space for a piece of cardio equipment such as a treadmill, stationary bike, stair climber or an elliptical machine and something for muscle building—a multigym, a trainer or a bench with weights.

"It's important to have about 30 inches clearance between each apparatus so exercisers won't scrape their limbs on a neighboring machine. If possible, it's nice to have some extra space to do lunges and other stretches. People who choose to do aerobics with a video or a routine with a big balance ball will need a fairly large, empty space.

"Especially in the smaller rooms, homeowners often like to mirror one wall. It not only makes the room seem bigger, but it lets them check their form as they're exercising.

Location

"In the Midwest, fitness rooms are often located in the lower level. Bonus rooms over garages are probably the most common spots in homes that don't have basements. These are both particularly good locations because pounding on a treadmill can cause noise and vibrations in adjacent rooms or rooms that may be underneath a fitness room.

"A standard floor should support a couple typical pieces of conventional equipment without any problems. But a fitness room on a second level, especially above a large, open living space, may produce some vibrations. (I-joists used for long spans may deflect more than joists supporting smaller rooms. If this is a concern, it's best to consult a structural engineer who may suggest using I-joists that are 12 or 14 inches deep, rather than the usual 10 inch.)"

"Another important factor to consider in locating a fitness room is to ensure the space is very accessible when it is time to bring the equipment in," notes Grant Gribble of Gribble Interior Group in Orlando and a national spokesperson for the American Society of Interior Designers.

Walls and Floors

"Interestingly, we frequently attempt to make our commercial spaces look somewhat residential while we try to make certain areas of our homes feel more commercial," Gribble

This large lower level fitness room is bordered by a TV area with a colorful world map.

muses. "Homeowners often want their kitchen to look industrial and their home gym to look like a professional gym.

"A washable commercial wall covering can be one way to accomplish this. It's also a practical choice for walls that may be subjected to perspiration oils and grease from equipment. My next choice would be a scrubbable paint with sheen.

"To promote energy, I usually recommend lighter colors, perhaps with some bold accent walls to keep heart rates up or some fun wall graphics, like some 'speed lines'—horizontal stripes that create a sense of motion.

"Machinery won't damage rubberized flooring, which also offers some cushioning and sound absorption, but it can be rather pricey.

Lighting and Ventilation

"I often recommend fluorescent recessed lights for fitness rooms," Gribble continues, "because color rendition is not as important in an exercise space as it is to keep the space cool. Incandescent and halogen lights create more heat than fluorescent. And there are more decorative fluorescent fixtures available now for those who wish to supplement the recessed lights.

"Where possible, operable windows can bring in welcome fresh air to an area that can get rather stale, but window treatments

A mirrored wall visually enlarges the fitness room.

that allow residents to screen bright sunlight and offer privacy are essential.

Amenities

"When it comes to extra amenities, entertainment is the primary feature that comes to mind," Gribble continues.

"To make exercising at home enjoyable, it's important to make sure the room is wired for television, a DVD player or stereo equipment. Since flat screen TVs have become more affordable, hanging a set on the wall doesn't take up much more space than a piece of artwork would.

"I've included a ballet bar for stretching, a small refrigerator for juices and health drinks, racks or hooks for towels, and occasionally, space for a massage table."

"A final feature I sometimes incorporate," adds Cuozzo, "is a sauna. They're not as

popular here as they are in Europe, but they are becoming more common."

SMARTtip

The New Must-Have Room

"Home fitness rooms are becoming a standard feature in nearly all of the custom homes I design," notes home designer Carl Cuozzo. "Homeowners enjoy the convenience of not having to drive to a gym and wait in line to use a machine, and the freedom to select their entertainment and to exercise privately."

A wall-mounted television entertains exercisers.

Ornamental Grasses: Laid Back Landscaping

Until recently, my clients rarely listed ornamental grasses on their "must have" landscaping lists. Today, roses and lilacs still top most lists, but more and more people are also requesting ornamental grasses as they recognize the beautiful textures, colors, and movements they contribute.

Of course, smart landscape designers have long been privy to the benefits of incorporating grasses into their designs—but not just for their good looks. On a continent that once contained the largest grassland prairie on earth, these plants readily thrive in our landscapes.

In addition to being virtually pest and disease free, they require little fertilizing, maintenance, or water. (Compare that to ever-thirsty turf lawns that cost Americans an estimated 30 billion a year to plant, maintain, and promote.)

An Eclectic Cast

From a petite 2 inches to a towering 15 feet in height, ornamental grasses grow in every nook and cranny of the globe. While most grasses prefer sunnier locales, a few varieties tolerate shade. For landscaping purposes, rushes, sedges, and bamboos are generally included when referring to ornamental grasses.

Two main categories define and help determine how ornamental grasses are used in the landscape. Running grasses are those that spread by underground stems called rhizomes or above ground stems called stolons. Most running grasses are invasive and can overwhelm a garden. However, they can be quite valuable in a large, open spot, where their spreading ground cover can control erosion. The common ribbon grass with its variegated foliage is one such example.

Clumping grasses are a better behaved lot. This group, which contains a wide variety of shapes and forms, from upright to mounded, stay where you plant them—making them a more ideal choice for the home landscape.

Supporting and Starring Roles

The strong, vertical nature of many ornamental grasses makes them a terrific partner to other perennials. They group especially well with shrub roses and more "airy" perennials such as Russian sage, baby's breath, and yarrow. They also look great next to denser perennials such as rudbekia, autumn joy sedum, and asters.

While ornamental grasses play a supporting role for much of the season, they become the star of the garden show when autumn's curtain goes up. This is when most grasses "bloom" or show what is properly known as their "inflorescence." As fall turns into winter, the stalks and inflorescence give the landscape structure after other plants have gone to bed. For many gardeners, the sight of frost or a snow dusting on the feathery plumes of a Miscanthus grass can be every bit as beautiful as a blooming rose in June.

Ornamental grasses don't need to be restricted to naturalistic or informal settings. On the contrary, the uniform habit and dramatic structure of most ornamental grasses allow novel adaptations to more traditional plant choices in formal settings. Planted as matching pairs on either side of a door, ornamental grasses can create a look every bit as formal as

Think of ornamental grasses as the workhorses of the landscape. Use them in plant borders, to enclose a seating area, and to fill in among other plants.

Ornamental grasses require little in the way of upkeep and maintenance. You can find grasses for most climate zones.

Keep the rest of your landscape in mind when selecting ornamental grasses. They can range from 2 in. to over 15 ft. in height.

boxwood topiaries—with a lot less upkeep. As a traditional "spike" is used in the center of a container planting, ornamental grasses can be thought of as the "spike" in the landscape.

Colorful Sets

While ornamental grasses aren't the first plants most people think of when adding color to the landscape, they are certainly not without color. It is the subtle and ever-changing color of their foliage that defines the species. Much like trees, grasses undergo changes that reflect the passing seasons. A plant that is a luxuriant green in May can turn rich gold or barn red by the time the kids are out trick-or-treating.

Variegated varieties add a long season of color to the garden palette. The popular 'Zebrinas' *Miscanthus* grass features gold stripes while 'Elijah Blue' fescue adds a blue hue to the garden year round. 'Bowles Golden' carex features bright yellow tufts and Japanese blood grass, is—you guessed it—red.

The most commonly planted ornamental grass has come to be 'Karl Forester' *Calamagrostis* (feather reed grass), in part because of its vigorous early season growth compared with other grasses. Loose, feathery pink "flowers" appear in June. As the seed heads mature, they become a golden tan color that lasts through the fall season. Both the leaves and flowers of 'Karl Forester' grass are

very upright, giving it an architectural quality. While it can be used in tight spaces, it is often planted in mass as well.

A Stunning Performance

Two bonuses of ornamental grasses that are often overlooked are movement and sound. Their vertical nature captures the breeze, lending a sense of animation to the landscape and producing a rushing sound.

Ornamental grasses are also extraordinarily translucent. When side-lit or back-lit by the sun (early or late in the day) grasses take on a luminous quality unsurpassed by other landscape plants. This ability to shine is even more valuable come late autumn and winter when flowering perennials have gone to bed for the season and the annuals have been tossed out with the fallen leaves.

Also, with the growing popularity of outdoor lighting, few plants provide as much drama as grasses when featured with accent lighting. If you have a large piece of ground, consider incorporating larger varieties into your privacy barrier. A variety of deciduous and evergreen shrubs and grasses makes for a much more intriguing border than a standard straight hedge. Pampas grasses can reach as high as 14 feet but, remember, they need to be cut down in the spring, so carefully site them where you won't mind sacrificing some early spring privacy.

Even if you don't have any ground at all, many ornamental grass varieties look outstanding when used in container plantings. Although it's an annual where I live, purple fountain grass is a mainstay in my container-planting designs. Grasses usually look best when they can have a whole pot to themselves that can be grouped with other pots filled with flowering annuals or perennials.

Clearing the Stage

Ornamental grasses along the side of the house, especially on the south or west side, are a terrific choice for a low-maintenance foundation planting. While shrubs can require hours to extract all the dead leaves they've caught, grasses provide little opportunity for leaves to catch—making both fall and spring cleanup a breeze.

Drawbacks to grasses include the "dead period" between cutting them back in early spring and the emergence of new growth. Planting early spring bulbs, such as daffodils, nearby can help to fill this void.

Check with your local extension office for advice on the type of ornamental grasses that grow best in your region. Visit your local nursery to ask questions and peruse plants firsthand. Keep in mind that grasses —even more than most perennials—look much better once established in the ground, rather than restricted in a pot waiting for purchase. If you haven't given them a chance in your landscape yet—what are you waiting for?

Plan #161002

Dimensions: 64'2" W x 44'2" D
Levels: 1
Heated Square Footage: 1,860
Bedrooms: 3
Bathrooms: 2
Foundation: Basement
Materials List Available: Yes
Price Category: D

Images provided by designer/architect.

The brick, stone, and cedar shake facade provides color and texture to the exterior, while the unique nooks and angles inside this delightful one-level home give it character.

Features:

- **Great Room/Dining Room:** This spacious great room is furnished with a wood-burning fireplace, a high ceiling, and French doors. Wide entrances to the breakfast room and dining room expand its space to comfortably hold large gatherings.

- **Kitchen:** The breakfast bar offers additional seating. The covered porch lets you enjoy a view of the landscape and is conveniently located for outdoor meals off this kitchen and breakfast area.

- **Master Suite:** The master suite is a private retreat. An alcove creates a comfortable sitting area, and an angled entry leads to the bath with whirlpool and a double-bowl vanity.

Left Side Elevation

Right Side Elevation

Rear Elevation

Copyright by designer/architect.

Dining Room

Living Room / Dining Room

Great Room/Breakfast Area

Great Room

Installing Rods and Poles

The way to install a rod or pole depends on the type it is, the brackets that will hold it, the weight of the window treatment, and the surface to which it is being fastened. Given below are some general guidelines, but for specific installation procedures, refer to the instructions that accompany the rod or pole.

- Use a stepladder to reach high places.

- Use the proper tools.

- Take accurate measurements.

- Work with a helper.

- If attaching a bracket to wood, first drill small pilot holes to avoid splitting the wood.

- Consider using wall anchors, particularly for the heavier window treatments.

- Use a level as needed to help you position the brackets for the pole or rod.

- Take care not to drill or hammer into any pipes or electrical wiring.

Because they're designed to stand out, decorative poles and their finials require more room for installation than conventional drapery rods. Finials add inches to the ends of a window treatment, so make sure you have enough wall room to display your hardware to its full advantage. And because decorative rods are often heavy, be certain your window frames and walls can support the weight.

Plan #121110

Dimensions: 52' W x 45'4" D
Levels: 1.5
Heated Square Footage: 1,855
Main Level Sq. Ft.: 1,297
Upper Level Sq. Ft.: 558
Bedrooms: 4
Bathrooms: 2½
Foundation: Full basement; crawl space for fee
Materials List Available: Yes
Price Category: D

Images provided by designer/architect.

If bright and sunny rooms make you happy, you'll love the open design of this home.

Features:

- Great Room: With its spectacular 13-ft.-high ceiling, this great room is sure to impress your family and friends. Its large size and cozy fireplace make it perfect for entertaining.

- Breakfast Room: A handy snack bar connects this room to the kitchen. The counter is the perfect place to leave a note for a family member or grab a bite to go. Large windows allow the sunshine to stream through at meal times.

- Master Suite: This master suite features a large walk-in closet, a whirlpool bath, a skylight, his and her sinks, and a 9-ft. stepped ceiling.

- Secondary Bedrooms: Upstairs, three additional bedrooms share a bathroom. This is the perfect setup for siblings.

Main Level Floor Plan

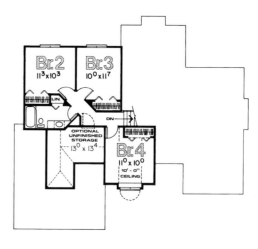

Upper Level Floor Plan

Copyright by designer/architect.

Plan #131015

Dimensions: 57'4" W x 56'10" D

Levels: 1

Heated Square Footage: 1,860

Bedrooms: 3

Bathrooms: 2

Foundation: Crawl space, slab, or basement

Materials List Available: Yes

Price Category: E

This home, as shown in the photograph, may differ from the actual blueprints. For more detailed information, please check the floor plans carefully.

Images provided by designer/architect.

The mixture of country charm and formal elegance is sure to thrill any family looking for a distinctive and comfortable home.

Features:

- Great Room: Separated from the dining room by a columned arch, this spacious room has a stepped ceiling, a built-in media center, and a fireplace. French doors within a rear bay lead to the large backyard patio at the rear of the house.

- Dining Room: Graced by a bay window, this formal room has an impressive 11-ft. 6-in.-high stepped ceiling.

- Breakfast Room: With a 12-ft. sloped ceiling, this room shares an eating bar with the kitchen.

- Master Bedroom: The 10-ft. tray ceiling and bay window contribute elegance, and the walk-in closet and bath with a bayed nook, whirlpool tub, and separate shower make it practical.

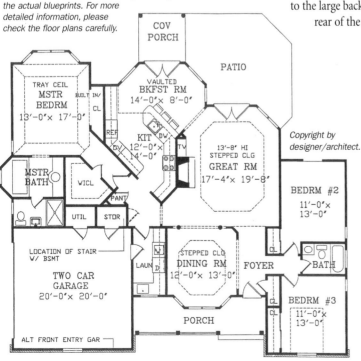

Copyright by designer/architect.

Rear Elevation

Great Room

Plan #121141

Dimensions: 54' W x 45'4" D
Levels: 1.5
Heated Square Footage: 1,865
Main Level Sq. Ft.: 1,301
Upper Level Sq. Ft.: 564
Bedrooms: 4
Bathrooms: 2½
Foundation: Basement;
crawl space for fee
Materials List Available: Yes
Price Category: D

CAD FILE AVAILABLE

Images provided by designer/architect.

This lovely home has an interior designed with daily living in mind — and ideal environment for a growing family.

Features:

- Porch: Walk into the house through this covered porch, perfect for relaxing during the heat of the day or the cool of the evening.

- Breakfast Room: This room lets in the morning sunshine while you enjoy a meal at the table or at the breakfast bar. A desk ensures that stray papers and forms have an easy-to-find home.

- Master Suite: This large master suite features a considerable walk-in closet, his and her sinks, and separate toilet room.

- Secondary Bedrooms: Additional bedrooms are upstairs, the three of which share a bathroom. Also upstairs is a large storage space for those extra items.

Main Level Floor Plan

TRANS.   TRANS.

Mbr.
13⁰ x 14⁰

Grt. rm.
14⁰ x 18⁷
17'-0" CEILING

Bfst.
11⁰ x 12⁴

Kit.
10⁸ x 11³

SNACK BAR
DESK   PANT.
UP   DN

E.

Din.
11⁰ x 11⁰

Gar.
22⁰ x 22⁴

W.
D.

COVERED
PORCH

45'-4"
54'-0"

Upper Level Floor Plan

Br. 2
10⁰ x 11⁶

Br. 3
11³ x 10³

OPEN TO BELOW

L
DN

Br. 4
11⁰ x 10⁰

UNFINISHED
Sto.
18⁰ x 21⁸

Copyright by designer/architect.

Plan #121194

Dimensions: 49' W x 60' D
Levels: 1.5
Heated Square Footage: 1,867
Main Level Sq. Ft.: 1,375
Upper Level Sq. Ft.: 492
Bedrooms: 3
Bathrooms: 2½
Foundation: Slab; basement for fee
Materials List Available: Yes
Price Category: D

Images provided by designer/architect.

You'll be happy to have this magnificent home welcoming you after a long day.

Features:

- Porches: The front porch is perfect for relaxing or playing board games with family or friends. The porches in the back are wonderful for entertaining, especially the screened-in porch, which provides outdoor living space rain or shine.

- Great Room: The open space that encompasses the living room, great room, and dining room is wonderful for the creative decorator, as the space is suitable for many

layouts. The gorgeous 14-ft.-high ceiling adds to the beauty of the room and the house as a whole.

- Master Suite: This expansive master suite has a 9-ft.-high ceiling, his and her sinks, and a large closet area.

- Optional Game Room: This space on the second floor can be turned into a game room, which is fun for the kids and the kids at heart.

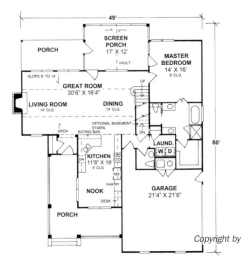

Main Level Floor Plan

Upper Level Floor Plan

Copyright by designer/architect.

Plan #121014

Dimensions: 52' W x 47'4" D
Levels: 1.5
Heated Square Footage: 1,869
Main Level Sq. Ft.: 1,421
Upper Level Sq. Ft.: 448
Bedrooms: 3
Bathrooms: 2½
Foundation: Basement;
crawl space or slab available for fee
Materials List Available: Yes
Price Category: D

Images provided by designer/architect.

This compact home is packed with all the amenities you'll need for a gracious lifestyle.

Features:

- Ceiling Height: 8 ft. except as noted.

- Great Room: A soaring ceiling and six tall transom-topped windows make this a light and airy spot for entertaining.

- Formal Dining Room: This elegant room is ideal for entertaining dinner guests.

- Breakfast Area: This sunny area shares a see-through fireplace with the great room. It's the perfect place to start the day.

- Master Suite: Here are all the features you expect to find in large luxury homes. Wake up to tall, sloped ceilings, and enjoy the corner whirlpool, separate shower, and vanity. A large walk-in closet provides plenty of wardrobe storage.

- Attached Garage: The garage provides two bays of parking plus plenty of storage space.

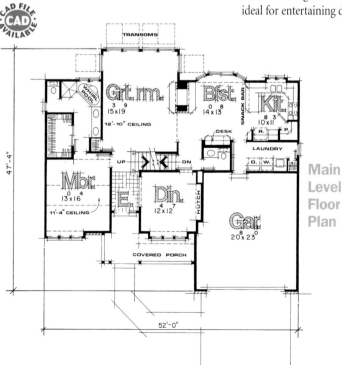

Main Level Floor Plan

Upper Level Floor Plan

Copyright by designer/architect.

Plan #141012

Dimensions: 44'4" W x 38' D

Levels: 2

Heated Square Footage: 1,870

Main Level Sq. Ft.: 1,159

Upper Level Sq. Ft.: 711

Bedrooms: 3

Bathrooms: 2½

Foundation: Basement

Materials List Available: Yes

Price Category: D

Country charm comes to mind with this classic two story design.

Features:

- Ceiling Height: 8 ft.

- Porch: This full shed porch with dormers creates a look few can resist.

- Living/Dining: This open living/dining area invites you to come in and sit a spell.

- Kitchen: This kitchen allows the host to see their guests from the sink through the opening in the angled walls.

- Breakfast Area: The cathedral ceiling in this breakfast area creates a sunroom effect at the rear of the house.

- Master Suite: This spacious master suite has all the amenities, including a double bowl vanity, corner tub, walk in closet, and 5-ft. shower.

- Bedrooms: Two large bedrooms upstairs share a hall bath.

- Balcony: This upstairs balcony is lit by the center dormer, creating a cozy study alcove.

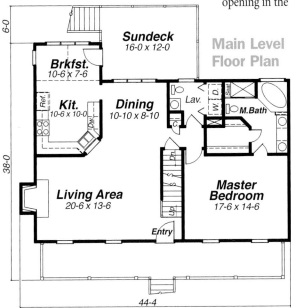

Main Level Floor Plan

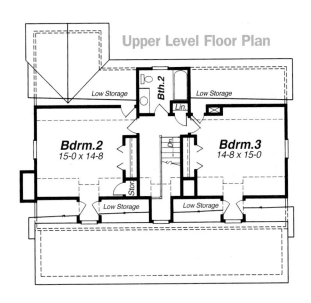

Upper Level Floor Plan

Plan #481151

Dimensions: 79'6" W x 66' D

Levels: 1

Heated Square Footage: 1,873

Bedrooms: 1

Bathrooms: 1½

Foundation: Walkout

Materials List Available: No

Price Category: D

Images provided by designer/architect.

CAD FILE AVAILABLE

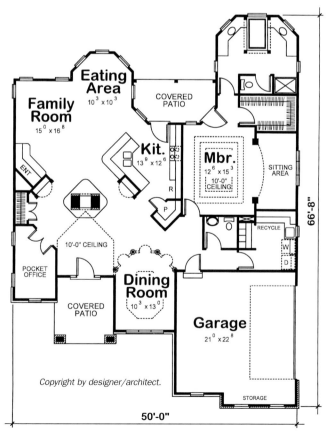

Copyright by designer/architect.

Plan #121399

Images provided by designer/architect.

CAD FILE AVAILABLE

Dimensions: 50' W x 66'8" D

Levels: 1

Heated Square Footage: 1,888

Bedrooms: 1

Bathrooms: 1½

Foundation: Slab; crawl space or basement for fee

Materials List Available: Yes

Price Category: D

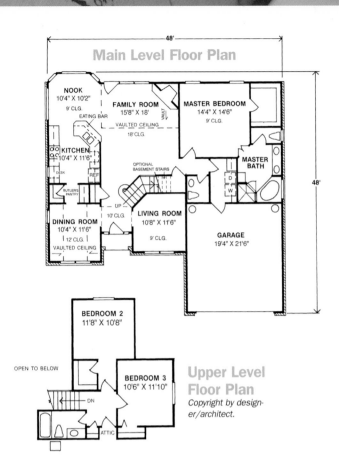

Main Level Floor Plan

NOOK
10'4" X 10'2"
9' CLG.

FAMILY ROOM
15'8" X 18'
VAULTED CEILING
18' CLG.

MASTER BEDROOM
14'4" X 14'6"
9' CLG.

EATING BAR

KITCHEN
10'4" X 11'6"

DESK

REF

OPTIONAL BASEMENT STAIRS

MASTER BATH

BUTLER'S PANTRY

UP

LIVING ROOM
10'8" X 11'6"
9' CLG.

W

D

DINING ROOM
10'4" X 11'6"
12' CLG.
VAULTED CEILING

10' CLG.

GARAGE
19'4" X 21'6"

48'

48'

Plan #121172

Dimensions: 48' W x 48' D
Levels: 1.5
Heated Square Footage: 1,897
Main Level Sq. Ft.: 1,448
Upper Level Sq. Ft.: 449
Bedrooms: 3
Bathrooms: 2½
Foundation: Slab; basement for fee
Material List Available: Yes
Price Category: D

Images provided by designer/architect.

This home, as shown in the photograph, may differ from the actual blueprints. For more detailed information, please check the floor plans carefully.

BEDROOM 2
11'8" X 10'8"

OPEN TO BELOW

BEDROOM 3
10'6" X 11'10"

DN

ATTIC

Upper Level Floor Plan

Copyright by designer/architect.

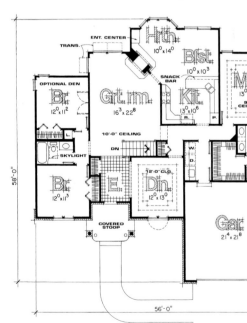
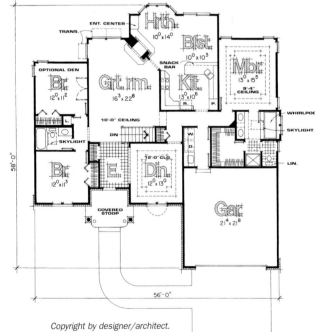

ENT. CENTER

TRANS.

Hrth.
10'0 x 14'0

Bfst.
10'0 x 10'3

OPTIONAL DEN

Br.
12'0 x 11'2

Grt. rm.
16'3 x 22'8

SNACK BAR

Kit.
13'0 x 10'6

R.

P.

Mbr.
13'0 x 15'5
9'-4" CEILING

WHIRLPOOL

SKYLIGHT

10'-0" CEILING

SKYLIGHT

DN

W.

D.

LIN.

Br.
12'0 x 11'3

Dn.
12'0 x 13'0
12'-0" CLG.

Gar.
21'4 x 21'8

COVERED STOOP

58'-0"

56'-0"

Plan #121001

Dimensions: 56' W x 58' D
Levels: 1
Heated Square Footage: 1,911
Bedrooms: 3
Bathrooms: 2
Foundation: Basement
Materials List Available: Yes
Price Category: D

Images provided by designer/architect.

CAD FILE AVAILABLE

Copyright by designer/architect.

Plan #151068

Dimensions: 57' W x 61'8" D
Levels: 1
Heated Square Footage: 1,880
Bedrooms: 4
Bathrooms: 2
Foundation: Crawl space, slab, or basement
CompleteCost List Available: Yes
Price Category: D

Images provided by designer/architect.

The graceful front porch sets the tone for this well-designed home with open, airy spaces.

Features:

- **Great Room:** This spacious great room has a 10-ft. boxed ceiling and opens to the rear grilling porch.

- **Dining Room:** This room is perfect for a formal dinner party or a gathering of family and friends.

- **Kitchen:** The family cook will love the step-saving layout in this kitchen, and everyone will appreciate the convenient snack bar.

- **Breakfast Room:** The bay window lets morning sunshine cheer the whole family.

- **Master Suite:** At the end of the day, you can relax by the fireplace or enjoy the luxurious bath with a whirlpool tub, separate shower, walk-in closet, and split vanities.

- **Study:** Turn bedroom 4 into a study where family members can spend some quiet reading time.

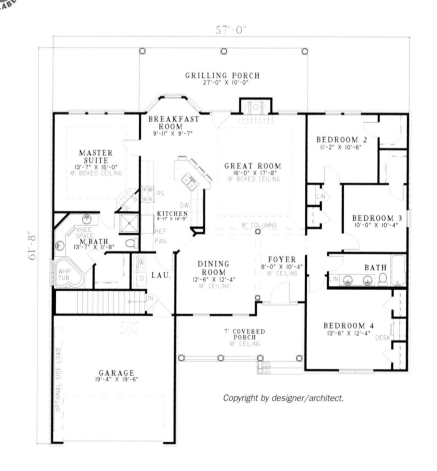

Copyright by designer/architect.

Plan #121092

Dimensions: 65'4" W x 52'8" D
Levels: 1
Heated Square Footage: 3,225
Main Level Sq. Ft.: 1,887
Basement Level Sq. Ft.: 1,338
Bedrooms: 3
Bathrooms: 2½
Foundation: Basement
Materials List Available: Yes
Price Category: D

Images provided by designer/architect.

This is the design if you want a home that will be easy to expand as your family grows.

Features:

- Entry: Both the dining room and great room are immediately accessible from this lovely entry.
- Great Room: The transom-topped bowed windows highlight the spacious feeling here.
- Gathering Room: Also with an angled ceiling, this room has a fireplace as well as a built-in entertainment center and bookcases.
- Dining Room: This elegant room features a 13-ft. boxed ceiling and majestic window around which you'll love to decorate.
- Kitchen: Designed for convenience, this kitchen includes a lovely angled ceiling and gazebo-shaped breakfast area.
- Basement: Use the plans for finishing a family room and two bedrooms when the time is right.

Main Level Floor Plan

Basement Level Floor Plan

Copyright by designer/architect.

Plan #131035

Dimensions: 65'4" W x 45'10" D
Levels: 1
Heated Square Footage: 1,892
Bedrooms: 3
Bathrooms: 2½
Foundation: Crawl space, slab, or basement
Materials List Available: Yes
Price Category: E

Images provided by designer/architect.

Families who love a mixture of traditional — a big front porch, simple roofline, and bay windows—and contemporary—an open floor plan—will love this charming home.

Features:

- Great Room: Central to this home, the open living and entertaining areas allow the family to gather effortlessly and create the perfect spot for entertaining.

- Dining Room: Volume ceilings both here and in the great room further enhance the spaciousness the open floor plan creates.

- Master Suite: Positioned on the opposite end of the other two bedrooms in the split-bedroom plan, this master suite gives an unusual amount of privacy and quiet in a home of this size.

- Bonus Room: Located over the attached garage, this bonus room gives you a place to finish for a study or a separate game room.

Rear Elevation

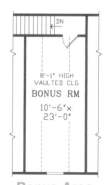

Bonus Area

Copyright by designer/architect.

Plan #351191

Dimensions: 69' W x 61'8" D

Levels: 1

Heated Square Footage: 1,919

Bedrooms: 3

Bathrooms: 2½

Foundation: Basement

Materials List Available: Yes

Price Category: D

This home is packed with all the features that you've always wanted, all designed within a small footprint.

Features:

- **Great Room:** This beautiful room includes vaulted ceilings, built-in cabinets, and a gas-log fireplace.

- **Kitchen:** You'll love the location of this room — it is close to the breakfast area, dining room, and garage entrance.

- **Master Suite:** Filled with amenities, this room boasts a trayed ceiling, dual lavatories, a separate toilet room, a whirlpool tub, separate shower, and his and her closets.

- **Bonus Room:** The flexibility of this area is perfect, as it can be a playroom, a home office, a guest room, or whatever you choose.

Images provided by designer/architect.

Main Level Floor Plan

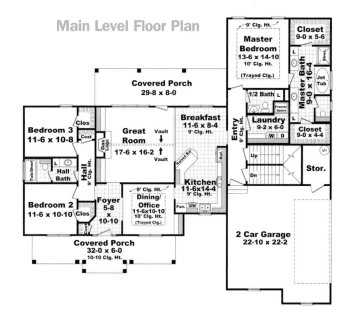

Bonus Area Floor Plan

Copyright by designer/architect.

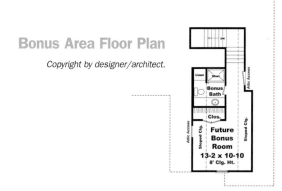

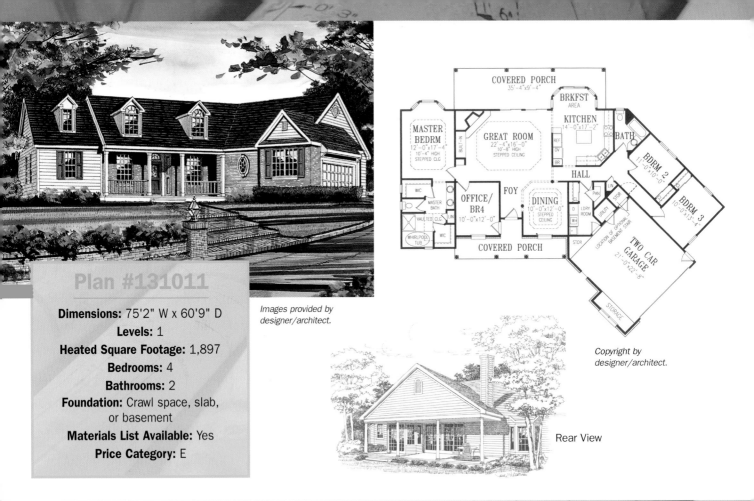

Images provided by designer/architect.

Copyright by designer/architect.

Rear View

Plan #131011

Dimensions: 75'2" W x 60'9" D

Levels: 1

Heated Square Footage: 1,897

Bedrooms: 4

Bathrooms: 2

Foundation: Crawl space, slab, or basement

Materials List Available: Yes

Price Category: E

Images provided by designer/architect.

Copyright by designer/architect.

CAD FILE AVAILABLE

Bonus Area Floor Plan

Plan #151089

Dimensions: 84' W x 55'6" D

Levels: 1

Heated Square Footage: 1,921

Bedrooms: 3

Bathrooms: 3

Foundation: Crawl space, slab, or basement

CompleteCost List Available: Yes

Price Category: D

Main Level Floor Plan

Copyright by designer/architect.

SPA

MASTER
12/10 X 16/0
9' CLG

VAULTED
GREAT RM.
14/6 X 17/8

VAULTED
PORCH

VAULTED
DINING
13/0 x 12/0

3RD CAR/
SHOP
11/0 x 16/6

VAULTED
OFFICE
10/2 x 11/6

UP

VAULTED

GARAGE
19/0 X 21/0

REF

STOR

SHELVES

55'

◀ 45' ▶

Images provided by designer/architect.

Rear Elevation

CAD FILE AVAILABLE CAD

Upper Level Floor Plan

BR. 3
11/0 10/1

STOR

NICHE
DN

BR. 2
12/0 X 10/1

LINEN

OPEN TO BELOW

Plan #441032

Dimensions: 45' W x 55' D
Levels: 2
Heated Square Footage: 1,944
Main Level Sq. Ft.: 1,514
Upper Level Sq. Ft.: 430
Bedrooms: 3
Bathrooms: 2½
Foundation: Crawl space; slab or basement available for fee
Materials List Available: No
Price Category: D

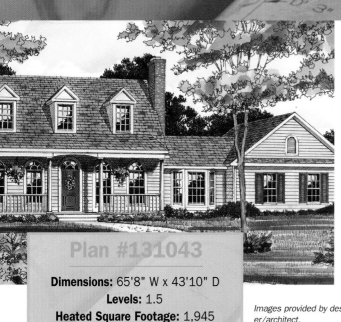

COVERED PORCH
18'-0" x 10'-0"

PASS-THRU

9'-4"
TRAY CEIL
MSTR BEDRM
12'-0" X 17'-0"

LAV

9'-4"
STEPPED CLG

PANTRY W D

LAUN UTIL

CLOS OR
BUILT-IN

STOR/DN TO
OPT. BSMT

VAULTED CLG

REF

CL

WICL

9'-4"
STEPPED CLG
GREAT RM
14'-4" X 28'-8"

COUNTRY
KITCHEN
12'-0" x
24'-0"

TWO CAR GARAGE
20'-0" X 20'-0"

MSTR
BATH

UP

CL

COVERED
PORCH
29'-0" X 8'-0"

Main Level Floor Plan

Images provided by designer/architect.

BATH

VAULTED
CLG

LIN

9'-0" HIGH

BEDRM #2
12'-0" x
13'-4"

DN

BEDRM #3
12'-0" x
13'-4"

CL

CL

Upper Level Floor Plan

Copyright by designer/architect.

Plan #131043

Dimensions: 65'8" W x 43'10" D
Levels: 1.5
Heated Square Footage: 1,945
Main Level Sq. Ft.: 1,375
Upper Level Sq. Ft.: 570
Bedrooms: 3
Bathrooms: 2½
Foundation: Crawl space, slab, or basement
Materials List Available: Yes
Price Category: E

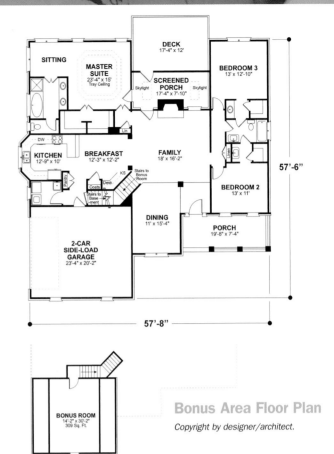

Images provided by designer/architect.

CAD FILE AVAILABLE

Plan #101028

Dimensions: 57'8" W x 57'6" D

Levels: 1

Heated Square Footage: 1,963

Bedrooms: 3

Bathrooms: 2

Foundation: Basement

Materials List Available: No

Price Category: D

Floor Plan Labels (Plan #101028)

- SITTING
- MASTER SUITE 23'-4" x 15' Tray Ceiling
- DECK 17'-4" x 12'
- BEDROOM 3 13' x 12'-10"
- SCREENED PORCH 17'-4" x 7'-10" Skylight Skylight
- KITCHEN 12'-9" x 10'
- BREAKFAST 12'-3" x 12'-2"
- FAMILY 18' x 16'-2"
- DW
- Lin
- BEDROOM 2 13' x 11'
- KS
- Stairs to Bonus Room
- Coats Desk
- Stairs to Basement
- DINING 11' x 15'-4"
- PORCH 19'-8" x 7'-4"
- 2-CAR SIDE-LOAD GARAGE 23'-4" x 20'-2"

57'-6"

57'-8"

BONUS ROOM 14'-2" x 30'-2" 309 Sq. Ft.

Bonus Area Floor Plan

Copyright by designer/architect.

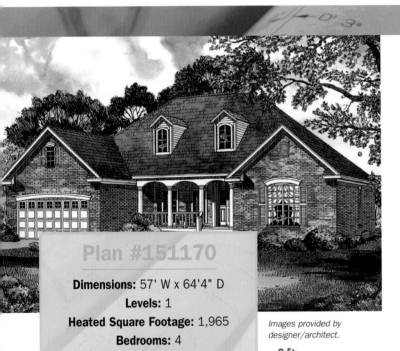

Plan #151170

Dimensions: 57' W x 64'4" D

Levels: 1

Heated Square Footage: 1,965

Bedrooms: 4

Bathrooms: 2

Foundation: Crawl space, slab; basement or daylight basement for fee

CompleteCost List Available: Yes

Price Category: D

Images provided by designer/architect.

CAD FILE AVAILABLE

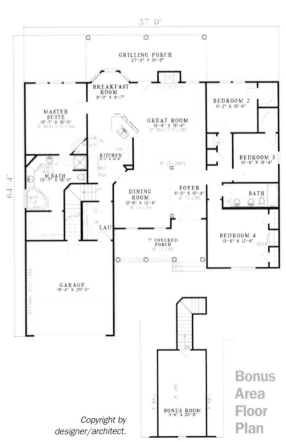

Floor Plan Labels (Plan #151170)

57' 0"

64'-4"

- GRILLING PORCH 27'-0" X 10'-0"
- BREAKFAST ROOM 9'-11" X 9'-7"
- MASTER SUITE 13'-7" X 16'-0"
- GREAT ROOM 15'-6" X 19'-4"
- BEDROOM 2 11'-2" X 10'-6"
- KITCHEN 9'-11" X 14'-8"
- M. BATH 13'-7" X 10'
- BEDROOM 3 10'-0" X 10'-4"
- DINING ROOM 12'-6" X 12'-4"
- FOYER 8'-0" X 10'-4"
- BATH
- LAU
- 7' COVERED PORCH
- BEDROOM 4 13'-6" X 12'-4"
- GARAGE 19'-4" X 20'-0"

BONUS ROOM 11'-6" X 20'-0"

Bonus Area Floor Plan

Copyright by designer/architect.

order direct: 1-800-523-6789

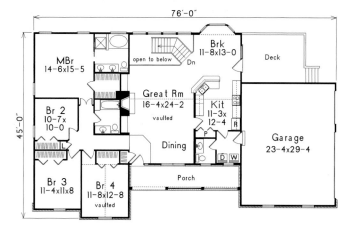

Plan #321006

Dimensions: 76' W x 45' D

Levels: 1, optional lower

Heated Square Footage: 1,977

Optional Basement Level

Sq. Ft.: 1,416

Bedrooms: 4

Bathrooms: 2½

Foundation: Basement

Materials List Available: Yes

Price Category: D

Images provided by designer/architect.

Optional Basement Level Floor Plan

Copyright by designer/architect.

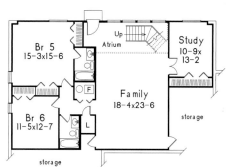

Plan #211048

Dimensions: 66' W x 60' D

Levels: 1

Heated Square Footage: 2,002

Bedrooms: 3

Bathrooms: 2

Foundation: Crawl space, slab

Materials List Available: Yes

Price Category: D

Images provided by designer/architect.

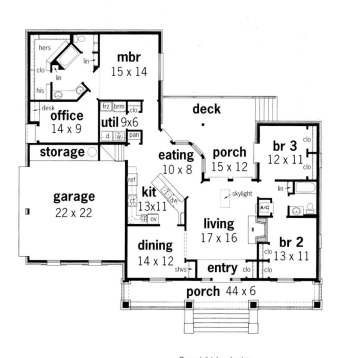

Copyright by designer/architect.

**Main Level
Floor Plan**

*Images provided by
designer/architect.*

Plan #321313

Dimensions: 50'8" W x 47' D

Levels: 1.5

Heated Square Footage: 1,980

Main Level Sq. Ft.: 1,337

Upper Level Sq. Ft.: 643

Bedrooms: 3

Bathrooms: 2½

Foundation: Basement

Material List Available: Yes

Price Category: D

Upper Level Floor Plan

Copyright by designer/architect.

Plan #101006

Dimensions: 63' W x 58' D

Levels: 1

Heated Square Footage: 1,982

Bedrooms: 3

Bathrooms: 2½

Foundation: Crawl space, slab,
basement, or walkout

Materials List Available: Yes

Price Category: D

*Images provided by
designer/architect.*

Copyright by designer/architect.

SMARTtip

Art in Pools

The tiled walls and floor of a pool make great canvases for art,
so incorporate a serious or whimsical design. Also, make the
stairs wide and shallow to form a wading area for kids.

Plan #121153

Dimensions: 62' W x 42'6" D

Levels: 1.5

Heated Square Footage: 1,984

Main Level Sq. Ft.: 1,487

Upper Level Sq. Ft.: 497

Bedrooms: 3

Bathrooms: 2½

Foundation: Slab; basement for fee

Material List Available: Yes

Price Category: D

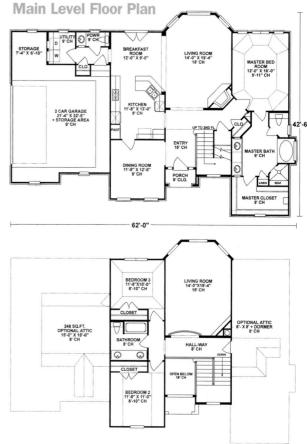

Main Level Floor Plan

Images provided by designer/architect.

CAD FILE AVAILABLE

Upper Level Floor Plan

Copyright by designer/architect.

Plan #121322

Dimensions: 44'8" W x 70'8" D

Levels: 1.5

Heated Square Footage: 1,991

Main Level Sq. Ft.: 1,619

Upper Level Sq. Ft.: 372

Bedrooms: 3

Bathrooms: 3

Foundation: Basement

Materials List Available: Yes

Price Category: D

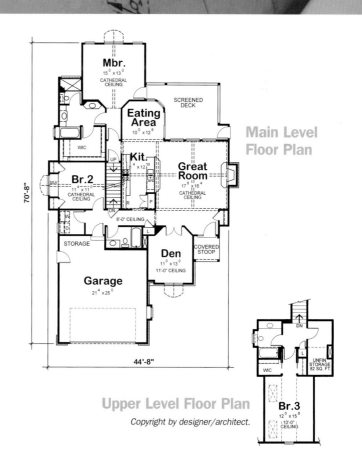

Images provided by designer/architect.

CAD FILE AVAILABLE

Main Level Floor Plan

Upper Level Floor Plan

Copyright by designer/architect.

Plan #101005

Dimensions: 63' W x 57'2" D

Levels: 1

Heated Square Footage: 1,992

Bedrooms: 3

Bathrooms: 2½

Foundation: Crawl space, slab, or basement

Materials List Available: Yes

Price Category: D

Images provided by designer/architect.

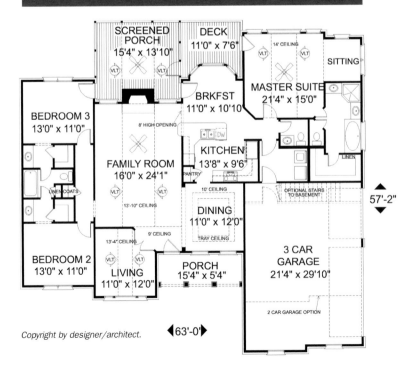

Rear View

This midsized ranch is accented with Palladian windows and inviting front porch.

Features:

- Ceiling Height: 9 ft. unless otherwise noted.

- Special Ceilings: Tray or vaulted ceilings adorn the living room, family room, dining room, and master suite.

- Kitchen: This bright and airy kitchen is designed to be a pleasure in which to work. It shares a big bay window with the contiguous breakfast room.

- Breakfast Room: The light streaming in from the bay window makes this the perfect place to linger with coffee and the Sunday paper.

- Master Suite: This lovely suite is exceptional, with its sitting area and direct access to the deck, as well as a full-featured bath, and spacious walk-in closet.

- Secondary Bedrooms: The other bedrooms each measure about 13 ft. x 11 ft. They have walk-in closets and share a "Jack-and-Jill" bath.

SCREENED PORCH 15'4" x 13'10"

DECK 11'0" x 7'6"

14' CEILING

SITTING

MASTER SUITE 21'4" x 15'0"

BEDROOM 3 13'0" x 11'0"

BRKFST 11'0" x 10'10

8' HIGH OPENING

KITCHEN 13'8" x 9'6"

LINEN

FAMILY ROOM 16'0" x 24'1"

PANTRY

10' CEILING

OPTIONAL STAIRS TO BASEMENT

13'-10" CEILING

DINING 11'0" x 12'0"

TRAY CEILING

9' CEILING

57'-2"

BEDROOM 2 13'0" x 11'0"

13'-4" CEILING

LIVING 11'0" x 12'0"

PORCH 15'4" x 5'4"

3 CAR GARAGE 21'4" x 29'10"

2 CAR GARAGE OPTION

Copyright by designer/architect.

◄63'-0"►

Kitchen

Living Room

Dining Room

Family Room

Master Bedroom

Master Bath

Plan #121290

Dimensions: 66' W x 58' D

Levels: 1

Heated Square Footage: 1,995

Bedrooms: 3

Bathrooms: 2

Foundation: Basement

Materials List Available: Yes

Price Category: D

Images provided by designer/architect.

This home, as shown in the photograph, may differ from actual blueprints. For more detailed information, please check the floor plans carefully.

The exterior of this home boasts several porches that are wonderful for relaxing with a book or with some friends.

Features:

• **Porches:** Two covered porches located at the front and side of the home, and one screened-in porch at the rear, are perfect for entertaining or relaxing, rain or shine.

• **Living Room:** Gather around the fireplace in this living room where you can easily entertain a group of dinner guests or watch a movie with the kids.

• **Kitchen:** You'll love to cook in this beautiful kitchen, which includes a center island, an eating bar, and a desk to keep papers and recipes organized.

• **Master Suite:** Tucked away from the busier areas of the home, you can relax in this master suite, which has a large walk-in closet, dual vanity, and tub.

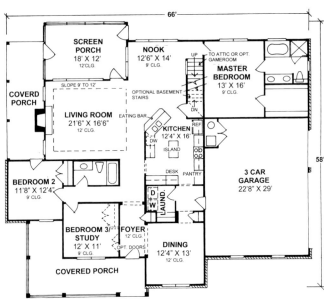

Optional Bonus Area

Copyright by designer/architect.

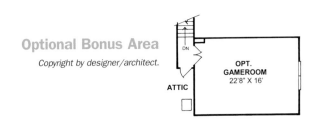

Plan #121015

Dimensions: 52' W x 47'4" D
Levels: 1.5
Heated Square Footage: 1,999
Main Level Sq. Ft.: 1,421
Upper Level Sq. Ft.: 578
Bedrooms: 4
Bathrooms: 2½
Foundation: Basement
Materials List Available: Yes
Price Category: D

This home, as shown in the photograph, may differ from the actual blueprints. For more detailed information, please check the floor plans carefully.

Images provided by designer/architect.

Hipped roofs and a trio of gables bring distinction to this plan.

Features:

- Ceiling Height: 8 ft.

- Open Floor Plan: The rooms flow into each other and are flanked by an abundance of windows. The result is a light and airy space that seems much larger than it really is.

- Formal Dining Room: Here is the perfect room for elegant entertaining.

- Breakfast Nook: This bright, bayed nook is the perfect place to start the day. It's also great for intimate get-togethers.

- Great Room: The family will enjoy gathering in this spacious area.

- Bedrooms: This large master suite, along with three secondary bedrooms and an extra room, provides plenty of room for a growing family.

- Attached Garage: The garage provides two bays of parking plus plenty of storage space.

Main Level Floor Plan

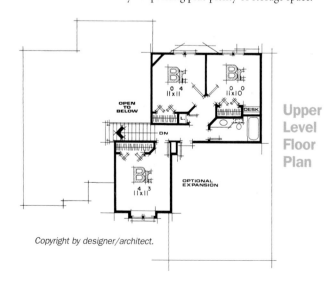

Upper Level Floor Plan

Copyright by designer/architect.

Images provided by designer/architect.

Plan #211005

Dimensions: 68' W x 64' D
Levels: 1
Heated Square Footage: 2,000
Bedrooms: 3
Bathrooms: 2
Foundation: Slab
Materials List Available: Yes
Price Category: D

A brick veneer exterior complements the columned porch to make this a striking home.

Features:

- Ceiling Height: 9 ft. unless otherwise noted.

- Living Room: From the front porch, the foyer unfolds into this expansive living room. Family and friends will be drawn to the warmth of the living room's cozy fireplace.

- Formal Dining Room: This elegant room is designed for dinner parties of any size.

- Kitchen: Located between the formal dining room and the dinette, the kitchen can serve formal meals as easily as quick family repasts.

- Master Suite: There's plenty of room to unwind at the end of a long day in the huge master bedroom. Luxuriate in the private bath, with its spa tub, separate shower, dual sinks, and two walk-in closets.

- Home Office: The home office, accessible from the master bedroom, is the perfect quiet spot to work, study, or pay the bills.

Copyright by designer/architect.

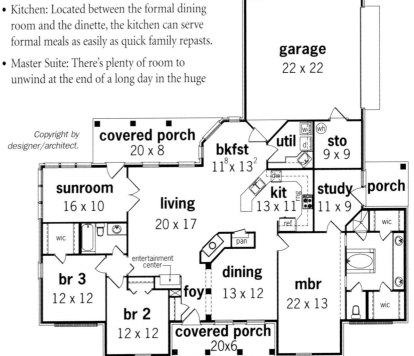

Plan #351008

Dimensions: 64'6" W x 61'4" D
Levels: 1
Heated Square Footage: 2,002
Bedrooms: 3
Bathrooms: 2
Foundation: Crawl space or basement
Materials List Available: Yes
Price Category: E

This home has the charming appeal of a quaint cottage that you might find in an old village in the English countryside. It's a unique design that maximizes every inch of its usable space.

Features:

• **Great Room:** This room has a vaulted ceiling and built-in units on each side of the fireplace.

• **Kitchen:** This kitchen boasts a raised bar open to the breakfast area; the room is also open to the dining room.

• **Master Suite:** This bedroom retreat features a raised ceiling and a walk-in closet. The bathroom has a double vanity, large walk-in closet, and soaking tub.

• **Bedrooms:** Two bedrooms share a common bathroom and have large closets.

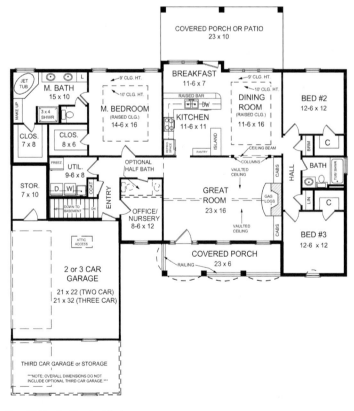

Copyright by designer/architect.

Plan #101022

Dimensions: 66'2" W x 62' D

Levels: 1

Heated Square Footage: 1,992

Bedrooms: 3

Bathrooms: 3

Foundation: Crawl space, slab, or basement

Materials List Available: Yes

Price Category: D

The exterior of this lovely home is traditional, but the unusually shaped rooms and amenities are contemporary.

Features:

- **Foyer:** This two-story foyer is open to the family room, but columns divide it from the dining room.

- **Family Room:** A gas fireplace and TV niche, flanked by doors to the covered porch, sit at the rear of this seven-sided, spacious room.

- **Breakfast Room:** Set off from the family room by columns, this area shares a snack bar with the kitchen and has windows looking over the porch.

- **Bedroom 3:** Use this room as a living room if you wish, and transform the guest room to a media room or a family bedroom.

- **Master Suite:** The bedroom features a tray ceiling, has his and her dressing areas, and opens to the porch. The bath has a large corner tub, separate shower, linen closet, and two vanities.

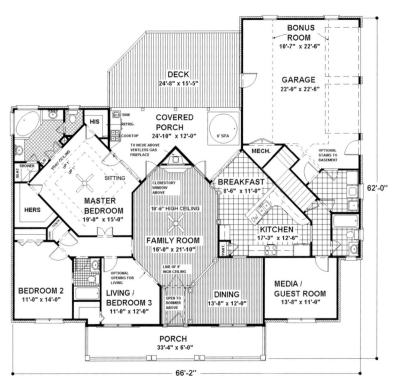

Kitchen

Living Room

Dining Room

Family Room

Master Bedroom

Master Bath

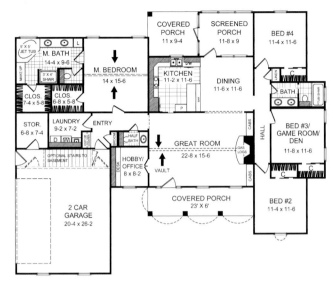

Images provided by designer/architect.

Plan #351044

Dimensions: 68' W x 55'8" D

Levels: 1

Heated Square Footage: 2,000

Bedrooms: 4

Bathrooms: 2½

Foundation: Crawl space, slab, or basement

Materials List Available: Yes

Price Category: E

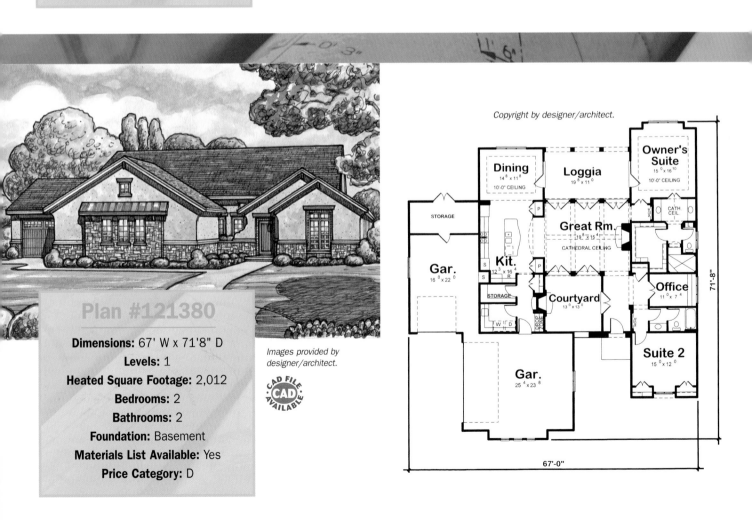

Plan #121380

Dimensions: 67' W x 71'8" D

Levels: 1

Heated Square Footage: 2,012

Bedrooms: 2

Bathrooms: 2

Foundation: Basement

Materials List Available: Yes

Price Category: D

Images provided by designer/architect.

CAD FILE AVAILABLE

Plan #121320

Dimensions: 43'4" W x 60'8" D

Levels: 1.5

Heated Square Footage: 2,019

Main Level Sq. Ft.: 1,503

Upper Level Sq. Ft.: 516

Bedrooms: 3

Bathrooms: 2½

Foundation: Basement

Materials List Available: Yes

Price Category: D

Images provided by designer/architect.

CAD FILE AVAILABLE

Main Level Floor Plan

Upper Level Floor Plan

Copyright by designer/architect.

Plan #211049

Dimensions: 73' W x 661' D

Levels: 1

Heated Square Footage: 2,023

Bedrooms: 3

Bathrooms: 2

Foundation: Slab

Materials List Available: Yes

Price Category: D

Images provided by designer/architect.

CAD FILE AVAILABLE

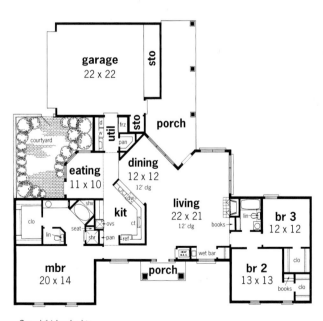

Copyright by designer/architect.

Main Level Floor Plan

Grt. rm.
15⁴ x 19⁹

Kit.
11³ x 12⁰

Bfst.
12⁴ x 11³

13'-6" CEILING

Gar.
31⁴ x 23⁰

Din.
11⁴ x 12⁴

E.

Mbr.
13⁰ x 15⁰

COVERED PORCH

47'-4"

62'-8"

Plan #121271

Dimensions: 62'8" W x 47'4" D

Levels: 1.5

Heated Square Footage: 2,029

Main Level Sq. Ft.: 1,411

Upper Level Sq. Ft.: 618

Bedrooms: 4

Bathrooms: 2½

Foundation: Basement

Materials List Available: Yes

Price Category: D

Images provided by designer/architect.

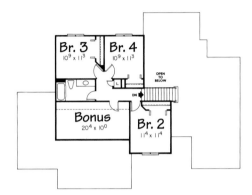

Upper Level Floor Plan

Copyright by designer/architect.

Br. 3
10⁹ x 11³

Br. 4
10⁹ x 11³

OPEN TO BELOW

Bonus
20⁴ x 10⁰

Br. 2
11⁴ x 11⁴

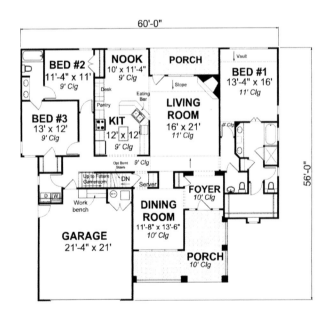

Plan #121415

Dimensions: 60' W x 56' D

Levels: 1

Heated Square Footage: 2,056

Bedrooms: 3

Bathrooms: 2½

Foundation: Slab; crawl space or basement for fee

Materials List Available: Yes

Price Category: D

Images provided by designer/architect.

60'-0"

BED #2
11'-4" x 11'
9' Clg

NOOK
10' x 11'-4"
9' Clg

PORCH

BED #1
13'-4" x 16'
11' Clg

BED #3
13' x 12'
9' Clg

KIT
12' x 12'
9' Clg

LIVING ROOM
16' x 21'
11' Clg

9' Clg

GARAGE
21'-4" x 21'

DINING ROOM
11'-8" x 13'-6"
10' Clg

FOYER
10' Clg

PORCH
10' Clg

56'-0"

Copyright by designer/architect.

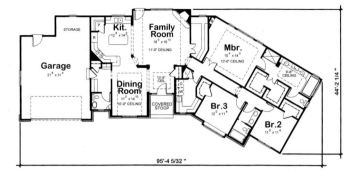

Plan #121338

Dimensions: 95'4" W x 44'2" D

Levels: 1

Heated Square Footage: 2,069

Bedrooms: 3

Bathrooms: 2½

Foundation: Basement

Material List Available: Yes

Price Category: D

Images provided by designer/architect.

Bonus Area Floor Plan

Copyright by designer/architect.

Plan #311001

Dimensions: 65'11" W x 67'9" D

Levels: 1

Heated Square Footage: 2,085

Bedrooms: 3

Bathrooms: 2½

Foundation: Crawl space, slab, or basement

Materials List Available: No

Price Category: D

Images provided by designer/architect.

Copyright by designer/architect.

Rear View

Optional Bonus Area

Plan #391001

Dimensions: 32' W x 40' D
Levels: 2
Heated Square Footage: 2,015
Main Level Sq. Ft.: 1,280
Upper Level Sq. Ft.: 735
Bedrooms: 3
Bathrooms: 2½
Foundation: Crawl space
Materials List Available: Yes
Price Category: D

- **Kitchen:** This L-shaped kitchen features an expansive cooktop/lunch counter.
- **Utility Areas:** A utility room handles the laundry and storage, and a half bath with linen closet takes care of other necessities.
- **Master Suite:** This main-floor master suite is just that—sweet! The spa-style bath features a corner tub nestled against a greenhouse window. Plus, there are double sinks and a separate shower.
- **Upstairs:** The sun-washed loft overlooks the activity below while embracing two dreamy bedrooms and a sizable bath with double sinks.

Follow your dream to this home surrounded with decking. The A-frame front showcases bold windowing (on two levels), and natural lighting fills the house.

Features:

- **Dining Room:** This dining room and the family room are completely open to each other, perfect for hanging out in the warmth of the hearth.

Main Level Floor Plan

Upper Level Floor Plan

Copyright by designer/architect.

Plan #131009

Dimensions: 64'10" W x 57'8" D
Levels: 1
Heated Square Footage: 2,018
Bedrooms: 3
Bathrooms: 2
Foundation: Crawl space, slab, or basement
Materials List Available: Yes
Price Category: E

The pavilion-styled great room at the heart of this H-shaped ranch gives it an unusual elegance that you're sure to enjoy.

Features:

- Great Room: The tray ceiling sets off this room, and a fireplace warms it on chilly nights and cool days. Two sets of sliding glass doors leading to the backyard terrace let in natural light and create an efficient traffic flow.

- Kitchen: Designed for a gourmet cook, this kitchen features a snack bar that everyone will enjoy and easy access to the breakfast room.

- Breakfast Room: Open to the columned rear porch, this breakfast room is an ideal spot for company or family brunches.

- Master Suite: A sitting area and access to the porch make the bedroom luxurious, while the private bath featuring a whirlpool tub creates a spa atmosphere.

Images provided by designer/architect.

Copyright by designer/architect.

Great Room

Images provided by designer/architect.

Plan #161020

Dimensions: 60' W" x 50'4" D

Levels: 2

Heated Square Footage: 2,082; 2,349 with bonus space

Main Level Sq. Ft.: 1,524

Upper Level Sq. Ft.: 558

Bedrooms: 3

Bathrooms: 2½

Foundation: Basement

Materials List Available: Yes

Price Category: D

You'll love the textured exterior finish and interesting roofline of this charming home.

Features:

- **Great Room:** Here you can enjoy the cozy fireplace, 12-ft. ceilings, and stylish French doors.

- **Dining Room:** A grand entry prepares you for the sloped ceiling that gives charm to this room.

- **Kitchen:** Natural light floods both the well-designed kitchen and adjacent breakfast room.

- **Master Suite:** Located on the first floor, this area boasts a whirlpool tub, a double-bowl vanity, and a large walk-in closet.

- **Upper Level:** Split stairs lead to a balcony over the foyer, a computer/study area, and two additional bedrooms.

- **Bonus Room:** Use this 267-sq.-ft. area over the garage for storage or a fourth bedroom.

Main Level Floor Plan

Upper Level Floor Plan

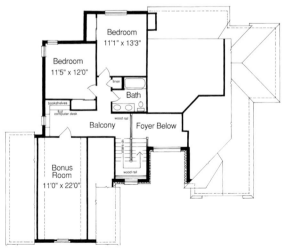

Copyright by designer/architect.

Plan #171015

Dimensions: 79' W x 46' D

Levels: 1

Heated Square Footage: 2,089

Bedrooms: 3

Bathrooms: 2½

Foundation: Crawl space or slab

Materials List Available: Yes

Price Category: D

Images provided by designer/architect.

This lovely three-bedroom country home, with a bonus room above the garage, is a perfect family home.

Features:

• **Dining Room:** This formal room and the great room form a large gathering space with a 12-ft.-high ceiling.

• **Kitchen:** The raised bar defines this kitchen and offers additional seating.

• **Master Suite:** This suite, located on the opposite side of the home from the secondary bedrooms, enjoys a luxurious bath with his and her walk-in closets.

• **Bedrooms:** Two secondary bedrooms have large closets and share a hall bathroom.

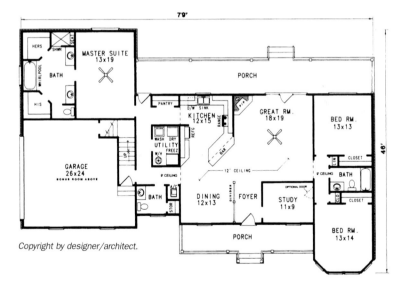

Copyright by designer/architect.

Bonus Area Floor Plan

Plan #151050

Dimensions: 69'2" W x 74'10" D

Levels: 1

Heated Square Footage: 2,096

Bedrooms: 3

Bathrooms: 2½

Foundation: Crawl space, slab, basement, or walkout

CompleteCost List Available: Yes

Price Category: D

You'll love this spacious home for both its elegance and its convenient design.

Features:

- Ceiling Height: 8 ft.

- Great Room: A 9-ft. boxed ceiling complements this large room, which sits just beyond the front gallery. A fireplace and door to the rear porch make it a natural gathering spot.

- Kitchen: This well-designed kitchen includes a central work island and shares an angled eating bar with the adjacent breakfast room.

- Breakfast Room: This room's bay window is gorgeous, and the door to the garage is practical.

- Master Suite: You'll love the 9-ft. boxed ceiling in the bedroom and the vaulted ceiling in the bath, which also includes two walk-in closets, a corner whirlpool tub, split vanities, a shower, and a separate toilet room.

- Workshop: A huge workshop with half-bath is ideal for anyone who loves to build or repair.

Images provided by designer/architect.

CAD FILE AVAILABLE

Optional Front View

Plan #101009

Dimensions: 70'2" W x 59' D
Levels: 1
Heated Square Footage: 2,097
Bedrooms: 3
Bathrooms: 3
Foundation: Crawl space, slab, or basement
Materials List Available: Yes
Price Category: E

Round columns enhance this country porch design, which will nestle into any neighborhood.

Features:

- Ceiling Height: 9 ft. unless otherwise noted.

- Family Room: This large family room seems even more spacious, thanks to the vaulted ceiling. It's the perfect spot for all kinds of family activities.

- Dining Room: This elegant dining room is adorned with a decorative round column and a tray ceiling.

- Kitchen: You'll love the convenience of this enormous 14-ft.-3-in. x 22-ft.-6-in. country kitchen, which is open to the family room.

- Screened Porch: A French door leads to this breezy porch, with its vaulted ceiling.

- Master Suite: This sumptuous suite includes a double tray ceiling, a sitting area, a large walk-in closet, and a luxurious bath.

- Patio or Deck: This area is accessible from both the screened porch and master suite.

Images provided by designer/architect.

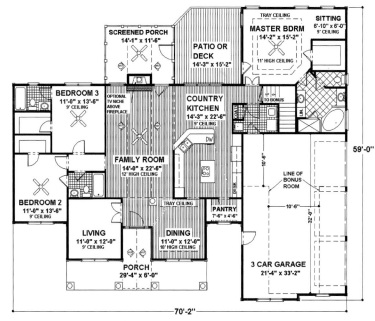

Copyright by designer/architect.

SMARTtip

Single-Level Decks

A single-level deck can use a strong vertical element, such as a pergola or a gazebo, to make it interesting. A simple and less-expensive option is a potted conical shrub or a clematis growing on a trellis.

Plan #351176

Dimensions: 69' W x 59' D

Levels: 1

Heated Square Footage: 2,100

Bedrooms: 4

Bathrooms: 2½

Foundation: Crawl space, slab

Material List Available: Yes

Price Category: D

The many available features and flexibility of this home make it the perfect choice for you and your family.

Features:

- **Great Room:** This great room features vaulted ceilings, built-in cabinets, a fireplace, and direct access to the rear covered porch.

- **Kitchen:** Mornings are made easy in this kitchen, which features a raised eating bar, a breakfast area, and ample counter space.

- **Master Suite:** You'll never want to leave this beautiful master suite with its coffered ceiling, two walk-in closets, whirlpool tub, and separate vanity areas.

- **Secondary Bedrooms:** Three additional bedrooms share a separate area of the home, each with its own walk-in closet.

Images provided by designer/architect.

Main Level Floor Plan

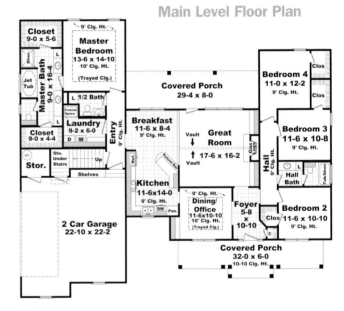

Bonus Area Floor Plan

Copyright by designer/architect.

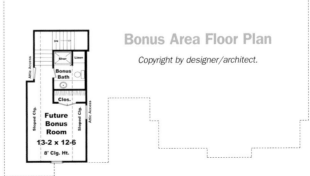

Plan #161016

Dimensions: 59'4" W x 58'8" D

Levels: 1.5

Heated Square Footage: 2,101

Main Level Sq. Ft.: 1,626

Upper Level Sq. Ft.: 475

Bedrooms: 3

Bathrooms: 2½

Foundation: Basement;
crawl space option available for fee

Materials List Available: Yes

Price Category: D

Note: Home in photo reflects a modified garage entrance.

Images provided by designer/architect.

Features:

- **Great Room:** Made for relaxing and entertaining, the great room is sunken to set it off from the rest of the house. A balcony from the second floor looks down into this spacious area, making it easy to keep track of the kids while they are playing.

- **Kitchen:** Convenience marks this well laid-out kitchen where you'll love to cook for guests and for family.

- **Master Suite:** A vaulted ceiling complements the unusual octagonal shape of the master

bedroom. Located on the first floor, this room allows some privacy from the second floor bedrooms. It is also ideal for anyone who no longer wishes to climb stairs to reach a bedroom.

Rear Elevation

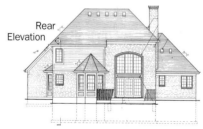

You'll love the exciting roofline that sets this elegant home apart from its neighbors as well as the embellished, solid look that declares how well-designed it is—from the inside to the exterior.

CAD FILE AVAILABLE

Main Level Floor Plan

Deck

Breakfast 9-2 x 16

Sunken Great Room 16-10 x 21

Kitchen 8 x 13-4

Bath

Walk-in closet

Stairs up

Dining Room 16 x 11-8

Foyer

Master Bedroom 14 x 17-4

Slope ceiling   Slope ceiling

Bath

Hall

Laundry

Two-car Garage 21 x 20-8

Copyright by designer/architect.

58'-8"

59'-4"

Upper Level Floor Plan

Bedroom 15x 10-8

Great Room Below

Bath

Bedroom 14x 10-6

Foyer Below

Plan #151004

Dimensions: 64'8" W x 62'1" D

Levels: 1

Heated Square Footage: 2,107

Bedrooms: 4

Bathrooms: 2½

Foundation: Crawl space, slab, or basement

CompleteCost List Available: Yes

Price Category: D

Images provided by designer/architect.

You'll love the spacious feeling in this comfortable home designed for a family.

Features:

- Foyer: A 10-ft. ceiling greets you in this home.

- Great Room: A 10-ft. ceiling complements this large room, with its fireplace, built-in cabinets, and easy access to the rear covered porch.

- Dining Room: The 9-ft. boxed ceiling in this large room helps to create a beautiful formal feeling.

- Kitchen: The island in this kitchen is open to the breakfast room for true convenience.

- Breakfast Room: Morning light will stream through the bay window here.

- Master Suite: A 9-ft. pan ceiling adds a distinctive note to this room with access to the rear porch. In the bath, you'll find a whirlpool tub, separate shower, double vanities, and two walk-in closets.

Copyright by designer/architect.

Plan #121114

Dimensions: 64' W x 52' D
Levels: 1.5
Heated Square Footage: 2,115
Main Level Sq. Ft.: 1,505
Upper Level Sq. Ft.: 610
Bedrooms: 4
Bathrooms: 2½
Foundation: Basement; crawl space for fee
Materials List Available: Yes
Price Category: D

This contemporary home is not only beautifully designed on the outside; it has everything you need on the inside. It will be the envy of the neighborhood.

Images provided by designer/architect.

Features:

• Great Room: The cathedral ceiling and cozy fireplace strike a balance that creates the perfect gathering place for family and friends. An abundance of space allows you to tailor this room to your needs.

• Kitchen/Breakfast Room: This combined area features a flood of natural light, workspace to spare, an island with a snack bar, and a door that opens to the backyard, creating an ideal space for outdoor meals and gatherings.

• Dining Room: A triplet of windows projecting onto the covered front porch creates a warm atmosphere for formal dining.

• Master Bedroom: Away from the busy areas of the home, this master suite is ideal for shedding your daily cares and relaxing in a romantic atmosphere. It includes a full master bath with skylight, his and her sinks, a stall shower, a whirlpool tub, and a walk-in closet.

• Second Floor: Three more bedrooms and the second full bathroom upstairs give you plenty of room for a large family. Or if you only need two extra rooms, use the fourth bedroom as a study or entertainment area for the kids.

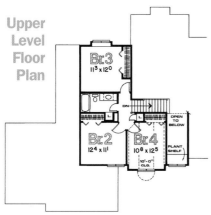

Copyright by designer/architect.

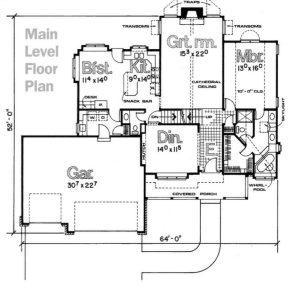

Plan #181061

Dimensions: 56' W x 53'2" D
Levels: 2
Heated Square Footage: 2,111
Main Level Sq. Ft.: 1,545
Upper Level Sq. Ft.: 565
Bedrooms: 2
Bathrooms: 2½
Foundation: Crawl space, basement
Materials List Available: Yes
Price Category: D

Images provided by designer/architect.

Main Level Floor Plan

Upper Level Floor Plan

Copyright by designer/architect.

Plan #121408

Dimensions: 48' W x 74' D
Levels: 1
Heated Square Footage: 2,116
Bedrooms: 3
Bathrooms: 2
Foundation: Slab; crawl space or basement for fee
Materials List Available: Yes
Price Category: D

Images provided by designer/architect.

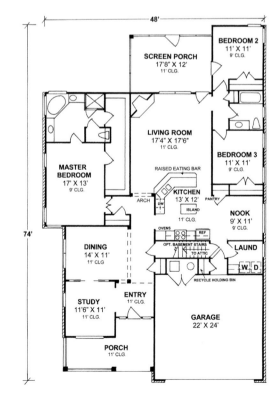

Copyright by designer/architect.

Plan #121407

Dimensions: 50' W x 59' D

Levels: 1

Heated Square Footage: 2,116

Bedrooms: 1

Bathrooms: 2

Foundation: Slab; crawl space or basement for fee

Materials List Available: Yes

Price Category: D

Images provided by designer/architect.

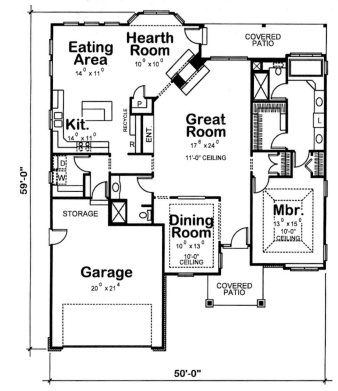

Copyright by designer/architect.

Plan #351193

Dimensions: 69' W x 61'8" D

Levels: 1

Heated Square Footage: 2,118

Bedrooms: 4

Bathrooms: 2½

Foundation: Basement

Materials List Available: Yes

Price Category: D

Images provided by designer/architect.

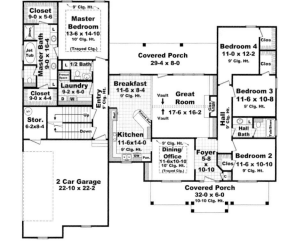

Bonus Area Floor Plan

Copyright by designer/architect.

Plan #441039

Dimensions: 50' W x 56' D

Levels: 2

Heated Square Footage: 2,120

Main Level Sq. Ft.: 1,603

Upper Level Sq. Ft.: 517

Bedrooms: 3

Bathrooms: 2½

Foundation: Crawl space; slab or basement for fee

Materials List Available: No

Price Category: D

Images provided by designer/architect.

Rear Elevation

Main Level Floor Plan

Copyright by designer/architect.

Upper Level Floor Plan

Plan #121328

Dimensions: 71' W x 62' D

Levels: 1

Heated Square Footage: 2,099

Bedrooms: 3

Bathrooms: 2½

Foundation: Basement

Materials List Available: Yes

Price Category: D

Images provided by designer/architect.

Copyright by designer/architect.

Plan #151034

Dimensions: 58'6" W x 64'6" D
Levels: 1
Heated Square Footage: 1,593
Bedrooms: 3
Bathrooms: 2
Foundation: Crawl space, slab, basement, or walkout
Materials List Available: Yes
Price Category: D

Images provided by designer/architect.

This home, as shown in the photograph, may differ from the actual blueprints. For more detailed information, please check the floor plans carefully.

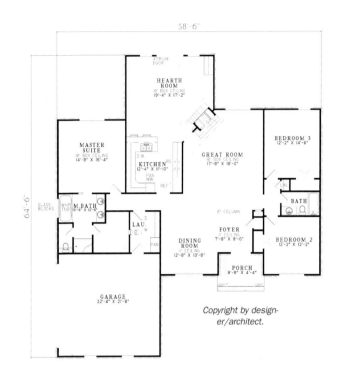

Copyright by designer/architect.

Plan #161607

Dimensions: 58' W x 44'4" D
Levels: 2
Heated Square Footage: 2,160
Main Level Sq. Ft.: 1,541
Upper Level Sq. Ft.: 619
Bedrooms: 3
Bathrooms: 2½
Foundation: Basement
Materials List Available: Yes
Price Category: D

Images provided by designer/architect.

Main Level Floor Plan

Upper Level Floor Plan

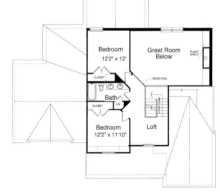

Kitchen Cabinets

Of all the rooms in a house, kitchens present unique decorating challenges because so much tends to happen in these spaces. In addition to preparing meals, most families use kitchens as gathering and entertaining areas. Kitchens need to be functional, comfortable, and inviting.

Who can't relate to this scenario: you turn on the oven to preheat it, but wait, did you take out the large roasting pan first?

How about the lasagna dish, muffin tins, pizza stone, and cookie sheets that are in there, too? Now where can you put everything that was in the oven while the casserole is baking and the countertop is laden with the rest of tonight's dinner ingredients? Good cabinetry outfitted with an assortment of organizing options can help you there. It can make your kitchen more efficient and a whole lot neater while establishing a style, or "look," for the room.

Cabinet Construction

Basically, cabinets are constructed in one of two ways: framed or frameless. Framed cabinets have a traditional look, with a full frame across the face of the cabinet box that may show between closed doors. This secures adjacent cabinets and strengthens wider cabinet boxes with a center rail. Hinges on framed cabinets may or may not be visible around doors when they are closed. The door's face may be ornamented with raised or recessed panels, trimmed or framed panels, or a framed-glass panel with or without muntins (the narrow vertical and horizontal strips of wood that divide panes of glass).

Frameless Cabinets. Also known as European-style cabinets, although American manufacturers also make them, frameless cabinets are built without a face frame and sport a clean, contemporary look, often not befitting a Southern or Country style. There's no trim or molding with this simple design. Close-fitting doors cover the entire front of the box, no ornamentation appears on the face of the doors, and hinges are typically hidden inside the cabinet box.

Selecting Cabinets

Choosing one type over another is generally a matter of taste, although framed units offer slightly less interior space. But the quality of construction is a factor that should always be taken into consideration. How do you judge it? Solid wood is too expensive for most of today's budgets, but it might be used on just the doors and frames. More typical is plywood box construction, which offers good structural support and solid wood on the doors and frames. To save money, cabinetmakers sometimes use strong plywood for support elements, such as the box and frame, and medium-density fiberboard for other parts, such as doors and drawer fronts. In

yet another alternative, good-quality laminate cabinets can be made with high-quality, thick particleboard underneath the laminate finish.

Quality Points. There are other things to look for in cabinet construction. They include dovetail or mortise-and-tenon joinery and solidly mortised hinges. Also, make sure that the interior of every cabinet is well finished, with adjustable shelves that are a minimum ⅝ inch thick to prevent bowing.

Bead-board paneled doors, opposite, are at home in Southern-style kitchens.

Framed cabinets, above, offer a traditional look to an otherwise modern kitchen.

Country-style designs have many attributes of Cottage decor, right.

Unless you have the time and skill to build the cabinets yourself or can hire someone else to do it, you'll have to purchase them in one of four ways. **Knockdown cabinetry** (also known as RTA, ready to assemble) is shipped flat and, sometimes, unfinished because you put the pieces together. **Stock cabinetry** comes in standard sizes but limited styles and colors; it is often available on the spot or can be delivered quickly. Like stock, **semicustom cabinetry** comes in standard styles, but it is manufactured to fit a homeowner's specific size and finish needs. **Custom cabinetry** is not limited in terms of style or size because it is built to the designer's specifications.

The Decorative Role of Cabinets

The look you create in your kitchen will be largely influenced by the cabinetry you select. Finding a style that suits you and how you will use your new kitchen is similar to shopping for furniture. In fact, don't be surprised to see many furniture details dressing up the cabinets on view in showrooms and home centers today.

Details That Stand Out. Besides architectural elements such as fluted pilasters, corbels, moldings, and bull's-eye panels, look for details such as fretwork, rope motifs, gingerbread trim, balusters, composition ornamentation (it looks like carving), even footed cabinets that mimic separate furniture pieces. If your taste runs toward less fussy design, you'll also find handsome door and drawer styles that feature minimal decoration, if any. Woods and finishes are just as varied, and range from informal looks in birch, oak, ash, and maple to rich mahogany and cherry. Laminate finishes, though less popular than they were a decade ago, haven't completely disappeared from the marketplace, but an array of colors has replaced the once-ubiquitous almond and white finishes.

Color

Color is coming on strong on wood cabinetry, too. Accents in one, two, or more hues are pairing with natural wood tones. White-painted cabinets take on a warmer

glow with tinted shades of this always popular neutral. Special "vintage" finishes, such as translucent color glazes, continue to grow in popularity, as do distressed finishing techniques such as wire brushing and rubbed-through color that add both another dimension and the appeal of handcraftmanship, even on mass-produced items.

If you're shy about using color on such a high-ticket item as cabinetry, try it as an accent on molding, door trim, or island cabinetry. Just as matched furniture suites have become passé in other rooms of the house, the same is true for the kitchen,

where mixing several looks can add sophistication and visual interest.

Cabinet Hardware

Another way to emphasize your kitchen's style is with hardware. From exquisite reproductions in brass, pewter, wrought iron, or ceramic to handsome bronze, chrome, nickel, glass, steel, plastic, rubber, wood, or stone creations, a smorgasbord of shapes and designs is available. Some pieces are highly polished; others are matte-finished, smooth, or hammered. Some are abstract or geometrical; others are simple,

elegant shapes. Whimsical designs take on the forms of animals or teapots, vegetables or flowers. Even just one or two great-looking door or drawer pulls can be showstoppers in a kitchen that may otherwise be devoid of much personality. Like mixing cabinet finishes, a combination of two hardware styles—perhaps picked up from other materials in the room—makes a big design statement. As the famed architect Mies Van der Rohe once stated, "God is in the details," and the most perfect detail in your new kitchen may be the artistic hardware that you select.

Cabinet style will set the tone for the design of the entire kitchen. The simple door styles keeps the room at left airy and casual.

The rustic look of the cabinets above is tailor-made for any Country style kitchen.

Color accents, such as the splash of color on the kitchen island shown right, can customize any simple cabinet design.

Cabinet hardware should complement the cabinet door and drawer designs, but it should also be easy for everyone in the household to grasp, above.

Kitchen storage comes in a variety of forms, including cabinets, drawers, pullout extensions, and the glass-front bins shown to the right.

Besides looks, consider the function of a pull or knob. You have to be able to grip it easily and comfortably. If your fingers or hands get stiff easily, or if you have arthritis, select C- or U-shaped pulls. If you like a knob, try it out in the showroom to make sure it isn't slippery or awkward when you grab it. Knobs and pulls can be inexpensive if you can stick to unfinished ones that you can paint in an accent color picked up from the tile or wallpaper. If you don't plan to buy new cabinets, changing the hardware on old ones can redefine their style. The right knob or pull can suggest any one of a number of vintage looks or decorative styles, from Colonial to Victorian, and reinforce your decor.

Types of Storage

Storage facilities can make or break a kitchen, so choose the places you'll put things with care. Here's a look at a few alternatives:

Pantries. How often you shop and how many groceries you typically bring home determine the amount of food storage space your family needs. If you like to stock up or take advantage of sales, add a pantry

to your kitchen. To maximize a pantry's convenience, plan shallow, 6-inch-deep shelves so that cans and packages will never be stored more than two deep. This way, you'll easily be able to see what you've got on hand. Pantries range in size from floor-to-ceiling models to narrow units designed to fit between two standard-size cabinets.

Appliance Garages. Appliance garages make use of dead space in a corner, but they can be installed anywhere in the vertical space between wall-mounted cabinets and the countertop. A tambour (rolltop) door hides small appliances like a food processor or anything else you want within reach but hidden from view.

Lazy Susans and Carousel Shelves. Rotating shelves like lazy Susans and carousels maximize dead corner storage and put items like dishes or pots and pans within easy reach. A lazy Susan rotates 360 degrees, so just spin it to find what you're looking for. Carousel shelves, which attach to two right-angled doors, rotate 270 degrees; open the doors, and the shelves swing out allowing you to reach items easily.

Pivoting Shelves. Door-mounted shelves and in-cabinet swiveling shelf units offer easy access to kitchen supplies. Taller units serve as pantries that hold a great deal in minimal space.

Pullout Tables and Trays. In tight kitchens, pullout tables and trays are excellent ways to gain eating space or an extra work surface. Pullout cutting boards come in handy near cooktops, microwaves, and food prep areas. Pullout tea carts are also available.

Customized Organizers. If you decide to use value-priced cabinets or choose to forego the storage accessories offered by manufacturers, consider refitting their interiors with cabinet organizers you purchase yourself. These plastic, plastic-coated wire, or enameled-steel racks and hangers are widely available at department stores, hardware stores, and home centers.

Some of these units slide in and out of base cabinets, similar to the racks in a dishwasher. Others let you mount shallow drawers to the undersides of wall cabinets. Still others consist of stackable plastic bins with plenty of room to hold kitchen sundries.

Beware of the temptation to over-specialize your kitchen storage facilities. Sizes and needs for certain items change, so be sure to allot at least 50 percent of your kitchen's storage to standard cabinets with one or more movable shelves. And don't forget to allow for storing recyclable items.

Today's cabinets can be customized with storage accessories, right.

Full-height pantries, above, provide a number of different types of storage near where you need the items. This pantry is next to the food-prep area.

Base cabinets can be outfitted with accessories for kitchen storage or for wet bar storage as shown in the cabinet below.

fer to have frequently used machines sitting on the counter, ready to go, plan enough space, along with conveniently located electrical outlets.

■ **Do you plan to store large quantities of food?**
Be sure to allow plenty of freezer, bin, and shelf space for the kind of food shopping you do.

■ **Do you intend to do a lot of freezing or canning?**
Allow a work space and place to stow equipment. Also plan adequate storage for the fruits of your labor—an extra stand-alone freezer, a good-sized food safe in the kitchen, or a separate pantry or cellar.

■ **Do you bake often?**
Consider a baking center that can house your equipment and serve as a separate baking-ingredients pantry.

■ **Do you collect pottery, tinware, or anything else that might be displayed in the kitchen?**
Soffits provide an obvious place to hang small objects like collectible plates. Eliminating soffits provides a shelf on top of the wall cabinets for larger lightweight objects like baskets. Open shelving, glass-front cupboards, and display cabinets are other options.

■ **Do you collect cookbooks?**
If so, you'll need expandable shelf space and perhaps a bookstand.

Personal Profile of You and Your Family

■ **How tall are you and everyone else who will use your kitchen?**
Adjust your counter and wall-cabinet heights to suit. Multilevel work surfaces for special tasks are a necessity for good kitchen design.

■ **Do you or any of your family members use a walker, leg braces, or a wheelchair?**
Plan a good work height, knee space, grab bars, secure seating, slide-out work

Storage Checklist

Here's a guide to help you get your storage needs in order.

■ **Do you like kitchen gadgets?**
Plan drawer space, countertop sorters, wall magnets, or hooks to keep these items handy near where you often use them.

■ **Do you own a food processor, blender, mixer, toaster oven, electric can opener, knife sharpener, juicer, coffee maker, or coffee mill?**
If you're particularly tidy, you may want small appliances like these tucked away in an appliance garage or cupboard to be taken out only when needed. If you pre-

boards, and other convenience features to make your kitchen comfortable for all who will use it.

■ Are you left- or right-handed?

Think about your natural motion when you choose whether to open cupboards or refrigerator doors from the left or right side, whether to locate your dishwasher to the left or right of the sink, and so on.

■ How high can you comfortably reach?

If you're tall, hang your wall cabinets high. If you're petite, you may want to hang the cabinets lower and plan a spot to keep a step stool handy.

■ Can you comfortably bend and reach for something in a base cabinet? Can you lift heavy objects easily and without strain or pain?

If your range is limited in these areas, be sure to plan roll-out shelving on both upper and lower tiers of your base cabinets. Also, look into spring-up shelves designed to lift mixer bases or other heavy appliances to counter height.

■ Do you frequently share cooking tasks with another family member?

If so, you may each prefer to have your own work area.

Fold-down ironing boards, above left, are a true luxury. If you have the space, install one near the kitchen or laundry room.

Corner cabinets often contain storage space you can't reach. Make it accessible by installing swing-out shelves, above right, or a lazy Susan.

Glass doors put your kitchen items on display. The owners of the kitchen below chose distinctive pottery and glassware for their glass-door cabinets.

Plan #101011

Dimensions: 71'2" W x 58'1" D

Levels: 1

Heated Square Footage: 2,184

Bedrooms: 3

Bathrooms: 3

Foundation: Crawl space, slab, basement, or walkout

Materials List Available: Yes

Price Category: E

A classic design and spacious interior add up to a flexible design suitable to any modern lifestyle.

Features:

• Ceiling Height: 9 ft. unless otherwise noted.

• Dining Room: A decorative square column and a tray ceiling adorn this elegant dining room.

• Screened Porch: Enjoy summer breezes in style by stepping out of the French doors into this vaulted screened porch.

• Kitchen: Does everyone want to hang out in the kitchen while you are cooking? No problem. True to the home's country style, this huge 14-ft.-3-in. x 22-ft.-6-in. kitchen has plenty of room for helpers. This area is open to the vaulted family room.

• Patio or Deck: This pleasant outdoor area is accessible from both the screened porch and the master bedroom.

• Master Suite: This luxurious suite includes a double tray ceiling, a sitting area, two walk-in closets, and an exquisite bath.

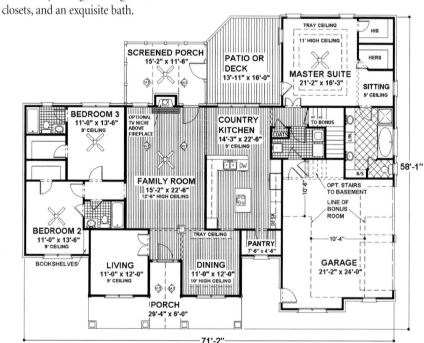

Kitchen

Dining Room

Family Room

Living Room

Master Bath

Master Bedroom

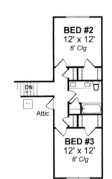

Main Level Floor Plan

Inside plan labels:
LIVING ROOM 20' x 15'-6" 12' Clg
NOOK 12' x 11' 9' Clg
BED #1 12'-8" x 17' 9' Clg
STUDY 15' x 11" 9' Ceiling
KIT 12' x 14' 9' Clg
2 CAR GARAGE 22'-8" x 22'
DINING ROOM 12' x 14' 9' Clg
PORCH
Slope
64'-0"
46'-0"

Plan #121412

Dimensions: 64' W x 46' D

Levels: 1.5

Heated Square Footage: 2,190

Main Level Sq. Ft.: 1,667

Upper Level Sq. Ft.: 523

Bedrooms: 3

Bathrooms: 2½

Foundation: Slab; crawl space or basement for fee

Materials List Available: Yes

Price Category: D

Images provided by designer/architect.

Upper Level Floor Plan

Copyright by designer/architect.

BED #2 12' x 12' 8' Clg
BED #3 12' x 12' 8' Clg
Attic
DN

Plan #361004

Dimensions: 77' W x 81' D

Levels: 1

Heated Square Footage: 2, 191

Bedrooms: 3

Bathrooms: 2

Foundation: Basement, crawl space

Materials List Available: No

Price Category: D

Images provided by designer/architect.

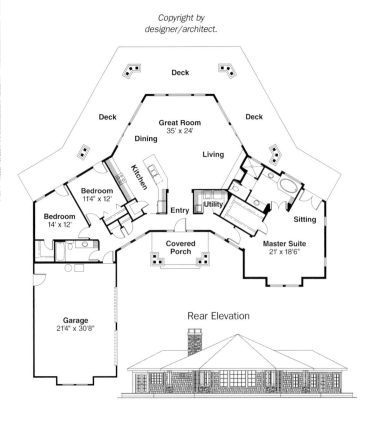

Copyright by designer/architect.

Deck
Deck
Deck
Great Room 35' x 24'
Dining
Living
Kitchen
Bedroom 11'4" x 12'
Bedroom 14' x 12'
Entry
Utility
Sitting
Master Suite 21' x 18'6"
Covered Porch
Garage 21'4" x 30'8"

Rear Elevation

Plan #191068

Dimensions: 70' W x 70' D

Levels: 1

Heated Square Footage: 2,197

Bedrooms: 3

Bathrooms: 2½

Foundation: Crawl space or slab

Material List Available: No

Price Category: D

Images provided by designer/architect.

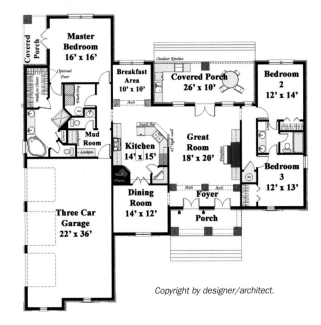

Copyright by designer/architect.

Rear View

Plan #121337

Dimensions: 68' W x 69' D

Levels: 1

Heated Square Footage: 2,200

Bedrooms: 3

Bathrooms: 2

Foundation: Basement

Materials List Available: Yes

Price Category: E

Images provided by designer/architect.

CAD FILE AVAILABLE

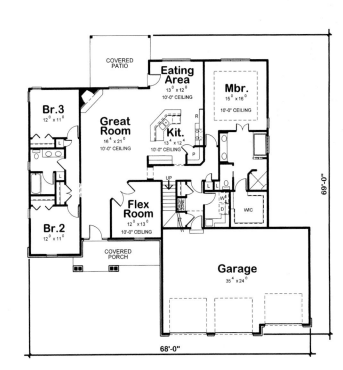

Copyright by designer/architect.

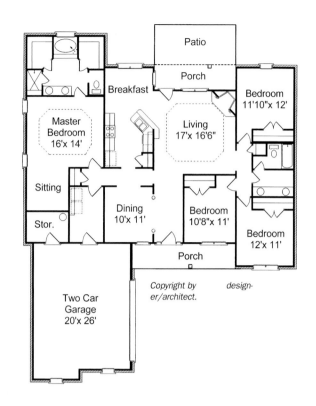

Plan #111015

Dimensions: 64' W x 58' D
Levels: 1
Heated Square Footage: 2,208
Bedrooms: 4
Bathrooms: 2
Foundation: Slab
Materials List Available: No
Price Category: F

Images provided by designer/architect.

Master Bedroom 16'x 14'
Sitting
Stor.
Breakfast
Patio
Porch
Living 17'x 16'6"
Dining 10'x 11'
Bedroom 10'8"x 11'
Bedroom 11'10"x 12'
Bedroom 12'x 11'
Porch
Two Car Garage 20'x 26'

Copyright by designer/architect.

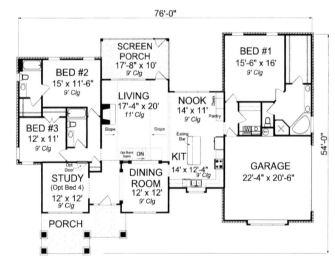

Plan #121416

Dimensions: 76' W x 54' D
Levels: 1
Heated Square Footage: 2,210
Bedrooms: 3
Bathrooms: 3
Foundation: Slab
Materials List Available: Yes
Price Category: E

Images provided by designer/architect.

76'-0"
54'-0"
SCREEN PORCH 17'-8" x 10' 9' Clg
BED #2 15' x 11'-6" 9' Clg
BED #3 12' x 11' 9' Clg
STUDY (Opt Bed 4) 12' x 12' 9' Clg
LIVING 17'-4" x 20' 11' Clg
DINING ROOM 12' x 12' 9' Clg
NOOK 14' x 11' 9' Clg
KIT 14' x 12'-4" 9' Clg
BED #1 15'-6" x 16' 9' Clg
GARAGE 22'-4" x 20'-6"
PORCH

Copyright by designer/architect.

Copyright by designer/architect.

Optional Basement Level Floor Plan

Plan #121034

Dimensions: 92'8" W x 59'4" D

Levels: 1

Heated Square Footage: 2,223

Bedrooms: 1

Bathrooms: 2½

Foundation: Basement; crawl space for fee

Materials List Available: Yes

Price Category: E

Images provided by designer/architect.

CAD FILE AVAILABLE

Plan #121425

Dimensions: 67'4" W x 71'8" D

Levels: 1

Heated Square Footage: 2,236

Bedrooms: 2

Bathrooms: 2½

Foundation: Slab; crawl space or basement for fee

Materials List Available: Yes

Price Category: E

Images provided by designer/architect.

Copyright by designer/architect.

Plan #131019

Dimensions: 83'6" W x 53'4" D

Levels: 1

Heated Square Footage: 2,243

Bedrooms: 3

Bathrooms: 2½

Foundation: Crawl space, slab, or basement

Materials List Available: Yes

Price Category: F

Images provided by designer/architect.

CAD FILE AVAILABLE

Copyright by designer/architect.

Plan #131046

Dimensions: 68' W x 57'6" D

Levels: 2

Heated Square Footage: 2,245

Main Level Sq. Ft.: 1,720

Upper Level Sq. Ft.: 525

Bedrooms: 3

Bathrooms: 21½

Foundation: Crawl space, slab, or basement

Materials List Available: Yes

Price Category: F

Images provided by designer/architect.

Copyright by designer/architect.

Main Level Floor Plan

80'

COVERED PORCH

SCREEN PORCH 17' X 16' 14' CLG.

COVERED PORCH

3 CAR GARAGE 21'4" X 28'4"

LAUND.

NOOK 12' X 12'6" 9' CLG.

LIVING ROOM 17' X 20' 18' CLG.

MASTER BEDROOM 16' X 13' 9' CLG.

EATING BAR

PANTRY

KITCHEN 12' X 14'

OPTIONAL BASEMENT STAIRS

REF

CAB.

DINING 12' X 12'8" 9' CLG.

FOYER 9' CLG.

STUDY/ BEDROOM 4 12' X 12'8" 9' CLG.

CAB.

COVERED PORCH

59'

Upper Level Floor Plan

Copyright by designer/architect.

Images provided by designer/architect.

OPT. GAMEROOM 16' X 25'-8" 8' CLG.

OPEN TO BELOW

JULIET BALCONY

ATTIC LIN

DN

BEDROOM 2 12' X 12'8" 8' CLG.

BEDROOM 3 12' X 12'8" 8' CLG.

Front View

Plan #121190

Dimensions: 80' W x 59' D
Levels: 1.5
Heated Square Footage: 2,252
Main Level Sq. Ft.: 1,736
Upper Level Sq. Ft.: 516
Bedrooms: 4
Bathrooms: 3
Foundation: Slab; crawl space for fee
Materials List Available: Yes
Price Category: E

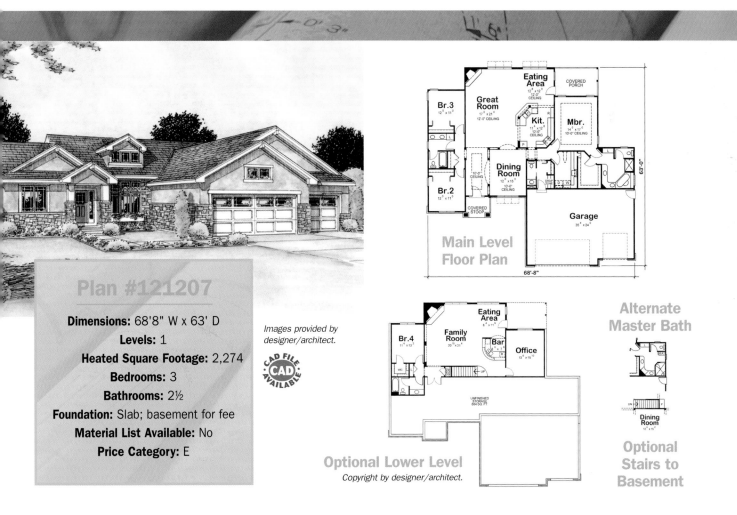

Br.3 13' x 11'

Great Room 17' x 21' 12'-0" CEILING

Eating Area 12' x 12'6" CEILING

COVERED PORCH

Kit. 11' x 12' 12'-0" CEILING

Mbr. 14' x 17' 10'-0" CEILING

Br.2 12' x 11'

Dining Room 12' x 16' 12'-0" CEILING

Garage 35' x 24'

Main Level Floor Plan

68'-8"

63'-0"

Br.4 11' x 13'

Family Room 20' x 21'

Eating Area

Bar

Office 13' x 15'

UNFINISHED STORAGE 884 SQ. FT.

Optional Lower Level
Copyright by designer/architect.

Alternate Master Bath

Optional Stairs to Basement

Dining Room 13' x 15'

Plan #121207

Dimensions: 68'8" W x 63' D
Levels: 1
Heated Square Footage: 2,274
Bedrooms: 3
Bathrooms: 2½
Foundation: Slab; basement for fee
Material List Available: No
Price Category: E

Images provided by designer/architect.

CAD FILE AVAILABLE

Plan #101017

Dimensions: 57' W x 51' D
Levels: 2
Heated Square Footage: 2,253
Main Level Sq. Ft.: 1,719
Upper Level Sq. Ft.: 534
Opt. Upper Level Bonus Sq. Ft.: 247
Bedrooms: 4
Bathrooms: 3
Foundation: Basement
Materials List Available: No
Price Category: E

Images provided by designer/architect.

This alluring two-story "master-down" design blends a spectacular floor plan with a lovely facade to create a home that's simply irresistible.

Features:

• Entry: You're welcomed by an inviting front porch and greeted by a beautiful leaded glass door leading to this two-story entry.

• Family Room: A corner fireplace and a window wall with arched transoms accent this dramatic room.

• Master Suite: This sumptuous suite includes a double tray ceiling, sitting area, and his and her walk-in closets. The master bathroom features dual vanities, a corner tub, and a shower.

• Bedrooms: Located upstairs, these two additional bedrooms share a Jack-and-Jill bathroom.

Main Level Floor Plan

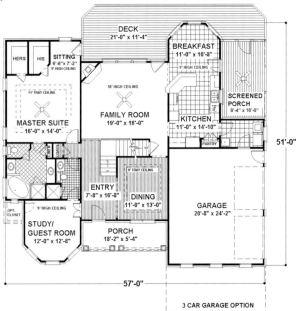

Upper Level Floor Plan

Copyright by designer/architect.

Kitchen

Dining Room

Study

Master Bath

Master Bedroom

Bedroom

Plan #121116

Dimensions: 72' W x 56' D
Levels: 1
Heated Square Footage: 2,276
Bedrooms: 3
Bathrooms: 2½
Foundation: Basement;
crawl space for fee
Material List Available: Yes
Price Category: E

Images provided by designer/architect.

This charming country home is filled with ingenious design and sumptuous spaces.

Features:

- Great Room: This spacious entertainment area can be kept formal for guests while the den holds all of the embarrassing family clutter.

- Kitchen: Uniquely laid out, this kitchen includes two pantries, a desk, a snack bar, and an adjacent wet bar. Transitioning right into the breakfast area means more natural light for the kitchen and simple shifting from meal preparation to dining.

- Master Suite: This master bedroom was planned with couples in mind. His and her closets and vanities simplify getting ready. A built-in entertainment center, whirlpool tub, and separate shower stall are added bonuses.

- Secondary Bedrooms: In a space all their own, these bedrooms have ample closet space, a nearby full bathroom, and are identically sized to keep siblings from squabbling.

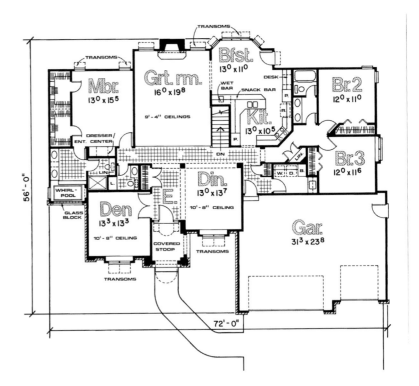

Copyright by designer/architect.

Plan #121233

Dimensions: 54' W x 50' D
Levels: 1.5
Heated Square Footage: 2,276
Main Level Sq. Ft.: 1,551
Upper Level Sq. Ft.: 725
Bedrooms: 4
Bathrooms: 2½
Foundation: Basement
Materials List Available: Yes
Price Category: E

Images provided by designer/architect.

This distinctive home has unique architectural details that are sure to make it stand out in your neighborhood.

CAD FILE AVAILABLE

Features:

- **Kitchen:** This well-designed kitchen with its spacious work area and center island will satisfy the family cook. The kitchen opens out to the breakfast room, which makes it a wonderful sunny place to enjoy a cup of coffee.

- **Great Room:** Sit back with friends and family in front of the fireplace in this great room. The 10-ft.-high ceiling gives the space a sense of openness.

- **Master Suite:** You'll appreciate the details in this master suite, with its stepped ceiling, separate toilet room, skylight, his and her sinks, whirlpool tub, and large walk-in closet.

- **Secondary Bedrooms:** The house's three supplemental bedrooms are perfect for the kids. The shared bathroom features two sinks and a clothes chute, cutting down on laundry-day trips.

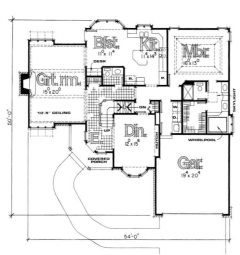

Main Level Floor Plan

Upper Level Floor Plan

Copyright by designer/architect.

Main Level Floor Plan

56'

48'

Plan #441043

Dimensions: 48' W x 56' D

Levels: 2

Heated Square Footage: 2,277

Main Level Sq. Ft.: 1,563

Upper Level Sq. Ft.: 714

Bedrooms: 3

Bathrooms: 2½

Foundation: Crawl space; slab or basement available for fee

Materials List Available: No

Price Category: E

Images provided by designer/architect.

Copyright by designer/architect.

Upper Level Floor Plan

Plan #121381

Dimensions: 68' W x 62'8" D

Levels: 1

Heated Square Footage: 2,279

Bedrooms: 2

Bathrooms: 2½

Foundation: Basement

Materials List Available: Yes

Price Category: E

Images provided by designer/architect.

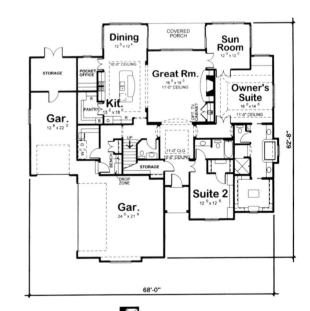

62'-8"

68'-0"

Bonus Area Floor Plan

Copyright by designer/architect.

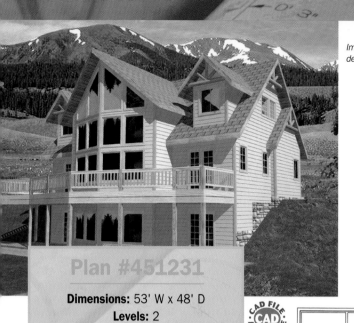

Images provided by designer/architect.

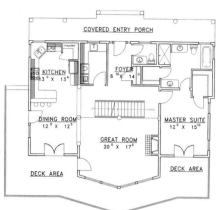

Main Level Floor Plan

COVERED ENTRY PORCH

PANTRY

KITCHEN
13'0" X 13'6"

FOYER
6'10" X 14'0"

DINING ROOM
12'0" X 12'5"

GREAT ROOM
20'0" X 17'0"

MASTER SUITE
12'0" X 15'10"

DECK AREA

DECK AREA

Lower Level Floor Plan

CAD FILE AVAILABLE CAD

UNFINISHED BASEMENT

CONC. PATIO

Upper Level Floor Plan

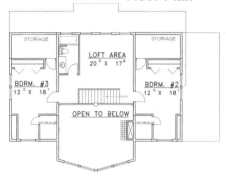

STORAGE

STORAGE

LOFT AREA
20'0" X 17'9"

BDRM. #3
12'0" X 18'0"

BDRM. #2
12'0" X 18'0"

STORAGE

OPEN TO BELOW

STORAGE

Plan #451231

Dimensions: 53' W x 48' D

Levels: 2

Heated Square Footage: 2,281

Main Level Sq. Ft.: 1,436

Upper Level Sq. Ft.: 845

Bedrooms: 3

Bathrooms: 2½

Foundation: Walkout

Materials List Available: No

Price Category: E

Plan #121095

Dimensions: 65'4" W x 48'8" D

Levels: 2

Heated Square Footage: 2,282

Main Level Sq. Ft.: 1,597

Upper Level Sq. Ft.: 685

Bedrooms: 4

Bathrooms: 2½

Foundation: Basement

Materials List Available: Yes

Price Category: E

Images provided by designer/architect.

CAD FILE AVAILABLE CAD

TRANSOMS

Kit.
10'0" X 13'0"

Bfst.
14'8" X 14'4"

Grt. rm.
16'0" x 20'0"
13'-0" CEILING

Mbr.
13'0" x 16'0"
10'-0" CEILING

PANT.

W. D.

Din.
12'0" x 14'0"

Gar.
31'4" x 22'4"

COVERED PORCH

WHIRLPOOL

48'-8"

65'-4"

Main Level Floor Plan

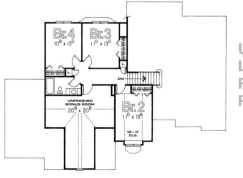

Br. 4
10'8" X 13'0"

Br. 3
11'0" X 13'0"

Br. 2
11'0" X 13'6"
10'-0" CLG.

UNFINISHED BONUS ROOM
20'8" X 20'8"

Upper Level Floor Plan

Plan #101012

Dimensions: 69'4" W x 62'9" D

Levels: 1

Heated Square Footage: 2,288

Bedrooms: 3

Bathrooms: 2½

Foundation: Crawl space, slab, basement, or walkout

Materials List Available: No

Price Category: E

Images provided by designer/architect.

This classic brick ranch boasts traditional styling and an exciting up-to-date floor plan.

Features:

• Ceiling Height: 9 ft. unless otherwise noted.

• Front Porch: Guests will be welcome by this inviting front porch, which features a 12-ft. ceiling.

• Family Room: This warm and inviting room measures 16 ft. x 19 ft. It features a 14-ft. ceiling and a rear wall of windows. French doors lead to an enormous deck.

• Kitchen: This unique angled kitchen is open to the hearth room and eating areas, all of which enjoy vaulted ceilings and are surrounded by windows. The hearth room has a TV niche.

• Master Suite: This 16-ft. x 15-ft. master suite is truly sumptuous, with its 12-ft. ceiling, sitting area, two walk-in closets, and full-featured bath.

• Bonus Room: Here is plenty of storage or room for future expansion. Just beyond the entry are stairs leading to a bonus room measuring approximately 12 ft. x 21 ft.

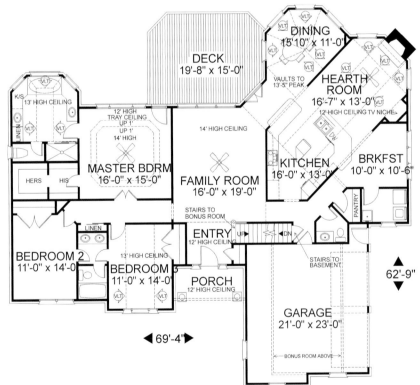

Copyright by designer/architect.

Kitchen

Dining Room

Living Room

Hearth Room

Master Bedroom

Bedroom

Plan #121406

Dimensions: 50' W x 80'4" D

Levels: 1

Heated Square Footage: 2,283

Bedrooms: 3

Bathrooms: 2

Foundation: Slab; basement for fee

Materials List Available: Yes

Price Category: E

Images provided by designer/architect.

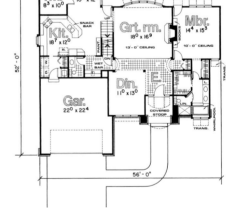

Plan #121389

Dimensions: 56' W x 52' D

Levels: 1.5

Heated Square Footage: 2,308

Main Level Sq. Ft.: 1,654

Upper Level Sq. Ft.: 654

Bedrooms: 4

Bathrooms: 2½

Foundation: Basement

Materials List Available: Yes

Price Category: E

Images provided by designer/architect.

This home, as shown in the photograph, may differ from actual blueprints. For more detailed information, please check the floor plans carefully.

Main Level Floor Plan

Upper Level Floor Plan

Copyright by designer/architect.

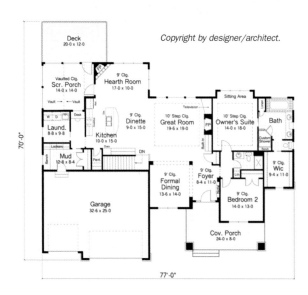

Plan #481158

Dimensions: 77' W x 70' D

Levels: 1

Heated Square Footage: 2,311

Bedrooms: 2

Bathrooms: 2

Foundation: Walkout

Materials List Available: No

Price Category: E

Images provided by designer/architect.

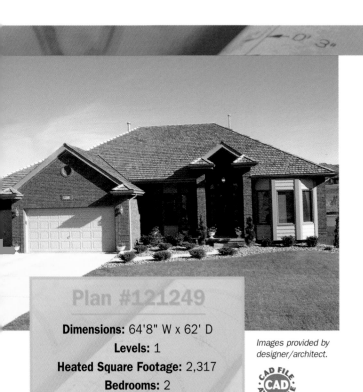

Plan #121249

Dimensions: 64'8" W x 62' D

Levels: 1

Heated Square Footage: 2,317

Bedrooms: 2

Bathrooms: 2½

Foundation: Basement

Materials List Available: Yes

Price Category: E

Images provided by designer/architect.

CAD FILE AVAILABLE

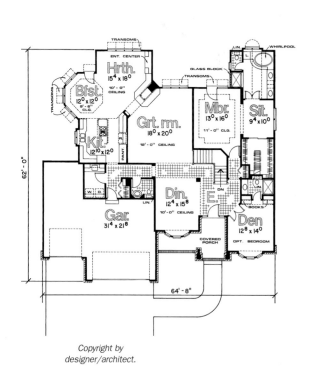

Plan #121123

Dimensions: 54' W x 52' D
Levels: 1.5
Heated Square Footage: 2,277
Main Level Sq. Ft.: 1,570
Upper Level Sq. Ft.: 707
Bedrooms: 4
Bathrooms: 2½
Foundation: Basement;
crawl space for fee
Material List Available: Yes
Price Category: E

This country-style home, with its classic wraparound porch, is just the plan you have been searching for.

Features:

- Entry: This two-story entry gives an open and airy feeling when you enter the home. A view into the dining room and great room adds to the open feeling.

- Great Room: This grand gathering area with cathedral ceiling is ready for your friends and family to come and visit. The fireplace, flanked by large windows, adds a cozy feeling to the space.

- Kitchen: The chef in the family will love how efficiently this island kitchen was designed. An abundance of cabinets and counter space is always a plus.

- Master Suite: This main level oasis will help you relieve all the stresses from the day. The master bath boasts dual vanities and a large walk-in closet.

- Secondary Bedrooms: Three generously sized bedrooms occupy the upper level. The full bathroom is located for easy access to all three bedrooms.

Main Level Floor Plan

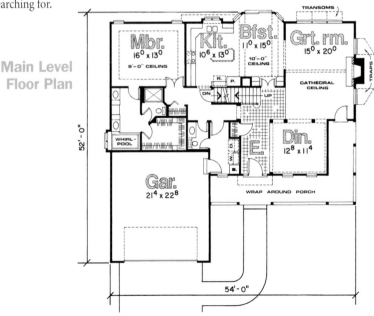

Upper Level Floor Plan

Copyright by designer/architect.

Plan #121032

Dimensions: 54' W x 45'4" D

Levels: 2

Heated Square Footage: 2,339

Main Level Sq. Ft.: 1,665

Upper Level Sq. Ft.: 674

Bedrooms: 4

Bathrooms: 2½

Foundation: Basement

Materials List Available: Yes

Price Category: E

Images provided by designer/architect.

This home is designed for gracious living and is distinguished by many architectural details.

Features:

- Ceiling Height: 8 ft. unless otherwise noted.

- Foyer: This is truly a grand foyer with a dramatic ceiling that soars to 18 ft.

- Great Room: The foyer's 18-ft. ceiling extends into the great room where an open staircase adds architectural windows. Warm yourself by the fireplace that is framed by windows.

- Kitchen: An island is the centerpiece of this handsome and efficient kitchen that features a breakfast area for informal family meals. The room also includes a handy desk.

- Private Wing: The master suite and study are in a private wing of the house.

- Room to Expand: In addition to the three bedrooms, the second level has an unfinished storage space that can become another bedroom or office.

Main Level Floor Plan

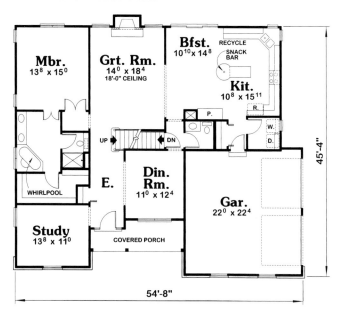

Upper Level Floor Plan

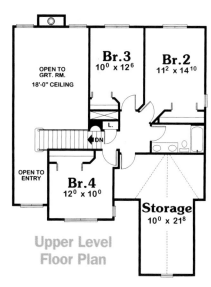

Copyright by designer/architect.

Plan #121088

Dimensions: 56'8" W x 48' D
Levels: 2
Heated Square Footage: 2,340
Main Level Sq. Ft.: 1,701
Upper Level Sq. Ft.: 639
Bedrooms: 4
Bathrooms: 2½
Foundation: Basement; slab for fee
Materials List Available: Yes
Price Category: E

Images provided by designer/architect.

You'll love this cheerful home, with its many large windows that let in natural light and cozy spaces that encourage family gatherings.

Features:

- **Entry:** Use the built-in curio cabinet here to display your best collector's pieces.

- **Den:** French doors from the entry lead to this room, with its built-in bookcase and triple-wide, transom-topped window.

- **Great Room:** The 14-ft. ceiling in this room accentuates the floor-to-ceiling windows that frame the raised-hearth fireplace.

- **Kitchen:** Both the layout and the work space make this room a delight for any cook.

- **Master Suite:** The bedroom has a tray ceiling for built-in elegance. A skylight helps to light the master bath, and an oval whirlpool tub, separate shower, and double vanity provide a luxurious touch.

Main Level Floor Plan

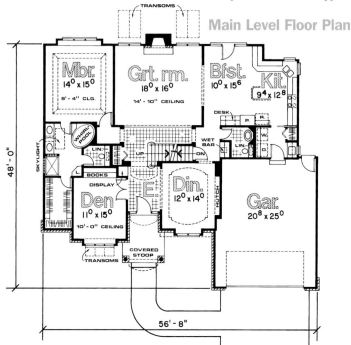

Upper Level Floor Plan

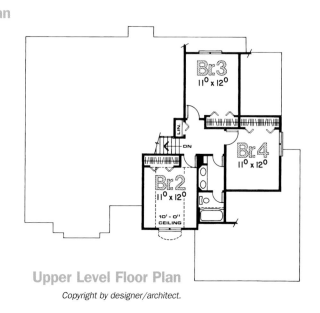

Copyright by designer/architect.

Plan #121017

Dimensions: 54' W x 50' D

Levels: 2

Heated Square Footage: 2,353

Main Level Sq. Ft.: 1,653

Upper Level Sq. Ft.: 700

Bedrooms: 4

Bathrooms: 2½

Foundation: Basement

Materials List Available: Yes

Price Category: E

The dramatic two-story entry with bent staircase is the first sign that this is a gracious home.

Features:

- Ceiling Height: 8 ft. except as noted.
- Great Room: A row of transom-topped windows and a tall, beamed ceiling add a sense of spaciousness to this family gathering area.
- Formal Dining Room: The bayed window helps make this an inviting place to entertain.
- See-through Fireplace: This feature spreads warmth and coziness throughout the informal areas of the home.
- Breakfast Area: This sunny area shares a see-through fireplace with the great room. It's the perfect place to start the day.
- Master Suite: Here are all the features you expect to find in large luxury homes. Wake up to tall, sloped ceilings, and enjoy the corner whirlpool, separate shower, and vanity. A large walk-in closet provides plenty of wardrobe storage.

Main Level Floor Plan

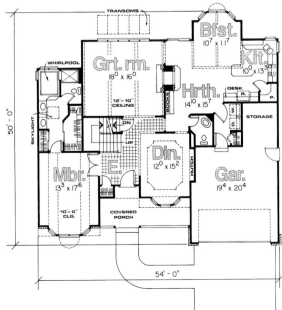

Upper Level Floor Plan

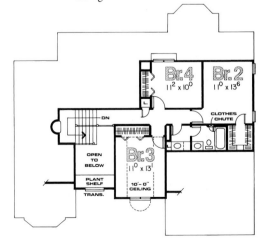

Copyright by designer/architect.

Plan #121340

Dimensions: 59' W x 62' D

Levels: 1

Heated Square Footage: 2,327

Bedrooms: 3

Bathrooms: 2½

Foundation: Basement

Materials List Available: Yes

Price Category: E

Images provided by designer/architect.

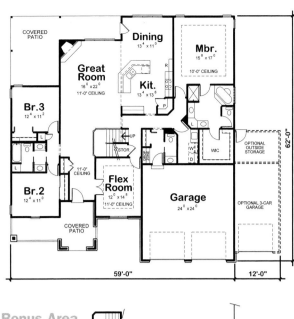

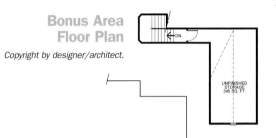

Bonus Area Floor Plan

Copyright by designer/architect.

Plan #121421

Dimensions: 40' W x 50' D

Levels: 2

Heated Square Footage: 2,338

Main Level Sq. Ft.: 1,203

Upper Level Sq. Ft.: 1,135

Bedrooms: 4

Bathrooms: 3½

Foundation: Basement; crawl space for fee

Materials List Available: Yes

Price Category: E

Images provided by designer/architect.

Main Level Floor Plan

Upper Level Floor Plan

Copyright by designer/architect.

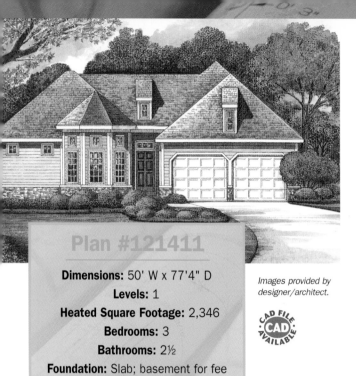

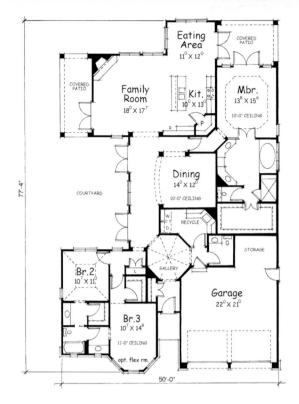

Images provided by designer/architect.

Plan #121411

Dimensions: 50' W x 77'4" D

Levels: 1

Heated Square Footage: 2,346

Bedrooms: 3

Bathrooms: 2½

Foundation: Slab; basement for fee

Materials List Available: Yes

Price Category: E

Copyright by designer/architect.

Images provided by designer/architect.

Plan #121325

Dimensions: 58' W x 68' D

Levels: 1

Heated Square Footage: 2,390

Bedrooms: 2

Bathrooms: 2½

Foundation: Basement

Materials List Available: Yes

Price Category: E

Copyright by designer/architect.

Plan #151172

Dimensions: 76'10" W x 53'4" D
Levels: 1.5
Heated Square Footage: 2,373
Main Level Sq. Ft.: 1,597
Upper Level Sq. Ft.: 776
Bedrooms: 4
Bathrooms: 3
Foundation: Crawl space, slab; basement or daylight basement for fee
Materials List Available: Yes
Price Category: E

This lovely home easily accommodates a busy family, but it also allows expansion should you want a larger home in the future.

Features:

• Great Room: A wall of windows, fireplace, and media center are highlights in this spacious area.

• Dining Room: This lovely room is separated from the foyer by columns, and it opens to the kitchen.

• Bedroom/Study: Use the walk-in closet here for a computer niche if you can turn this room into a study.

• Kitchen: You'll love the angled snack bar in this well-designed step-saving kitchen.

• Breakfast Room: Large windows let natural light pour in, and a door leads to the rear grilling porch.

• Master Suite: The bedroom has a door to the rear porch and large corner windows, and the bath includes a corner whirlpool tub, shower with seat, two vanities, and walk-in closet.

Main Level Floor Plan

Upper Level Floor Plan

Copyright by designer/architect.

Plan #121080

Dimensions: 56' W x 49' D

Levels: 2

Heated Square Footage: 2,384

Main Level Sq. Ft.: 1,616

Upper Level Sq. Ft.: 768

Bedrooms: 4

Bathrooms: 2½

Foundation: Slab; basement for fee

Materials List Available: Yes

Price Category: E

This home, as shown in the photograph, may differ from the actual blueprints. Images provided by designer/architect. For more detailed information, please check the floor plans carefully.

This design is ideal if you want a generously sized home now and room to expand later.

Features:

- Living Room: Your eyes will be drawn towards the ceiling as soon as you enter this lovely room. The ceiling is vaulted, giving a sense of grandeur, and a graceful balcony from the second floor adds extra interest to this room.

- Kitchen: Designed with lots of counter space to make your work convenient, this kitchen also shares an eating bar with the breakfast nook.

- Breakfast Nook: Eat here or go out to the adjoining private porch where you can enjoy your meal in the morning sunshine.

- Master Suite: The bayed area in the bedroom makes a picturesque sitting area. French doors in the bedroom open to a private bath that's fitted with a bathtub, separate shower, two vanities, and a walk-in closet.

Main Level Floor Plan

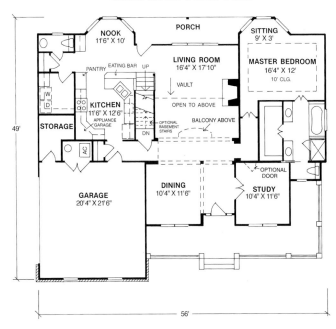

Upper Level Floor Plan

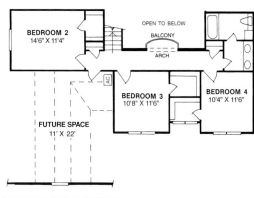

Copyright by designer/architect.

Plan #121068

Dimensions: 54' W x 49'10" D

Levels: 2

Heated Square Footage: 2,391

Main Level Sq. Ft.: 1,697

Upper Level Sq. Ft.: 694

Bedrooms: 4

Bathrooms: 2½

Foundation: Basement

Materials List Available: Yes

Price Category: E

This home, as shown in the photograph, may differ from the actual blueprints. Images provided by designer/architect. For more detailed information, please check the floor plans carefully.

This home allows you a great deal of latitude in the way you choose to finish it, so you can truly make it "your own."

Features:

• Living Room: Located just off the entryway, this living room is easy to convert to a stylish den. Add French doors for privacy, and relish the style that the 12-ft. angled ceiling and picturesque arched window provide.

• Great Room: The highlight of this room is the two-sided fireplace that easily adds as much design interest as warmth to this area. The three transom-topped windows here fill the room with light.

• Kitchen: A center island, walk-in pantry, and built-in desk combine to create this wonderful kitchen, and the attached gazebo breakfast area adds the finishing touch.

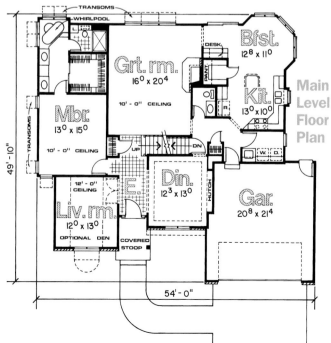

Main Level Floor Plan

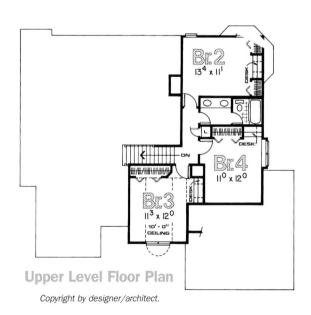

Upper Level Floor Plan

Copyright by designer/architect.

Plan #161040

Dimensions: 63'4" W x 48' D
Levels: 2
Heated Square Footage: 2,403
Main Level Sq. Ft.: 1,710
Upper Level Sq. Ft.: 695
Bedrooms: 4
Bathrooms: 3½
Foundation: Basement; slab for fee
Materials List Available: Yes
Price Category: E

Designed with attention to detail, this elegant home will please the most discriminating taste.

Features:

- Great Room: The high ceiling in this room accentuates the fireplace and the rear wall of windows. A fashionable balcony overlooks the great room.

- Dining Room: This lovely formal dining room is introduced by columns and accented by a boxed window.

- Kitchen: This wonderful kitchen includes a snack bar, island, and large pantry positioned to serve the breakfast and dining rooms with equal ease.

- Master Suite: This master suite features a dressing room, private sitting area with 11-ft.

ceiling, tub, double-bowl vanity, and large walk-in closet.

- Additional Bedrooms: Three additional bedrooms complete this spectacular home.

Rear Elevation

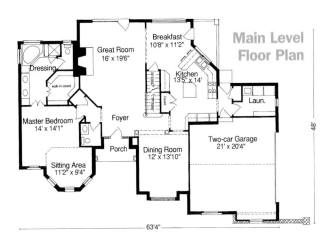

Main Level Floor Plan

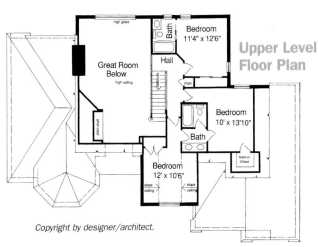

Upper Level Floor Plan

Copyright by designer/architect.

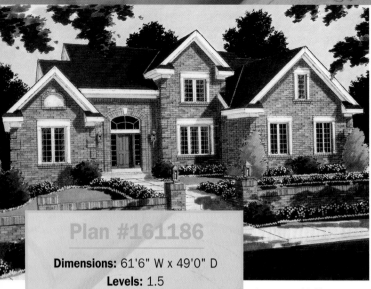

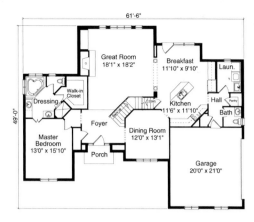

Main Level Floor Plan

Images provided by designer/architect.

Copyright by designer/architect.

Upper Level Floor Plan

Plan #161186

Dimensions: 61'6" W x 49'0" D

Levels: 1.5

Heated Square Footage: 2,397

Main Level Sq. Ft.: 1,730

Upper Level Sq. Ft.: 667

Bedrooms: 3

Bathrooms: 2½

Foundation: Basement; crawl space, slab, or walkout for fee

Materials List Available: Yes

Price Category: E

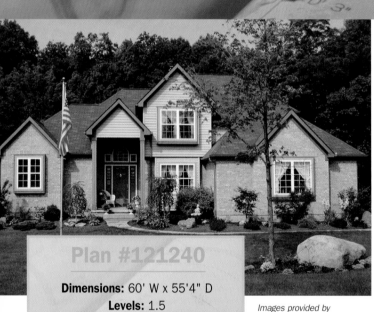

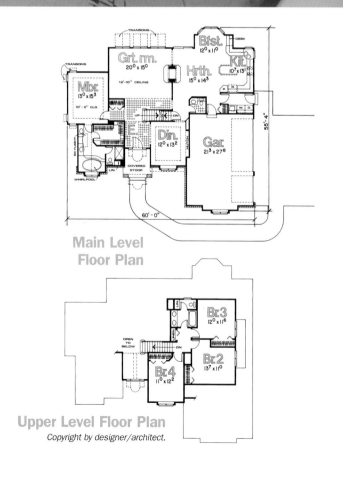

Main Level Floor Plan

Images provided by designer/architect.

Upper Level Floor Plan

Copyright by designer/architect.

Plan #121240

Dimensions: 60' W x 55'4" D

Levels: 1.5

Heated Square Footage: 2,405

Main Level Sq. Ft.: 1,733

Upper Level Sq. Ft.: 672

Bedrooms: 4

Bathrooms: 2½

Foundation: Basement

Materials List Available: Yes

Price Category: E

Plan #121418

Dimensions: 59' W x 58' D

Levels: 1.5

Heated Square Footage: 2,422

Main Level Sq. Ft.: 1,858

Upper Level Sq. Ft.: 564

Bedrooms: 4

Bathrooms: 3

Foundation: Slab; crawl space or basement for fee

Materials List Available: Yes

Price Category: E

Images provided by designer/architect.

CAD FILE AVAILABLE

Main Level Floor Plan

Upper Level Floor Plan

Copyright by designer/architect.

Plan #151002

Dimensions: 67' W x 66' D

Levels: 1

Heated Square Footage: 2,444

Bedrooms: 3

Bathrooms: 2½

Foundation: Crawl space, slab, or basement

CompleteCost List Available: Yes

Price Category: E

Images provided by designer/architect.

CAD FILE AVAILABLE

Copyright by designer/architect.

Plan #121336

Dimensions: 69' W x 68' D
Levels: 1
Heated Square Footage: 2,449
Bedrooms: 3
Bathrooms: 2½
Foundation: Basement
Materials List Available: Yes
Price Category: E

Images provided by designer/architect.

Copyright by designer/architect.

Main Level Floor Plan

Plan #161165

Dimensions: 55'8" W x 51'4" D
Levels: 2
Heated Square Footage: 2,454
Main Level Sq. Ft.: 1,622
Upper Level Sq. Ft.: 832
Bedrooms: 4
Bathrooms: 2½
Foundation: Basement; crawl space, slab, or walkout for fee
Materials List Available: Yes
Price Category: E

Images provided by designer/architect.

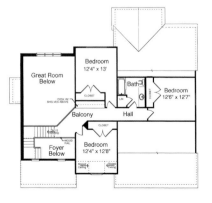

Upper Level Floor Plan

Copyright by designer/architect.

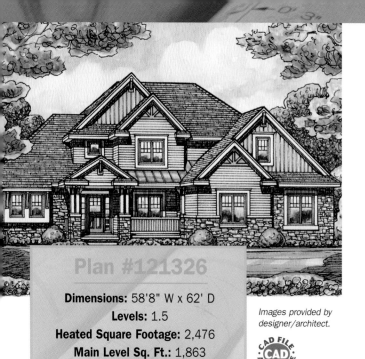

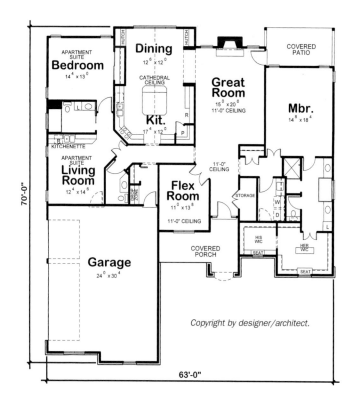

Main Level Floor Plan

Mbr.
15'0 x 18'0
10'-0" CEILING

Great Room
15'0 x 19'10

Eating Area
14'8 x 14'10

Kit.

Study
11'4 x 11'0

Garage
24'0 x 33'8

Covered Porch

58'-8"

62'-0"

Upper Level Floor Plan

OPEN TO BELOW

Br.3
12'0 x 11'10

Br.2
11'4 x 13'8

UNFINISHED STORAGE 450 SQ. FT.

Images provided by designer/architect.

Copyright by designer/architect.

Plan #121326

Dimensions: 58'8" W x 62' D

Levels: 1.5

Heated Square Footage: 2,476

Main Level Sq. Ft.: 1,863

Upper Level Sq. Ft.: 613

Bedrooms: 3

Bathrooms: 2½

Foundation: Basement

Materials List Available: Yes

Price Category: E

CAD FILE AVAILABLE

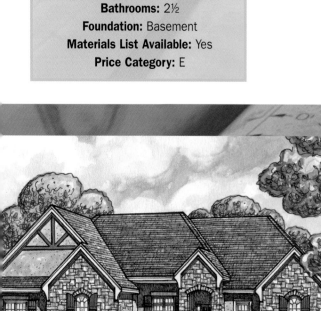

Plan #121339

Dimensions: 63' W x 70' D

Levels: 1

Heated Square Footage: 2,485

Bedrooms: 2

Bathrooms: 2½

Foundation: Basement

Materials List Available: Yes

Price Category: E

CAD FILE AVAILABLE

APARTMENT SUITE
Bedroom
14'4 x 13'0

Dining
12'8 x 12'0

CATHEDRAL CEILING

Kit.
17'4 x 12'0

Great Room
15'0 x 20'0
11'-0" CEILING

COVERED PATIO

Mbr.
14'8 x 18'4

KITCHENETTE

APARTMENT SUITE
Living Room
12'4 x 14'8

Flex Room
11'0 x 13'8
11'-0" CEILING

11'-0" CEILING

STORAGE

HIS WIC

HER WIC

SEAT

SEAT

Garage
24'0 x 30'4

COVERED PORCH

70'-0"

63'-0"

Images provided by designer/architect.

Copyright by designer/architect.

Plan #121074

Dimensions: 68'8" W x 47'8" D
Levels: 2
Heated Square Footage: 2,486
Main Level Sq. Ft.: 1,829
Upper Level Sq. Ft.: 657
Bedrooms: 4
Bathrooms: 2½
Foundation: Basement
Materials List Available: Yes
Price Category: E

Images provided by designer/architect.

Enjoy the natural light that streams through the many lovely windows in this well-designed home.

Features:

- Living Room: This room is sure to be your family's headquarters, thanks to the lovely 15-ft. ceiling, stacked windows, central location, and cozy fireplace.
- Dining Room: A boxed ceiling adds formality to this well-positioned room.
- Kitchen: The island cooktop in this kitchen is so large that it includes a snack bar area. A pantry gives ample storage space, and a built-in desk—where you can set up a computer station or a record-keeping area—adds efficiency.
- Master Suite: For the sake of privacy, this master suite is located on the opposite side of the home from the other living areas. You'll love the roomy bedroom and luxuriate in the private bath with its many amenities.

Main Level Floor Plan

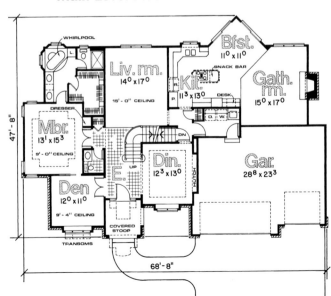

Upper Level Floor Plan

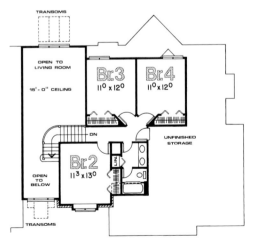

Copyright by designer/architect.

Plan #121334

Dimensions: 58'4" W x 54' D
Levels: 1.5
Heated Square Footage: 2,495
Main Level Sq. Ft.: 1,664
Upper Level Sq. Ft.: 831
Bedrooms: 4
Bathrooms: 3½
Foundation: Basement
Materials List Available: Yes
Price Category: E

This beautiful country home will look great in any neighborhood.

Features:

• Great Room: You and your guests will love this great room, with its central location in the home and its beautiful fireplace.

• Kitchen: Meals are made easy in this kitchen, with its open access to the dining room and center island for easy prep work.

• Master Suite: A dual vanity, a corner tub, a large walk-in closet with a dresser, and a beautiful bedroom area accentuate this large master suite.

• Secondary Bedrooms: Upstairs, three additional bedrooms share two bathrooms, and each has its own walk-in closet.

Images provided by designer/architect.

Main Level Floor Plan

Upper Level Floor Plan

Copyright by designer/architect.

Plan #121127

Dimensions: 58' W x 59'4" D
Levels: 1.5
Heated Square Footage: 2,496
Main Level Sq. Ft.: 1,777
Upper Level Sq. Ft.: 719
Bedrooms: 4
Bathrooms: 2½
Foundation: Basement; crawl space for fee
Material List Available: Yes
Price Category: E

Images provided by designer/architect.

• Master Bedroom: Featuring an entry to the backyard to continue relaxing outside, this master bedroom also includes a full master bath with standing shower, his and her sinks, a whirlpool tub, and a walk-in closet. Take some time for yourself.

• Second Floor: Bedrooms for three share the second full bathroom between them. If three is one too many, use the larger space for a study or entertainment area.

• Garage: A three-bay garage gives you room for every driver or for extra storage or a workshop.

Beautiful, unique architecture and classic brick combine to make a breathtaking welcome for friends and family alike.

CAD FILE AVAILABLE

Features:

• Great Room: Through the covered stoop and foyer is this welcoming space for coming home after a hard day of work or for entertaining guests. Whether in the brightness of the sun or the warm glow of the fireplace, this will be everyone's favorite place to gather.

• Kitchen: With utility space on one side and a window-surrounded breakfast room on the other, this kitchen is the height of convenience. With plenty of work and storage space, as well as a large snack bar, the room makes mealtimes simple.

• Den: If you're bringing your work home with you or just need a quiet place to use the computer, what you need is just on the other side of French doors in the foyer.

Main Level Floor Plan

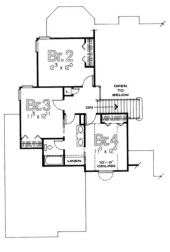

Copyright by designer/architect.

Upper Level Floor Plan

Plan #311005

Dimensions: 87' W x 57'3" D
Levels: 1
Heated Square Footage: 2,497
Bedrooms: 3
Bathrooms: 2½
Foundation: Crawl space, slab or basement
Material List Available: Yes
Price Category: E

You'll love this home, which mixes practical features with a gracious appearance.

Features:

- **Great Room:** A handsome fireplace and flanking windows that give a view of the back patio are the highlights of this gracious room.

- **Kitchen:** A curved bar defines the perimeter of this well-planned kitchen.

- **Breakfast Room:** Open to both the great room and the kitchen, this sunny spot leads to the rear porch, which in turn, leads to the patio beyond.

- **Master Suite:** Vaulted ceilings, a huge walk-in closet, and deluxe bath create luxury here.

- **Bonus Room:** Finish this 966-sq.-ft. area as a huge game room, or divide it into a game room, study, and sewing or craft room.

- **Additional Bedrooms:** Each bedroom has a private bath and good closet space.

Images provided by designer/architect.

Main Level Floor Plan

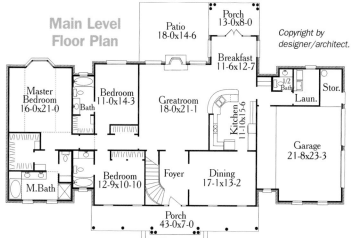

Copyright by designer/architect.

Bonus Area Floor Plan

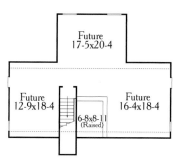

SMARTtip

Front Porch

A front porch proclaims you to the outside world, so furnish it in a way that expresses what you want the world to know about you. Use the walls of your porch to hang interesting items such as sundials or old shutters. Set a mirror into an old window to reflect a portion of the garden.

Have It Your Way: Creating a Home Office That's Right for You

It's no wonder millions of Americans are now working from home. Unlike a commercial office, a home office can reflect your personality. Having a completely individualized work space can make the difference between having to work and wanting to work. In fact, after moving home, you may find yourself staying at your desk a little longer, which balances out time-wise since there's no commuting!

The Ideal Location

Individual needs play a large part in determining a home office's location. Each possible location has pros and cons to consider. If you will be meeting with clients, an office near an exterior entry and a bathroom will allow the rest of the family to retain some degree of privacy. Many new homes include an office off the front entry, enclosed by stylish, glass French doors. However, such a public location may be undesirable if your work habits are less than tidy.

If you prefer a sense of community or need to keep a watch on children, you may prefer a loft overlooking the great room. However, even if you can tune out the distractions inherent to an open loft, you'll want to ensure clients on the other end of the phone don't hear children roughhousing in the background.

If, on the other hand, you function best in a quiet, secluded spot, you might choose to locate your office in the basement, the attic, your master suite, or a finished room over the garage.

Utilizing a sitting area off your master bedroom may interfere with your partner's sleep if you like to work at night – or interfere with yours when a difficult project remains in your field of vision. To provide visual separation, a bookcase on a track can close off the bedroom.

Home offices come in all shapes and sizes. This stately den would be right at home in a traditionally styled house. Floor-to-ceiling bookcases add a touch of elegance and provide plenty of open storage. Closed storage houses important items.

A converted spare bedroom offers natural light and a closet for storage. However, it's important to consider resale before making a bedroom a permanent office. According to a study by the National Association of Realtors, listing a "professional home office" in real-estate ads subtracted an average of 5 percent from the selling price, while mentioning a "den/study" added 7 percent to the selling price.

If your home has three or four other bedrooms, a permanent office probably won't hurt resale. If not, it's wise to keep the room flexible by not changing window and door configurations or covering walls with permanent cabinets or shelving. If you're building a home with fewer bedrooms, it's wise to include a closet so the room can easily convert back to a bedroom for future homeowners.

Attic Offices

With their sloped ceilings and interesting nooks, attics offer charm and isolation. "On the down side, vent stacks and low ceilings may limit how the space is used," notes Custom Home Designer Carl Cuozzo. "Most building codes require that at least 50 percent of the

Small spaces can be turned into efficient working areas with the help of movable storage and heavy duty wall-mounted storage shelves above a simple desk.

lightest tone on the ceiling), applying a satin paint on the ceiling, using uplighting, incorporating vertical stripes on the walls, or installing tall, thin bookcases.

Reducing Noise

Noise coming in or going out of the office can be a concern. You may not want your office next to the great room if your husband likes to crank up the volume when he watches movies. If you're particularly sensitive, you may be distracted by the dishwasher, washing machine, or furnace as well. Rooms that don't face the street will generally be quieter than those that do. On the other hand, frequent phone calls, a fax machine, and a printer may disturb the serenity of neighboring rooms.

Drapes and carpeting will help absorb sound. (Flat pile floor coverings produce less static and are easier to roll an office chair over.) Adding bookcases filled with books or turning an entire wall into a bulletin board by installing cork can also help.

"Other possibilities include adding two layers of dry wall or sound channels (corrugated rubber behind the dry wall) in interior walls and installing a threshold in the doorway with a solid, tight-fitting door and a weatherproof sweep on the bottom," advises Cuozzo. "If the room is highly insulated from the rest of the house, it may be wise for it to have its own thermostat. It's also important to remember that it's easier to keep sound in than to keep it out. So it will be most effective to insulate a space where the noise originates."

floor area have a ceiling height of 7 feet, 6 inches. In addition to installing wiring and ductwork, finishing an attic space may require structural changes to strengthen the floor and adding insulation to keep the space cool in the summer."

Offices over garages often have cold floors. To eliminate this problem, ensure the floor is very well-insulated and consider installing electric radiant heating grids.

Basement Offices

While naturally cool in the summer, basement offices often require a dehumidifier to control dampness and adequate insulation to be comfortable in cooler months in northern climates.

Basement offices may have small or no windows. While somewhat expensive, this can be remedied by installing a window well. If a low ceiling makes the space feel claustrophobic, consider painting the walls and ceiling in monotones (with the

Lighting and Wiring

Even with wireless networks, home offices require ample outlets that are conveniently located. If you're planning to have a desk away from the walls, you may want to consider having an outlet installed in the floor to eliminate stepping over cords. Some sources also recommend isolating the office on its own circuit to avoid tripping a circuit breaker.

A variety of light sources on separate switches will provide choices for different

When not in use, this small kitchen workspace is neatly hidden in special cabinets.

under a staircase, walk-in closet, or butler's pantry. Even a reach-in closet can accommodate a desk with shallow shelves above it.

The other solution is to share space in a room that serves another function. One possibility might be to add a stylish desk to one end of a great room. For added privacy, you may purchase a folding screen or create a room divider camouflaged as a bookcase.

A computer armoire in a dining room can also work quite well. Dining rooms aren't used on an everyday basis; they provide an attractive place for an occasional meeting with clients; and the table offers a large work surface.

Because they're used infrequently, guest rooms also often double as offices. A built-in wall unit can include office storage, a pull-down desk and a Murphy bed. On a smaller scale, a deep drawer under a captain's bed can be fitted with hanging files, a roll top desk can keep projects out of sight, or a computer on a trolley can be wheeled into another room before guests arrive.

Configurations

The L, T and U work space designs mentioned in "Hobby Rooms: Creative Getaway Spaces" (page 172) are also common in offices. The most popular of the three, the L shape does not have to be anchored to a wall and can float in a large room. A T shape can work well for two people sharing an office.

An ideal work space is around 60 inches wide and 32 inches deep, offering space for a monitor and free space for writing or reading. According to Lorrie Mack, author of Calm Working Spaces, you should also allow at least 3 feet clearance between your chair and a wall or other furniture, a minimum of 2 feet between other furnishings and three feet or more in front of a filing cabinet.

Legal Matters

Before proceeding, it's important to ensure local zoning ordinances do not prohibit or restrict the home office you envision. This may be more likely if you

tasks. Because glare on white paper and computer screens can produce eye strain, indirect light is a welcome option.

Avoid having a computer screen face a window. The best position for a computer is at right angles to a window so that light falls on the working area but doesn't reflect off a screen. Blinds are a good window covering because they allow you to direct the sunlight to the ceiling to create a soft, ambient light.

Indirect lighting hidden in moldings will produce a similar effect. Accent lighting on decorative objects can add drama, and task lighting is important for reading printed matter.

Limited Space

In homes that don't have the luxury of a designated office, creative homeowners may "find" a suitable spot in a wide hallway, stair landing, recessed space

Traditional furniture, top, provides a comfortable setting for this home office. The desk is ideal for working on projects away from the main office.

French doors, middle, can be closed to provide privacy for anyone using this small office.

Beautiful paneled walls, bottom, and built-ins create the ultimate home office setting.

will be receiving regular deliveries, clients will be coming to your home, or you will be employing additional help. You should also review your homeowner's insurance policy to make sure you will be adequately covered.

On the plus side, if your home office will be your primary place of business, you may be able to deduct your equipment and furnishings, the cost of decorating the office, and even a percentage of your home's utility cost on your income taxes. By the same token, a designated office used only for business might attract a capital gains tax when you sell your home, according to Mack. She suggests this can often be avoided if the room has another household function (such as a guest room).

If there are no legal restrictions, it may be time to leave that gray cubicle and head home!

Hobby Rooms: Creative Get-Away Spaces

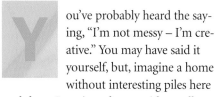

You've probably heard the saying, "I'm not messy – I'm creative." You may have said it yourself, but, imagine a home without interesting piles here and there. Imagine a home with a well-designed hobby room.

Hobby rooms come in different shapes, sizes, and locations. They are common in finished lower levels, bonus rooms over garages, and converted bedrooms (especially in empty nester homes). Oversized laundry room/craft studios are a relatively new phenomenon that is also catching on. In many homes, hobby rooms serve a dual purpose, as in the combination office/hobby room or guest room/hobby room. Where no other space is available, a converted closet can become an efficient hobby space.

Built-Ins

There are many factors that determine the best design for the space. If you plan to stay in your home for an extended time, special built-ins may be the best option.

Because this is a permanent arrangement, it's important to carefully plan how you want the room laid out. For sewing, quilting, scrapbooking, and crafts, activity centers in an L-, T- or U-shaped configuration will probably be more efficient than a single, straight-line surface. These arrangements can also accommodate more than one person, in case you like to work alongside a friend or family member.

Consider each activity you will be doing and the tools and supplies you will need for each. For instance, for sewing

This hobby room has it all: stacked bins, shelving, storage boxes, a roomy work surface, and a storage cart.

and quilting you will need a cutting table or island (ideally with fabric storage underneath), a sewing machine station with room for threads and bobbins, and an ironing board. A bulletin board can offer a convenient way to post pattern instructions. Hand finishing will be much nicer with an easy chair and a lamp on top of a small chest for scissors, needles, and gauge tools.

"You may want to vary the heights of your work surfaces," advises Custom Home Designer Carl Cuozzo. "Thirty-six inches is the norm for work you'll be doing while standing; 30-32 inches is preferable if you'll be sitting down."

Built-ins don't necessarily have to be custom made. Two base cabinets can be placed back to back to create an island wide enough to lay out 60-inch-wide fabric folded in half. Kitchen cabinets are generally 36 inches high; bath vanities are typically 32-33 inches. If a cabinet is still too tall to be comfortable, a few inches can be cut off the toe-kick space.

Casual, Open Storage

Some crafters and scrapbookers prefer to have their tools and supplies visible, with open wall shelving for fabric, paper supplies, and clear plastic tubs with smaller items. "There are so many organizational products available," notes Grant Gribble of Gribble Interior Group in Orlando and a national spokesperson for the American Society of Interior Designers.

"You can get specialized storage items at hobby stores, pick up nuts and bolt containers from a home improvement store, try a tackle box from a sporting store or shop online at www.TheContainerStore .com or www.WestElm.com for larger shelving units.

"In order to work most efficiently, arrange tools and supplies in the order you plan to use them, and label tubs and bins with samples or with a label maker. If you participate in quilting or scrapbooking groups, make sure you have at least one unit that's easy to transport."

"In a designated hobby room, you have the luxury of 'climbing the walls,'" adds Cuozzo. "A peg board framed with mold-

Orange walls and red containers create a lively, playful room.

ing and painted to match the walls keeps tools in easy reach, and a magnetic board holds clips with fabric swatches or paper scraps — without inflicting pin holes. Vinyl-coated grid systems can support hooks for hanging, baskets, clips, and racks. Another option is the type of slat wall system used by retailers (available through display houses)."

Hobby Spaces in Other Rooms

Some extra ingenuity may be necessary to create a hobby room that doubles as a welcoming guest room. A built-in wall bed, bookcase, and sewing armoire combination can make the most use of space and present a stylish, streamlined appearance.

"A nice, uncluttered desk is something a guest may also enjoy," Gribble observes. "A

wood filing cabinet or a small chest with drawers can be used for a night stand. You might find some unique furnishings that add warmth and character at antique shops, office super stores, or secondhand office furnishing stores.

"For instance, an old library card catalog file would work well for spools of thread, buttons, and other sewing notions. An architect's drawing cabinet's thin drawers could offer accessible storage for craft tools and supplies. The small drawers in an old dental cabinet would accommodate trinkets and stamps for scrapbooking. Antique printer's drawers can be hung on the wall for thread or stamps."

"Purchasing an organized closet system with shelves and drawers is a practical storage solution," suggests Cuozzo, "because

This trim sewing armoire keeps projects out of sight when guests are expected.

most guests don't stay long enough to need much closet space. Sewers and quilters may hang fabric and a rotary cutting mat from hangers.

"An armoire can look at home in a dining room, where you could use the table as a temporary work space. Sauder Wood Working Co. makes an armoire with a pull out work surface that's designed for sewing, crafts, or scrapbooking and keeps clutter out of sight.

"In a large shared room, a wall divider can be constructed with a bookcase on one side and a craft or sewing center on the other side."

Maximizing Small Spaces

Done right, a reach-in closet can become an efficient hobby space. Sliding doors should be replaced with bi-fold or swinging doors to keep side walls accessible for wall systems. A counter across the back of the closet with storage underneath and shallow shelves above it can provide a work space and a fair amount of storage. The back of a swing door can also be utilized by attaching a dowel system for lengths of fabric or spools of ribbon or a swing-down table. (Make sure the table is mounted above the inside countertop so the door will close.)

Still other possibilities include a wide linen closet, a pocket office, or a butler's pantry.

Last, But Not Least

To ensure your hobby room is a place you love to be, paint the walls a color that nourishes your spirit whether it's an energizing orange or a soothing blue or something in between.

Make sure you have adequate natural, ambient, and task lighting. Halogen bulbs provide the truest color rendering, followed by incandescent. If you prefer to use fluorescent bulbs, but you require true color rendering, choose a bulb with a color rendering index (CRI) around 80 and a Kelvin temperature around 2700.

Choose easy-care flooring. For designated hobby rooms, vinyl may be the simplest. In shared rooms, low-pile carpet will be easiest to vacuum, retrieve dropped pins, and roll a chair across. Small threads and paper snips can settle in grout lines in tile flooring, and dropped pins may scratch wood floors.

Finally, provide some form of entertainment a stereo and/or a television with a DVD player. Once you've created the ideal room, you can get started on countless other creations!

Planning for Pets

Plan for a pet by including products and materials that will keep them, and you, happy.

For many families, pets contribute some of the feelings of warmth and comfort they associate with their homes. More than half of all U.S. households have a pet of some kind. According to a survey done by the American Pet Products Manufacturers Association, these homes include 77.6 million cats and 65 million dogs.

Of course, some challenges come along with the companionship and loyalty pets provide. Your Golden Retriever does a great job of protecting your home but how do you protect your home from him?

Protecting Your Home

Julia Szabo, author of *Animal House Style: Designing a Home to Share with Your Pets*, advocates using semigloss paint to protect walls from oil stains from loose pet hair and pets rubbing against walls.

She also says bare floors (wood, tile, stone, or laminate) with area rugs are a better choice than wall-to-wall carpeting for homes with pets. Carpeting traps pet hair, stains, and odors. Bare floors are much easier to keep clean and won't be damaged by "accidents."

Katherine Salant, author of *The Brand New House Book*, warns the one place that your house should be carpeted is the stairs because dogs especially "seniors" and puppies can slip on them.

It's also wise to secure small area rugs with a nonstick mat or some heavy furniture or your pet's activities may turn them into "scatter" rugs.

The simpler window treatments now popular are a boon for pet owners. Sheer curtains, blinds, and shades harbor less dust and pet hair than heavy drapes.

Durable, washable slip covers help keep furniture clean. If your pet is trained to stay off the furniture, you may want to purchase some coordinating fabric to cover a large floor pillow just for him.

Special Pet Amenities:

In an article written for the Valley Humane Society in Pleasanton, California, pet owner Sue Jones shares the following practical ways to create an attractive, comfortable haven for families and pets.

"Some architectural elements to consider in your home might include:

- Built-in dog 'dens' beneath custom cabinets (to keep dogs from getting under foot during meal preparation)
- Indoor bathing and grooming stations (often in mud or laundry rooms)
- Pull out drawers acting as tuck-away feeding stations
- Gates that work like sliding pocket doors to limit a pet's access to another room
- Indoor structural ramps and beams for kitties to roam about the upper reaches of your ceiling; and
- Accessible, built-in food storage areas.

"Design materials," Jones continues, "include a new carpet that has a waterproof polyethylene backing that prevents urine from reaching the carpet pad. Decorating with imitation suede or 'ultra suede' discourages scratching. A tightly quilted, very durable fabric called matelasse is recommended for bed coverings.

"Backyard landscaping could include a separate dirt pit apart from your flower garden for the pet that needs to bury his treasures. Try a Kitty Aviary or a Kitty Walk for your indoor cats to safely enjoy the outdoors. Plan a garden path to include small bridges and tunnels for terriers to explore. Plant a beautiful garden with non toxic plants. Add a continuous water fountain for your pets to enjoy clean water and stay hydrated."

Protecting Your Pet

In her popular book *Beautiful Places, Spiritual Spaces*, author Sharon Hanby-Robie adds these suggestions to keep pets safe:

"Just like children, you must pet-proof your home. Lock cabinet doors to keep little paws from opening them. Keep trash cans covered or safely behind locked cabinet doors. Be sure your garage is safe by keeping rakes and shovels out of the way, so they don't get knocked over. Clean the floor of any oil or antifreeze puddles because one lick can be deadly. Consider installing an invisible fence. It works great for dogs and cats alike."

A little careful forethought inside and outside your home will make it easier for you and your four-legged friends to live harmoniously for years to come.

Plan #101013

Dimensions: 72' W x 66' D

Levels: 1

Heated Square Footage: 2,564

Bedrooms: 3

Bathrooms: 2½

Foundation: Basement; slab

Materials List Available: Yes

Price Category: F

Images provided by designer/architect.

This exciting design combines a striking classic exterior with a highly functional floor plan.

Features:

- Ceiling Height: 9 ft. unless otherwise noted.

- Family Room: This warm and inviting room measures 18 ft. x 22 ft. It features a 14-ft. ceiling and a rear wall of windows. French doors lead to an enormous deck.

- Kitchen: This unique angled kitchen is open to the hearth room and eating areas, all of which enjoy vaulted ceilings and are surrounded by windows. The hearth room has a TV niche.

- Master Suite: This 19-ft. x 18-ft. master suite is truly sumptuous, with its 12-ft. ceiling, sitting area, two walk-in closets, and full-featured bath.

- Secondary Bedrooms: Each of the secondary bedrooms measures 11 ft. x 14 ft. and has direct access to a shared bath.

- Bonus Room: Just beyond the entry are stairs leading to this bonus room, which measures approximately 12 ft. x 21 ft.—plenty of room for storage or future expansion.

Copyright by designer/architect.

Dining Room

Hearth Room

Kitchen

Family Room

Master Bedroom

Master Bath

Plan #211010

Dimensions: 81' W x 84' D
Levels: 1
Heated Square Footage: 2,503
Bedrooms: 3
Bathrooms: 2½
Foundation: Slab
Materials List Available: Yes
Price Category: E

A well-designed floor plan makes maximum use of space and creates convenience and comfort.

Features:

- Ceiling Height: 10 ft. unless otherwise noted.

- Living Room: A stepped ceiling gives this living room special architectural interest. There's a full-service wet bar designed to handle parties of any size. When the weather gets warm, step out of the living room into a lovely screened rear porch.

- Master Bedroom: You'll love unwinding at the end of a busy day in this master suite. It's located away from the other bedrooms for more privacy.

- Study: This charming study adjoins the master bedroom. It's the perfect quiet spot to get some work done, surf the internet, or pay the bills.

SMARTtip

Deck Railings

Install caps and post finials to your railings. A rail cap protects the cut ends of the posts from the weather. Finials add another decorative layer to your design, and the styles are endless—ball, chamfered, grooved, and top hat are a few.

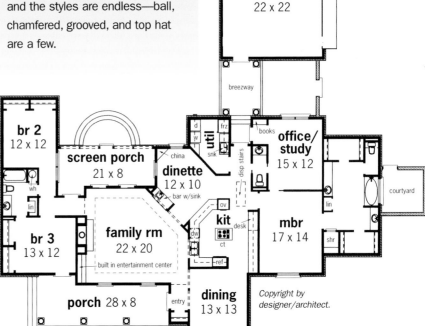

Copyright by designer/architect.

Plan #121007

Dimensions: 74' W x 67'8" D

Levels: 1

Heated Square Footage: 2,512

Bedrooms: 3

Bathrooms: 2½

Foundation: Basement

Materials List Available: Yes

Price Category: E

A series of arches brings grace to this home's interior and exterior.

Features:

- Ceiling Height: 8 ft.

- Formal Dining Room: Tapered columns give this dining room a classical look that lends elegance to any dinner party.

- Great Room: Just beyond the dining room is this light-filled room, with its wall of arched windows and see-through fireplace.

- Hearth Room: On the other side of the fire place you will find this cozy area, with its corner entertainment center.

- Dinette: A gazebo-shaped dinette is the architectural surprise of the house layout.

- Kitchen: This well-conceived working kitchen features a generous center island.

- Garage: With three garage bays you'll never be short of parking space or storage.

Images provided by designer/architect.

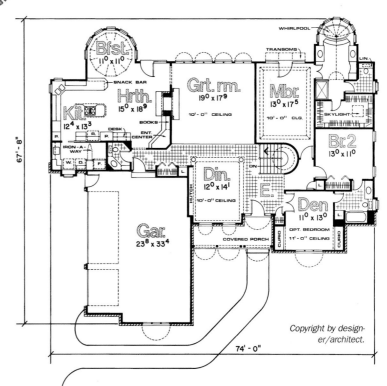

Copyright by designer/architect.

Optional Bedroom

Plan #151711

Dimensions: 64' W x 60'2" D
Levels: 1
Heated Square Footage: 2,554
Bedrooms: 4
Bathrooms: 2½
Foundation: Crawl space or slab
CompleteCost List Available: Yes
Price Category: E

Images provided by designer/architect.

An alluring arched entry welcomes guests into your home, giving them a taste of the lavishness they'll find once inside.

CAD FILE AVAILABLE

Features:

- **Kitchen:** Counter space on all sides and a center island provide ample space for the budding chef. This kitchen is located across the hall from the dining room and opens into the hearth room, providing easy transitions between preparing and serving. A snack bar acts as a shift between the kitchen and hearth room.

- **Hearth Room:** This spacious area is lined with windows on one side, shares a gas fire place with the great room, and opens onto the grilling porch, which makes it ideal for gatherings of all kinds and sizes.

- **Master Suite:** Larger than any space in the house, this room will truly make you feel like the master. The bedroom is a blank canvas waiting for your personal touch and has a door opening to the backyard. The compartmentalized master bath includes his and her walk-in closets and sinks, a glass shower stall, and a whirlpool bathtub.

- **Secondary Bedrooms:** If three bedrooms is one too many, the second bedroom can easily be used as a study with optional French doors opening from the foyer. Every additional bedroom has a large closet and access to the central full bathroom.

Front View

Copyright by designer/architect.

This home, as shown in the photograph, may differ from the actual blueprints. For more detailed information, please check the floor plans carefully.

Plan #121025

Dimensions: 60' W x 59'4" D
Levels: 2
Heated Square Footage: 2,562
Main Level Sq. Ft.: 1,875
Upper Level Square Footage: 687
Bedrooms: 4
Bathrooms: 2½
Foundation: Basement; slab for fee
Materials List Available: Yes
Price Category: E

Images provided by designer/architect.

Dramatic arches are the reoccurring architectural theme in this distinctive home.

Features:

- Ceiling Height: 8 ft. unless otherwise noted.
- Foyer: This is a grand two-story entrance. Plants will thrive on the plant shelf thanks to light streaming through the arched window.
- Great Room: The foyer flows into the great room through dramatic 15-ft.-high arched openings.

- Kitchen: An island is the centerpiece of this highly functional kitchen that includes a separate breakfast area.
- Office: French doors open into this versatile office that features a 10-ft. ceiling and transom-topped windows.
- Master Suite: The master suite features a volume ceiling, built-in dresser, and two closets. You'll unwind in the beautiful corner whirlpool bath with its elegant window treatment.

Main Level Floor Plan

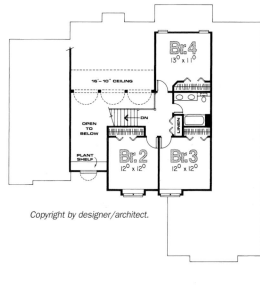

Upper Level Floor Plan

Copyright by designer/architect.

Plan #131027

Dimensions: 62'4" W x 53'6" D
Levels: 1.5
Heated Square Footage: 2,567
Main Level Sq. Ft.: 2,017
Upper Level Sq. Ft.: 550
Bedrooms: 4
Bathrooms: 3
Foundation: Crawl space, slab, or basement
Materials List Available: Yes
Price Category: F

This home, as shown in the photograph, may differ from the actual blueprints. For more detailed information, please check the floor plans carefully.

Images provided by designer/architect.

The features of this home are so good that you may have trouble imagining all of them at once.

Features:

- **Great Room:** Imagine a stepped ceiling, corner fireplace, built-media center, and wall of windows with a glass door to the backyard—in one room.

- **Dining Room:** A stepped ceiling and server with a sink add to the elegance of this formal room.

- **Breakfast Room:** Eat at the bar this room shares with the island kitchen, and admire the 12-ft. cathedral ceiling and bayed group of 8- and 9-ft. windows. Or go through the sliding glass door to the covered side porch.

- **Master Suite:** The bedroom has a tray ceiling and cozy sitting area, and a whirlpool tub, shower, and walk-in closet are in the skylighted bath.

- **Optional Study:** The private bath in bedroom 2 makes it ideal for a study or home office.

Breakfast Nook

Rear View

Great Room

Main Level Floor Plan

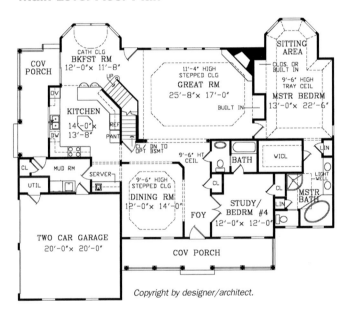

Copyright by designer/architect.

Upper Level Floor Plan

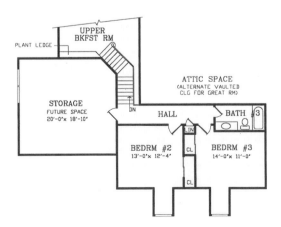

Painting Tips

As with any skill, there is a right and a wrong way to paint. There is a right way to hold a brush, a right way to maneuver a roller, a right way to spray a wall, etc. Follow these basic professional tips:

Brushing vs. Rolling. Some painters insist that only a brush-painted job looks right. However, most painters will "cut in" the edges with a brush, and then finish the main body of a wall or ceiling using a roller. Brushing alone can be time-consuming, and it is typically reserved for architectural woodwork.

Using the Right Brush. Use the largest brush with which you are comfortable. Professional painters seldom pick up anything smaller than a 4-inch brush. Most homeowners will achieve good results using a 4-inch brush for "cutting in" and for large surfaces, and an angled 2½- to 3-inch sash brush for trim around windows and doors. Be sure, also, to use brushes that are appropriate for the type of paint being applied. Oil-based paints require a natural bristle (also called "China bristles"), while water-based paints are applied with a synthetic bristle brush.

Handling a Brush. Many people grip a paintbrush as if they were shaking someone's hand. It is better to grip a brush more like a pencil, with the fingers and thumb wrapped around the metal ferrule. This grip provides the hand and wrist with a wider range of motion and therefore greater speed and precision. If your hand cramps, switch hands or switch temporarily to the handshake grip.

Wiping Rags. Before you begin painting, put a dust rag in your pocket. This is helpful for clearing away cobwebs and dust before painting. It is also handy for wiping off paint drips before they have a chance to dry.

Paint Hooks. When working on a ladder, use a good-quality paint hook to secure the paint bucket to your ladder. Avoid makeshift hooks made with wire or coat hangers. Paint hooks are inexpensive and available at virtually all paint and hardware stores.

Plan #121321

Dimensions: 59'4" W x 88' D

Levels: 1

Heated Square Footage: 2,506

Bedrooms: 3

Bathrooms: 2½

Foundation: Basement

Materials List Available: Yes

Price Category: E

Images provided by designer/architect.

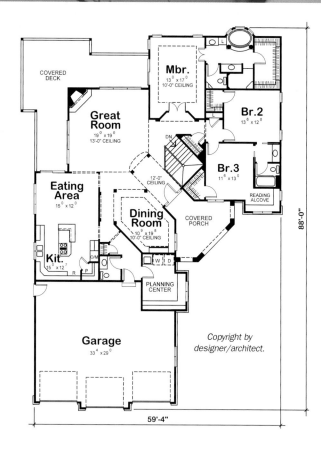

Copyright by designer/architect.

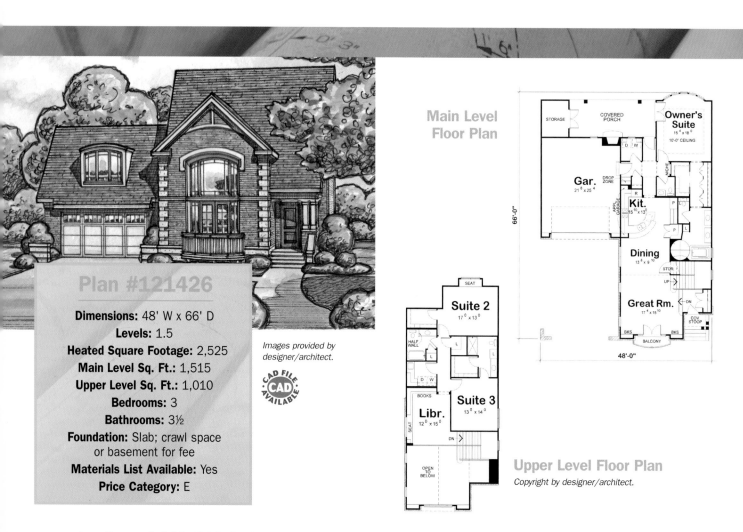

Plan #121426

Dimensions: 48' W x 66' D

Levels: 1.5

Heated Square Footage: 2,525

Main Level Sq. Ft.: 1,515

Upper Level Sq. Ft.: 1,010

Bedrooms: 3

Bathrooms: 3½

Foundation: Slab; crawl space or basement for fee

Materials List Available: Yes

Price Category: E

Images provided by designer/architect.

Main Level Floor Plan

Upper Level Floor Plan

Copyright by designer/architect.

Plan #321173

Dimensions: : 61'4" W x 48' D
Levels: 2
Heated Square Footage: 2,597
Main Level Sq. Ft.: 1,742
Upper Level Sq. Ft.: 855
Bedrooms: 4
Bathrooms: 3½
Foundation: Crawl space, slab, or walkout
Materials List Available: Yes
Price Category: E

Images provided by designer/architect.

CAD FILE AVAILABLE

Main Level Floor Plan

- Screened Porch (vaulted)
- Deck
- Hearth Rm 15-8x13-0
- Kitchen 14-0x13-0
- Great Rm 17-0x17-0 vaulted
- Dining 12-0x15-9
- Entry
- MBr 18-4x17-5 vaulted
- Garage 21-4x21-4

Upper Level Floor Plan
- Br 2 12-11x11-0
- Br 3 12-0x13-4
- Br 4 13-0x10-3
- open to below

Copyright by designer/architect.

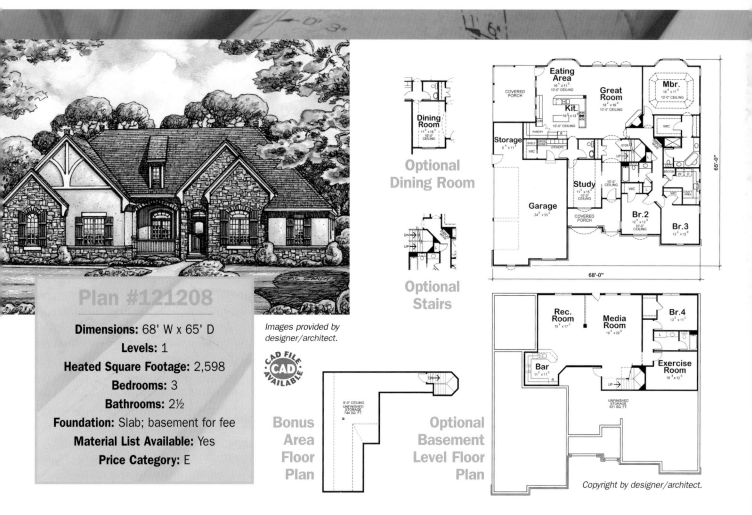

Plan #121208

Dimensions: 68' W x 65' D
Levels: 1
Heated Square Footage: 2,598
Bedrooms: 3
Bathrooms: 2½
Foundation: Slab; basement for fee
Material List Available: Yes
Price Category: E

Images provided by designer/architect.

CAD FILE AVAILABLE

Optional Dining Room

Dining Room 11' x 15' 10'-0" CEILING

Optional Stairs

Bonus Area Floor Plan

8'-0" CEILING UNFINISHED STORAGE 744 SQ. FT.

Optional Basement Level Floor Plan

- Eating Area 18' x 11' 10'-0" CEILING
- Kit. 16'5 x 13'5 10'-0" CEILING
- Great Room 18' x 18' 10'-0" CEILING
- Mbr. 16' x 17'5 10'-0" CEILING
- Storage 9'4 x 11'
- Study 11' x 15' 10'-0" CEILING
- Garage 24'8 x 33'5
- Br.2 13'5 x 12'5 10'-0" CEILING
- Br.3 12'4 x 12'
- Rec. Room 15' x 17'5
- Media Room 18' x 22'5
- Br.4 13'5 x 11'5
- Bar 11'5 x 11'
- Exercise Room 16'5 x 12'5
- UNFINISHED STORAGE 931 SQ. FT.

Copyright by designer/architect.

Plan #121029

Dimensions: 58'8" W x 54' D

Levels: 1.5

Heated Square Footage: 2,576

Main Level Sq. Ft.: 1,735

Upper Level Sq. Ft.: 841

Bedrooms: 4

Bathrooms: 2½

Foundation: Basement

Materials List Available: Yes

Price Category: E

Images provided by designer/architect.

This gracious home is designed with the contemporary lifestyle in mind.

Features:

- Ceiling Height: 8 ft. unless otherwise noted.

- Great Room: This room features a fireplace and entertainment center. It's equally suited for family gatherings and formal entertaining.

- Breakfast Area: The fireplace is two-sided so it shares its warmth with this breakfast area—the perfect spot for informal family meals.

- Master Suite: Halfway up the staircase you'll find double-doors into this truly distinctive suite featuring a barrel-vault ceiling, built-in bookcases, and his and her walk-in closets. Unwind at the end of the day by stretching out in the oval whirlpool tub.

- Computer Loft: This loft overlooks the great room. It is designed as a home office with a built-in desk for your computer.

- Garage: Two bays provide plenty of storage in addition to parking space.

CAD FILE AVAILABLE

Main Level Floor Plan

Upper Level Floor Plan

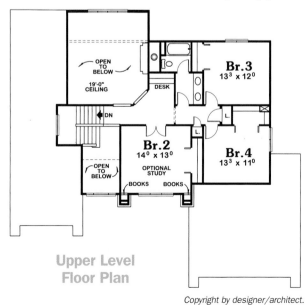

Copyright by designer/architect.

Plan #121073

Dimensions: 70' W x 52' D
Levels: 1.5
Heated Square Footage: 2,579
Main Level Sq. Ft.: 1,933
Upper Level Sq. Ft.: 646
Bedrooms: 4
Bathrooms: 2½
Foundation: Basement
Materials List Available: Yes
Price Category: E

Images provided by designer/architect.

Luxury will surround you in this home with contemporary styling and up-to-date amenities at every turn.

Features:

• Great Room: This large room shares both a see-through fireplace and a wet bar with the adjacent hearth room. Transom-topped windows add both light and architectural interest to this room.

• Den: Transom-topped windows add visual interest to this private area.

• Kitchen: A center island and corner pantry add convenience to this well-planned kitchen, and a lovely ceiling treatment adds beauty to the bayed breakfast area.

• Master Suite: A built-in bookcase adds to the ambiance of this luxury-filled area, where you're sure to find a retreat at the end of the day.

Main Level Floor Plan

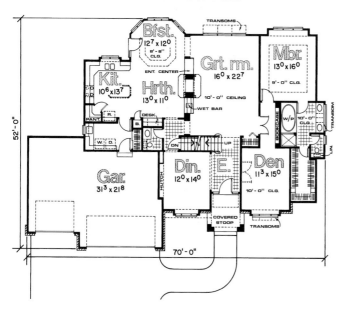

Upper Level Floor Plan

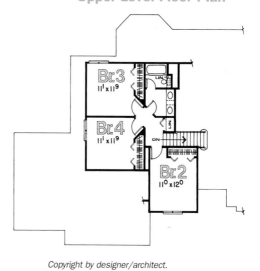

Copyright by designer/architect.

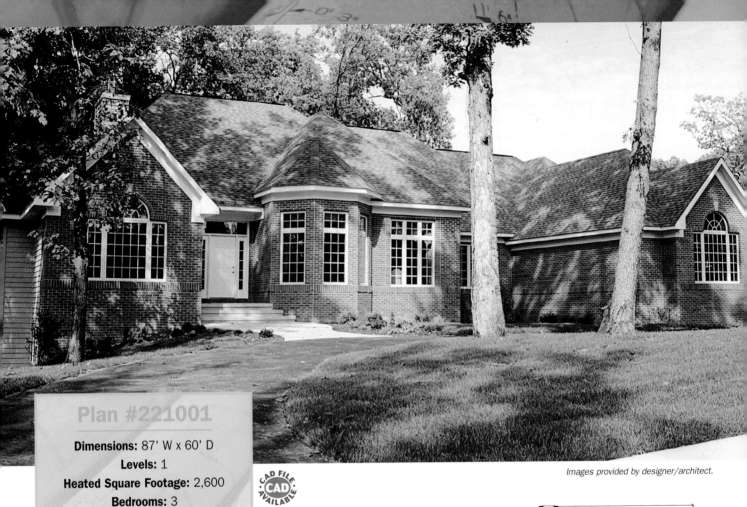

Plan #221001

Dimensions: 87' W x 60' D

Levels: 1

Heated Square Footage: 2,600

Bedrooms: 3

Bathrooms: 2½

Foundation: Basement

Materials List Available: No

Price Category: F

You'll love this traditional ranch for its unusual spaciousness and many comfortable amenities.

Features:

• **Great Room:** As you enter the home, you'll have a clear view all the way to the backyard through the many windows in this huge room. Built-ins here provide a practical touch, and the fireplace makes this room cozy when the weather's cool.

• **Kitchen:** This large kitchen has been thoughtfully designed to make cooking a pleasure. It flows into a lovely dining nook, so it's also a great place to entertain.

• **Master Suite:** Relaxing will come naturally in this lovely suite, with its two walk-in closets, private sitting area, and large, sumptuous bathroom that features a Jacuzzi tub.

• **Additional Bedrooms:** Located on the opposite side of the house from the master suite, these bedrooms are convenient to a full bath. You can also use one room as a den.

Images provided by designer/architect.

Copyright by designer/architect.

Rear Elevation

Plan #121093

Dimensions: 62' W x 60'8" D
Levels: 1.5
Heated Square Footage: 2,603
Main Level Sq. Ft.: 1,800
Upper Level Sq. Ft.: 803
Bedrooms: 4
Bathrooms: 3½
Foundation: Basement
Materials List Available: Yes
Price Category: F

Images provided by designer/architect.

If you love family life but also treasure your privacy, you'll appreciate the layout of this home.

Features:

• Entry: This two-story, open area features plant shelves to display your favorite plants and flowers.

• Dining Room: Open to the entry, this room features 12-ft. ceilings and corner hutches.

• Den: French doors lead to this quiet room, with its bowed window and spider-beamed ceiling.

• Gathering Room: A three-sided fireplace, shared with both the kitchen and the breakfast area, is the highlight of this room.

• Master Suite: Secluded for privacy, this suite also has a private covered deck where you can sit and recharge at any time of day. A walk-in closet is practical, and a whirlpool tub is pure comfort.

CAD FILE AVAILABLE

Main Level Floor Plan

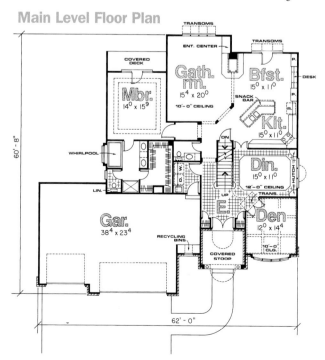

Upper Level Floor Plan

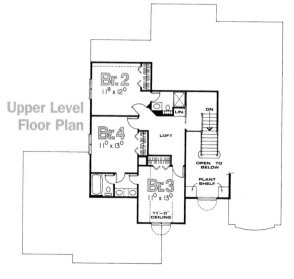

Copyright by designer/architect.

Plan #191017

Dimensions: 78' W x 51' D
Levels: 1
Heated Square Footage: 2,605
Bedrooms: 4
Bathrooms: 2½
Foundation: Crawl space, slab, or basement
Materials List Available: No
Price Category: F

You'll love the elegance of this gorgeous home, which includes every amenity you can imagine.

Features:

- Great Room: An archway from the foyer welcomes you to this expansive room, with its recessed ceiling, gas fireplace, custom cabinets, and French doors leading to the covered rear porch.

- Kitchen: This large room includes a pantry, stove on an island, angled sink, snack bar, and built-in desk close to the hall stairs.

- Laundry Room: You'll find a sink, storage closets, and wall-to-wall cabinets above the washer/dryer and freezer area in this practical spot.

- Master Suite: A wall of windows greets you in the bedroom, and built-in cabinets add storage space. The huge walk-in closet is close to the dressing area. The luxurious bath has a skylight over the dual sinks and is located so that one person can sleep while the other uses it.

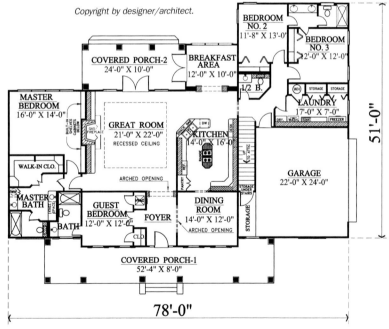

Entry

Kitchen

Plan #151144

Dimensions: 66'4" W x 64' D

Levels: 1

Heated Square Footage: 2,624

Bedrooms: 4

Bathrooms: 3

Foundation: Crawl space, slab; basement for fee

CompleteCost List Available: Yes

Price Category: F

Images provided by designer/architect.

The traditional exterior appearance of this home gives way to a surprisingly contemporary interior design and a wealth of lovely amenities.

Features:

- **Living Room:** The 8-inch columns create an elegant feeling in this well-lit room.

- **Dining Room:** An 11-ft. ceiling makes this room ideal for hosting dinner parties or entertaining a crowd.

- **Kitchen:** The kitchen features a pass-through to the living room for serving convenience and a snack bar where the kids are sure to gather.

- **Breakfast/Hearth Room:** The fireplace is the centerpiece in winter, but you'll love the access to the grilling porch when the weather's warm.

- **Master Suite:** The door to the rear porch is a special feature in this private retreat, and you'll love the bath with a walk-in closet, split vanities, and a glass shower.

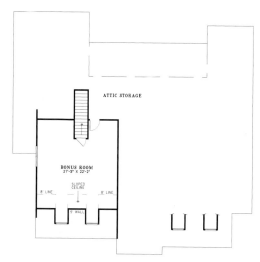

Bonus Area Floor Plan

Copyright by designer/architect.

Plan #321051

Dimensions: 69'8" W x 46' D
Levels: 2
Heated Square Footage: 2,624
Main Level Sq. Ft.: 1,774
Upper Level Sq. Ft.: 850
Bedrooms: 4
Bathrooms: 2½
Foundation: Basement
Materials List Available: Yes
Price Category: F

The dramatic exterior design allows natural light to flow into the spacious living area of this home.

Features:

- Entry: This two-story area opens into the dining room through a classic colonnade.

- Dining Room: A large bay window, stately columns, and doorway to the kitchen make this room both beautiful and convenient.

- Great Room: Enjoy light from the fireplace or the three Palladian windows in the 18-ft. ceiling.

- Kitchen: The step-saving design features a walk-in pantry as well as good counter space.

- Breakfast Room: You'll love the light that flows through the windows flanking the back door.

- Master Suite: The vaulted ceiling and bayed areas in both the bed and bath add elegance. You'll love the two walk-in closets and bath with a sunken tub, two vanities, and separate shower.

This home, as shown in the photograph, may differ from the actual blueprints. For more detailed information, please check the floor plans carefully.   *Images provided by designer/architect.*

Main Level Floor Plan

Copyright by designer/architect.

Master Bath

Upper Level Floor Plan

Plan #121155

Dimensions: 65'6" W x 56'10" D
Levels: 1.5
Heated Square Footage: 2,638
Main Level Sq. Ft.: 1,844
Upper Level Sq. Ft.: 794
Bedrooms: 4
Bathrooms: 3½
Foundation: Slab; basement for fee
Material List Available: Yes
Price Category: F

This home, as shown in the photograph, may differ from the actual blueprints. For more detailed information, please check the floor plans carefully.

Images provided by designer/architect.

This traditional home is so attractive that passersby will want to stop and visit.

Features:

- Study: Situated in close proximity to the entry, this study would function well as a home office. The triple-window unit adds light to the area.

- Kitchen: This gourmet peninsula kitchen offers a handy pantry. The attached breakfast room offers easy access to the veranda.

- Master Suite: This master suite boasts a vaulted ceiling and two walk-in closets. The private bath shows off a whirlpool tub and dual vanities.

- Secondary Bedrooms: Residing on the upper level are three family bedrooms. Bedroom 4 boasts its own private bath, while bedrooms 2 and 3 share a Jack-and-Jill bathroom.

Upper Level Floor Plan

Copyright by designer/architect.

Main Level Floor Plan

Plan #121333

Dimensions: 74' W x 68'8" D

Levels: 1

Heated Square Footage: 2,632

Bedrooms: 2

Bathrooms: 2½

Foundation: Basement

Materials List Available: Yes

Price Category: F

Images provided by designer/architect.

Copyright by designer/architect.

Plan #121150

Dimensions: 68'7" W x 57'4" D

Levels: 1.5

Heated Square Footage: 2,639

Main Level Sq. Ft.: 2,087

Upper Level Sq. Ft.: 552

Bedrooms: 4

Bathrooms: 3½

Foundation: Slab; basement for fee

Material List Available: Yes

Price Category: F

Images provided by designer/architect.

Main Level Floor Plan

Upper Level Floor Plan

Copyright by designer/architect.

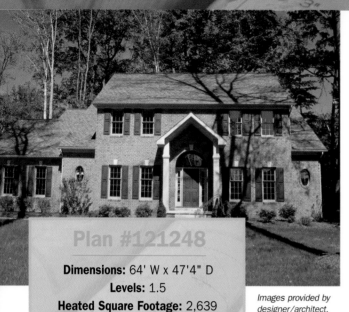

Plan #121248

Dimensions: 64' W x 47'4" D
Levels: 1.5
Heated Square Footage: 2,639
Main Level Sq. Ft.: 1,865
Upper Level Sq. Ft.: 774
Bedrooms: 4
Bathrooms: 3½
Foundation: Basement
Materials List Available: Yes
Price Category: F

Images provided by designer/architect.

Main Level Floor Plan

Upper Level Floor Plan

Copyright by designer/architect.

Plan #121324

Dimensions: 79'8" W x 57' D
Levels: 1
Heated Square Footage: 2,641
Bedrooms: 3
Bathrooms: 3½
Foundation: Basement
Materials List Available: Yes
Price Category: F

Images provided by designer/architect.

Copyright by designer/architect.

Plan #121090

Dimensions: 60' W x 58' D
Levels: 1.5
Heated Square Footage: 2,645
Main Level Sq. Ft.: 1,972
Upper Level Sq. Ft.: 673
Bedrooms: 4
Bathrooms: 2½
Foundation: Basement
Materials List Available: Yes
Price Category: F

You'll be amazed at the amenities that have been designed into this lovely home.

Features:

- Den: French doors just off the entry lead to this lovely room, with its bowed window and spider-beamed ceiling.

- Great Room: A trio of graceful arched windows highlights the volume ceiling in this room. You might want to curl up to read next to the see-through fireplace into the hearth room.

- Kitchen: Enjoy the good design in this room.

- Hearth Room: The shared fireplace with the great room makes this a cozy spot in cool weather.

- Master Suite: French doors lead to this well-lit area, with its roomy walk-in closet, sunlit whirlpool tub, separate shower, and two vanities.

Main Level Floor Plan

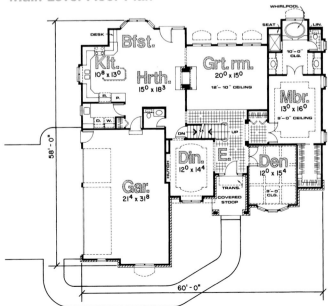

Upper Level Floor Plan

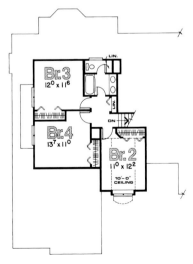

Copyright by designer/architect.

Plan #121046

Dimensions: 65'3" W x 57'1½" D

Levels: 2

Heated Square Footage: 2,655

Main Level Sq. Ft.: 1,906

Upper Level Sq. Ft.: 749

Bedrooms: 4

Bathrooms: 2½

Foundation: Slab; basement for fee

Materials List Available: Yes

Price Category: F

CAD FILE AVAILABLE

Images provided by designer/architect.

This home beautifully blends traditional architectural detail with modern amenities.

Features:

• Ceiling Height: 8 ft. unless otherwise noted.

• Entry: This two-story entry enjoys views of the uniquely shaped study, a second-floor balcony, and the formal dining room.

• Formal Dining Room: With its elegant corner column, this dining room sets the

stage for formal entertaining as well as family gatherings.

• Kitchen: This well-appointed kitchen features a center island for efficient food preparation. It has a butler's pantry near the dining room and another pantry in the service entry.

• Breakfast Area: Here's the spot for informal family meals or lingering over coffee.

• Rear Porch: Step out through French doors in the master bedroom and the breakfast area.

Main Level Floor Plan

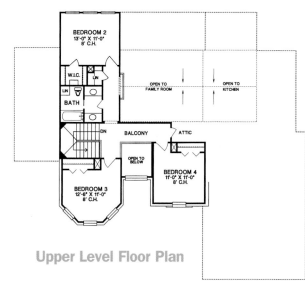

Upper Level Floor Plan

Copyright by designer/architect.

Plan #121163

Dimensions: 65'10" W x 75'6" D
Levels: 1
Heated Square Footage: 2,679
Bedrooms: 4
Bathrooms: 3
Foundation: Slab; basement for fee
Material List Available: Yes
Price Category: F

Large rooms give this home a spacious feel in a modest footprint.

Features:

- Family Room: This area is the central gathering place in the home. The windows to the rear fill the area with natural light. The fireplace take the chill off on cool winter nights.

- Kitchen: This peninsula kitchen with raised bar is open into the family room and the breakfast area. The built-in pantry is a welcomed storage area for today's family.

- Master Suite: This secluded area features large windows with a view of the backyard. The master bath boasts a large walk-in closet, his and her vanities and a compartmentalized lavatory area.

- Secondary Bedrooms: Bedroom 2 has its own access to the main bathroom, while bedrooms 3 and 4 share a Jack-and-Jill bathroom. All bedrooms feature walk-in closets.

Copyright by designer/architect.

Plan #211062

Dimensions: 96'6" W x 43' D
Levels: 1
Heated Square Footage: 2,719
Bedrooms: 4
Bathrooms: 21½
Foundation: Slab
Materials List Available: Yes
Price Category: F

If you're looking for a beautiful home that combines luxurious amenities with a separate, professional office space, this could be the one.

Features:

- Living Room: Enjoy an 11-ft. ceiling, brick fireplace, and built-in shelving in this room.

- Dining Room: A 2-story ceiling gives presence to this room.

- Kitchen: A breakfast bar here is open to the breakfast room beyond for ease of serving.

- Breakfast Room: A built-in corner china closet adds to the practicality you'll find here.

- Office: A separate entrance makes it possible to run a professional business from this home.

- Master Suite: Separated for privacy, this suite includes two vanities and a walk-in closet.

- Porch: The rear screened porch opens to a courtyard where you'll love to entertain.

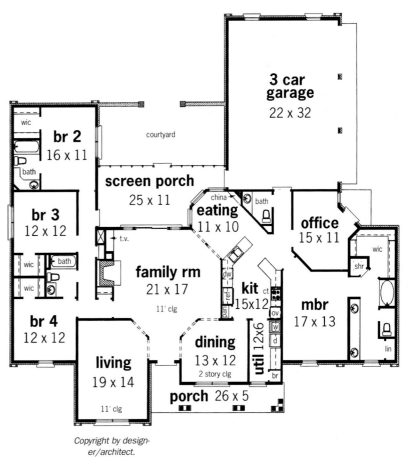

Copyright by designer/architect.

Main Level Floor Plan

Plan #161053

Dimensions: 58'6" W x 62'3" D
Levels: 2
Heated Square Footage: 2,679
Main Level Sq. Ft.: 1,905
Upper Level Sq. Ft.: 774
Bedrooms: 4
Bathrooms: 3½
Foundation: Basement; crawl space, slab, or walkout for fee
Materials List Available: Yes
Price Category: F

Images provided by designer/architect.

Upper Level Floor Plan

Copyright by designer/architect.

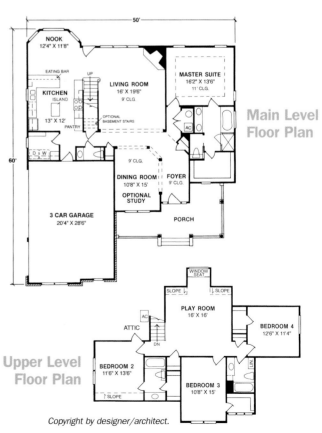

Main Level Floor Plan

Plan #121079

Dimensions: 50' W x 60' D
Levels: 2
Heated Square Footage: 2,688
Main Level Sq. Ft.: 1,650
Upper Level Sq. Ft.: 1,038
Bedrooms: 4
Bathrooms: 3½
Foundation: Slab
Materials List Available: Yes
Price Category: F

Images provided by designer/architect.

This home, as shown in the photograph, may differ from the actual blueprints. For more detailed information, please check the floor plans carefully.

Upper Level Floor Plan

Copyright by designer/architect.

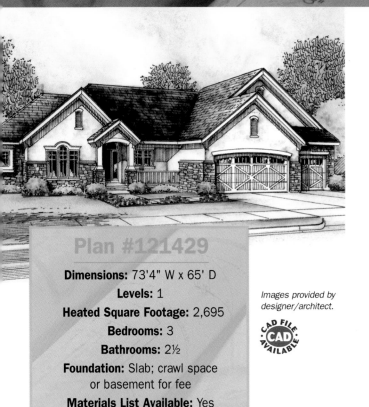

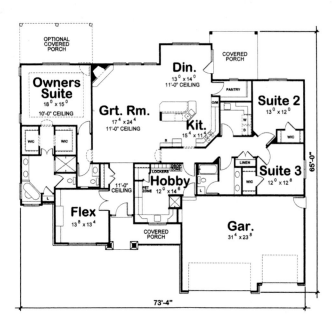

Plan #121429

Dimensions: 73'4" W x 65' D

Levels: 1

Heated Square Footage: 2,695

Bedrooms: 3

Bathrooms: 2½

Foundation: Slab; crawl space or basement for fee

Materials List Available: Yes

Price Category: F

Images provided by designer/architect.

CAD FILE AVAILABLE

Copyright by designer/architect.

Plan #321007

Dimensions: 76' W x 55'2" D

Levels: 1

Heated Square Footage: 2,695

Bedrooms: 3

Bathrooms: 2½

Foundation: Basement

Materials List Available: Yes

Price Category: F

Images provided by designer/architect.

CAD FILE AVAILABLE

Copyright by designer/architect.

SMARTtip

Decorative Poles

Drapery poles are supported by the brackets fastened to the window frame or wall. The brackets that are provided with the poles generally coordinate and blend in with the pole finish. Brackets can be simple but also decorative. If you opt for a spectacular, attention-grabbing bracket, consider choosing less showy finials for the ends of the pole.

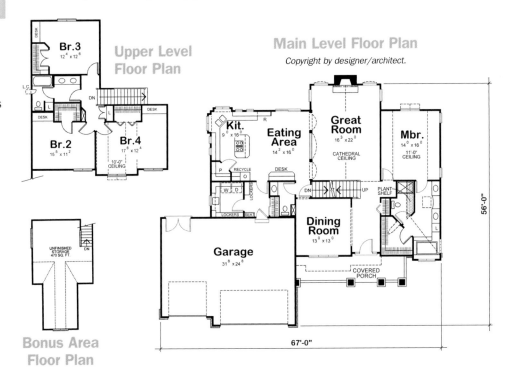

Plan #121203

Dimensions: 67' W x 56' D
Levels: 1.5
Heated Square Footage: 2,690
Main Level Sq. Ft.: 1,792
Upper Level Sq. Ft.: 898
Bedrooms: 4
Bathrooms: 2½
Foundation: Basement; crawl space or slab for fee
Materials List Available: Yes
Price Category: F

This traditional Craftsman-style home has a unique design to accommodate the needs of the growing family.

Features:

• Porch: A long covered porch welcomes guests out of the elements or gives you outdoor living space where you can sit and greet the neighbors while listening to the sounds of the day.

• Great Room: With its cathedral ceiling and glowing fireplace, this room welcomes you home comfortably. Relax with your family or entertain your friends.

• Kitchen: Long counters, a large pantry, a stovetop island and a snack bar make this efficiently designed kitchen ideal for the family cook and expert chef alike. An attached eating area and a nearby formal dining room mean you can cater to any kind of meal.

Images provided by designer/architect.

• Master Bedroom: Unwind in this private space, and enjoy its conveniences. The full master bath includes a standing shower, his and her sinks, a large tub, and a spacious walk-in closet.

• Secondary Bedrooms: Each of the three bedrooms upstairs has ample living space,

large closets, and a desk, and all share access to the second full bathroom, which is compartmentalized.

• Garage: This three-car garage allows for space for both established and budding drivers, or you can use one bay for storage or a workbench.

Upper Level Floor Plan

Br.3 12⁴ x 12⁶
Br.2 15⁵ x 11²
Br.4 17⁸ x 12⁴ 10'-0" CEILING

Main Level Floor Plan

Copyright by designer/architect.

Kit. 9⁰ x 16⁰
Eating Area 14² x 16⁰
Great Room 16³ x 22⁰ CATHEDRAL CEILING
Mbr. 14⁰ x 16⁰ 11'-0" CEILING
Dining Room 13⁰ x 13⁰
Garage 31⁸ x 24⁸
COVERED PORCH

56'-0"
67'-0"

Bonus Area Floor Plan

UNFINISHED STORAGE 470 SQ. FT.

Plan #121083

Dimensions: 72' W x 45'4" D
Levels: 2
Heated Square Footage: 2,695
Main Level Sq. Ft.: 1,881
Upper Level Sq. Ft.: 814
Bedrooms: 4
Bathrooms: 3½
Foundation: Basement
Materials List Available: Yes
Price Category: F

You'll love this home for its soaring entryway ceiling and well-designed layout.

Features:

- Entry: A balcony from the upper level looks down into this two-story entry, which features a decorative plant shelf.

- Great Room: Comfort is guaranteed in this large room, with its built-in bookcases framing a lovely fireplace and trio of transom-topped windows along one wall.

- Living Room: Save both this formal room and the formal dining room, both of which flank the entry, for guests and special occasions.

- Kitchen: This convenient work space includes a gazebo-shaped breakfast area where friends and family will gather at any time of day.

Upper Level Floor Plan

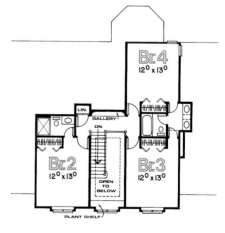

Copyright by designer/architect.

Main Level Floor Plan

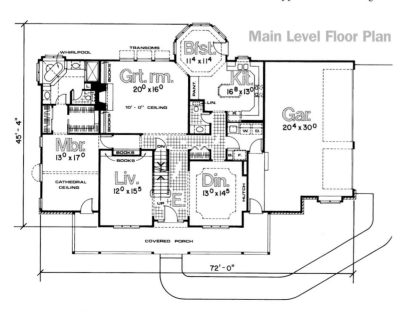

Plan #151014

Dimensions: 70'2" W x 51'4" D
Levels: 1.5
Heated Square Footage: 2,698
Main Level Sq. Ft.: 1,813
Upper Level Sq. Ft.: 885
Bedrooms: 5
Bathrooms: 3
Foundation: Crawl space, slab; basement for fee
CompleteCost List Available: Yes
Price Category: F

A comfortable front porch welcomes you into this home that features a balcony over the great room, a study, and a kitchen designed for gourmet cooks.

CAD FILE AVAILABLE

Images provided by designer/architect.

Features:

- Ceiling Height: 9 ft.
- Front Porch: Stately 12-in.-wide pillars form the entryway.
- Foyer: Open to upper story.
- Great Room: A fireplace, vaulted 9-ft. ceiling, and balcony from the second floor add character to this lovely room.
- Dining Room: Open to the kitchen for convenience.
- Kitchen: A large walk-in pantry, well-designed work areas, and eat-in bar make this room a treasure.
- Breakfast Room: Enjoy this spot that opens to both the kitchen and a large covered porch at the rear of the house.
- Study: This quiet room has French doors leading to the yard.
- Master Suite: This spacious area has cozy window seats as well as his and her walk-in closets. The master bathroom is fitted with a whirlpool tub, a glass shower, and his and her sinks.

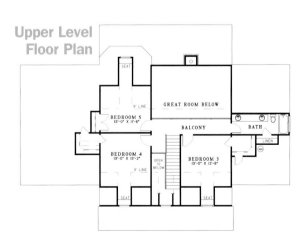

Upper Level Floor Plan

Main Level Floor Plan

Copyright by designer/architect.

Plan #121067

Dimensions: 56' W x 59'4" D
Levels: 1.5
Heated Square Footage: 2,708
Main Level Sq. Ft.: 1,860
Upper Level Sq. Ft.: 848
Bedrooms: 4
Bathrooms: 3½
Foundation: Basement
Materials List Available: Yes
Price Category: F

Images provided by designer/architect.

You'll love this home because it is such a perfect setting for a family and still has room for guests.

Features:

- **Family Room:** Expect everyone to gather in this room, near the built-in entertainment centers that flank the lovely fireplace.

- **Living Room:** The other side of the see-through fireplace looks out into this living room, making it an equally welcoming spot in chilly weather.

- **Kitchen:** This room has a large center island, a corner pantry, and a built-in desk. It also features a breakfast area where friends and family will congregate all day long.

- **Master Suite:** Enjoy the oversized walk-in closet and bath with a bayed whirlpool tub, double vanity, and separate shower.

Main Level Floor Plan

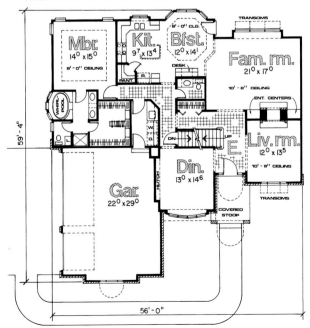

Upper Level Floor Plan

Copyright by designer/architect.

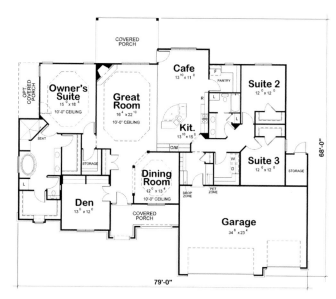

Copyright by designer/architect.

Plan #121428

Dimensions: 79' W x 68' D
Levels: 1
Heated Square Footage: 2,701
Bedrooms: 3
Bathrooms: 2
Foundation: Slab; crawl space or basement for fee
Materials List Available: Yes
Price Category: F

Images provided by designer/architect.

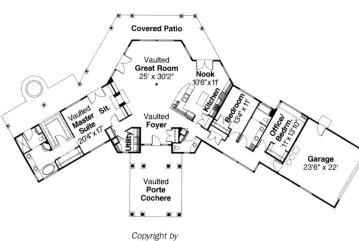

Copyright by designer/architect.

Plan #361064

Dimensions: 130'4" W x 70'6" D
Levels: 1
Heated Square Footage: 2,711
Bedrooms: 3
Bathrooms: 2½
Foundation: Slab
Material List Available: No
Price Category: F

Images provided by designer/architect.

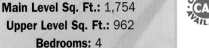

Plan #321176

Dimensions: 61'4" W x 46' D
Levels: 2
Heated Square Footage: 2,716
Main Level Sq. Ft.: 1,754
Upper Level Sq. Ft.: 962
Bedrooms: 4
Bathrooms: 4½
Foundation: Basement
Materials List Available: Yes
Price Category: F

Images provided by designer/architect.

Main Level Floor Plan

Upper Level Floor Plan

Copyright by designer/architect.

Plan #151184

Dimensions: 57'4" W x 55'10" D
Levels: 2
Heated Square Footage: 2,755
Main Level Sq. Ft.: 2,084
Upper Level Sq. Ft.: 671
Bedrooms: 4
Bathrooms: 3
Foundation: Crawl space, slab; basement or walkout basement option for fee
CompleteCost List Available: Yes
Price Category: F

Images provided by designer/architect.

Main Level Floor Plan

Upper Level Floor Plan

Copyright by designer/architect.

Plan #161018

Dimensions: 74'4" W x 69'11" D
Levels: 1.5
Heated Square Footage: 2,816
+ 325 Sq. Ft. bonus room
Main Level Sq. Ft.: 2,231
Upper Level Sq. Ft.: 624
Bedrooms: 3
Bathrooms: 2 full, 2 half
Foundation: Basement or walkout
Materials List Available: No
Price Category: F

Images provided by designer/architect.

If you love classic European designs, look closely at this home with its multiple gables and countless conveniences and luxuries.

Features:

- Foyer: Open to the great room, the 2-story foyer offers a view all the way to the rear windows.

- Great Room: A fireplace makes this room cozy in any kind of weather.

- Kitchen: This large room features an island with a sink, and an angled wall with French doors to the back yard.

- Dining Room: The furniture alcove and raised ceiling make this room both formal and practical.

- Master Suite: You'll love the quiet in the bedroom and the luxuries — a tub, separate shower, and double vanities — in the bath.

- Basement: The door from the basement to the side yard adds convenience to outdoor work.

Main Level Floor Plan

Upper Level Floor Plan

Copyright by designer/architect.

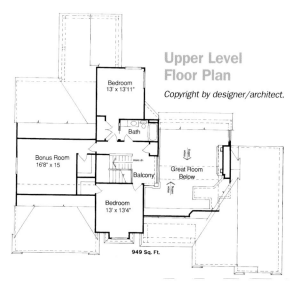

Rear View

Foyer/Dining Room

Rear Elevation

Living Room

Plan #271047

Dimensions: 68' W x 47' D

Levels: 2

Heated Square Footage: 2,729

Main Level Sq. Ft.: 1,778

Upper Level Sq. Ft.: 951

Bedrooms: 4

Bathrooms: 2½

Foundation: Basement

Materials List Available: No

Price Category: F

CAD FILE AVAILABLE / CAD

Constructed of materials chosen with your health in mind, this two-story home promises to pamper your body and soul.

Features:

- **Great Room:** Not only does this room host a media nook and a two-story ceiling, it also includes a sealed gas fireplace for zero emissions.

- **Kitchen:** Here, cultured-marble countertops replace traditional pressed-wood and laminate.

- **Master Suite:** Here's a lovely retreat. A tray ceiling, cavernous walk-in closet, and private bath are just the beginning.

- **Air Safety:** A radon-detection system and exhaust fan in the garage help to eliminate airborne irritants. Tile floors replace carpet in much of the home, too.

Main Level Floor Plan

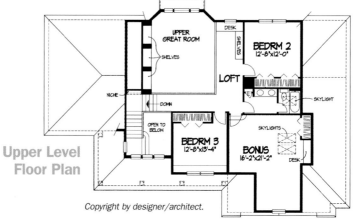

Upper Level Floor Plan

Copyright by designer/architect.

Plan #161025

Dimensions: 63'4" W x 48' D

Levels: 1.5

Heated Square Footage: 2,738

Main Level Sq. Ft.: 1,915

Upper Level Sq. Ft.: 823

Bedrooms: 4

Bathrooms: 3½

Foundation: Basement

Materials List Available: No

Price Category: F

This home, as shown in the photograph, may differ from the actual blueprints. For more detailed information, please check the floor plans carefully.

Images provided by designer/architect.

One look at the octagonal tower, boxed window, and wood-and-stone trim, and you'll know how much your family will love this home.

Features:

- **Foyer:** View the high windows across the rear wall, a fireplace, and open stairs as you come in.

- **Great Room:** Gather in this two-story-high area.

- **Hearth Room:** Open to the breakfast room, it's close to both the kitchen and dining room.

- **Kitchen:** A snack bar and an island make the kitchen ideal for family living.

- **Master Suite:** You'll love the 9-ft. ceiling in the bedroom and 11-ft. ceiling in the sitting area. The bath has a tub, double-bowl vanity, and walk-in closet.

- **Upper Level:** A balcony leads to a bedroom with a private bath and 2 other rooms with private access to a shared bath.

Main Level Floor Plan

Upper Level Floor Plan

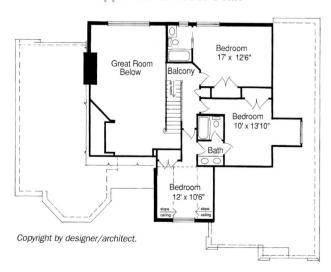

Copyright by designer/architect.

Plan #151015

Dimensions: 72'4" W x 48'4" D
Levels: 1.5
Heated Square Footage: 2,789
Main Level Sq. Ft.: 1,977
Upper Level Sq. Ft.: 812
Bedrooms: 4
Bathrooms: 3
Foundation: Crawl space, slab, or basement
CompleteCost List Available: Yes
Price Category: F

Images provided by designer/architect.

The spacious kitchen that opens to the breakfast room and the hearth room make this family home ideal for entertaining.

Features:

- Great Room: The fireplace will make a cozy winter focal point in this versatile space.
- Hearth Room: Enjoy the built-in entertainment center, built-in shelving, and fireplace here.
- Dining Room: A swing door leading to the kitchen is as attractive as it is practical.
- Study: A private bath and walk-in closet make this room an ideal spot for guests when needed.
- Kitchen: An island work area, a computer desk, and an eat-in bar add convenience and utility.
- Master Suite: Two vanities, two walk-in closets, a shower with a seat, and a whirlpool tub highlight this private space.

Upper Level Floor Plan

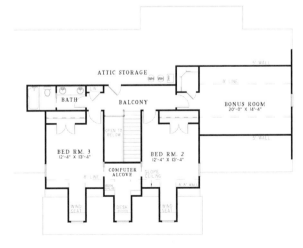

Main Level Floor Plan

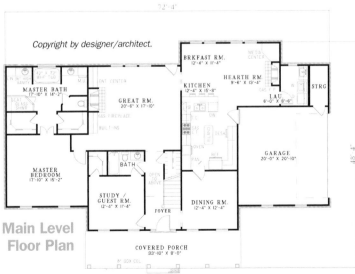

Copyright by designer/architect.

Plan #211011

Dimensions: 84' W x 54' D
Levels: 1
Heated Square Footage: 2,791
Bedrooms: 3 or 4
Bathrooms: 2
Foundation: Slab or crawl space
Materials List Available: Yes
Price Category: F

CAD FILE AVAILABLE

Images provided by designer/architect.

Plenty of room plus an open, flexible floor plan make this a home that will adapt to your needs.

Features:

- Ceiling Height: 8 ft. unless otherwise noted.
- Living Room: This distinctive room features a 12-ft. ceiling and is designed so that it can also serve as a master suite with a sitting room.
- Family Room: The whole family will want to gather in this large, inviting family room.
- Morning Room: The family room blends

into this sunny spot, which is perfect for informal family meals.

- Kitchen: This spacious kitchen offers a smart layout. It is also contiguous to the family room.
- Master Suite: You'll look forward to the end of the day when you can enjoy this master suite. It includes a huge, luxurious master bath with two large walk-in closets and two vanity sinks.
- Optional Bedroom: This optional fourth bedroom is located so that it can easily serve as a library, den, office, or music room.

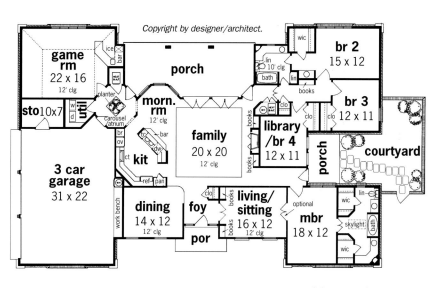

Copyright by designer/architect.

Plan #111031

Dimensions: 56' W x 53' D
Levels: 1.5
Heated Square Footage: 2,869
Main Level Sq. Ft.: 2,152
Upper Level Sq. Ft.: 717
Bedrooms: 4
Bathrooms: 3
Foundation: Basement; slab
Materials List Available: No
Price Category: G

Images provided by designer/architect.

This home is ideal for any family, thanks to its spaciousness, beauty, and versatility.

Features:

- Ceiling Height: 9 ft.
- Front Porch: The middle of the three French doors with circle tops here opens to the foyer.
- Living Room: Archways from the foyer open to both this room and the equally large dining room.
- Family Room: Also open to the foyer, this room features a two-story sloped ceiling and a balcony from the upper level. You'll love the fireplace, with its raised brick hearth and the

two French doors with circle tops, which open to the rear porch.

- Kitchen: A center island, range with microwave, built-in desk, and dining bar that's open to the breakfast room add up to comfort and efficiency.
- Master Suite: A Palladian window and linen closet grace this suite's bedroom, and the bath has an oversized garden tub, standing shower, two walk-in closets, and double vanity.

Copyright by designer/architect.

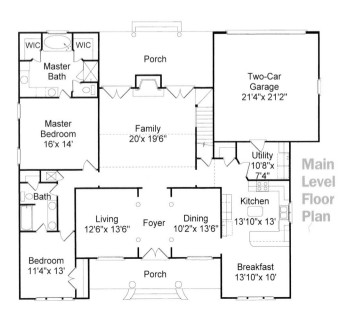

Main Level Floor Plan

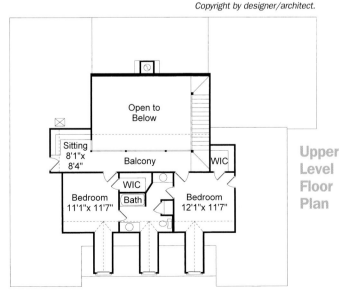

Upper Level Floor Plan

Entry

Kitchen

Living Room

Living Room

SMART tip

Preparing to Use a Clay Chiminea

Before getting started, there are a couple of general rules about using a clay chiminea. Make sure the chiminea is completely dry before lighting a fire, or else it will crack. Also, line the bottom of the pot with about 4 inches of sand. Finally, always build the fire slowly, and never use kerosene or charcoal lighter fluid.

To cure a new clay chiminea, follow these simple steps:

• Build a small paper fire inside the pot. For kindling, use strips of newspaper rolled into a few balls. Place one newspaper ball on the sand inside the chiminea. Ignite it with a match. Then add another ball, and another, one at a time, until the outside walls of the chiminea are slightly warm. Allow the fire to burn out; then let the pot cool completely before the next step.

• Once the chiminea feels cool, light another small fire, this time using wood. Again, let the fire burn out naturally, and then allow the unit to completely cool.

• Repeat the process of lighting a wood fire three more times, adding more kindling and building a larger fire with each consecutive attempt. Remember to let the chiminea cool completely between fires.

After the fifth fire, the chiminea should be cured and ready to use anytime you want a cozy fire.

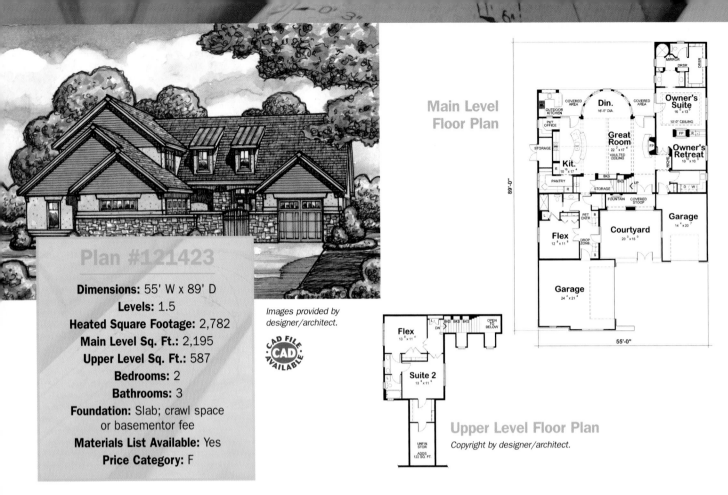

Plan #121423

Dimensions: 55' W x 89' D

Levels: 1.5

Heated Square Footage: 2,782

Main Level Sq. Ft.: 2,195

Upper Level Sq. Ft.: 587

Bedrooms: 2

Bathrooms: 3

Foundation: Slab; crawl space or basementor fee

Materials List Available: Yes

Price Category: F

Images provided by designer/architect.

Main Level Floor Plan

Upper Level Floor Plan

Copyright by designer/architect.

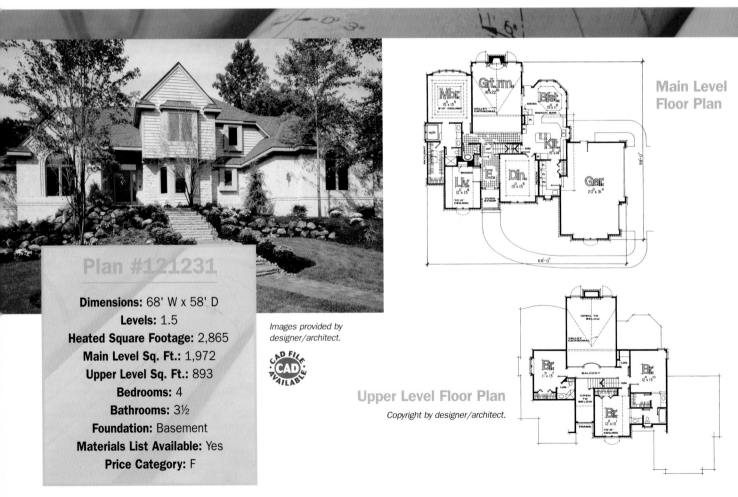

Plan #121231

Dimensions: 68' W x 58' D

Levels: 1.5

Heated Square Footage: 2,865

Main Level Sq. Ft.: 1,972

Upper Level Sq. Ft.: 893

Bedrooms: 4

Bathrooms: 3½

Foundation: Basement

Materials List Available: Yes

Price Category: F

Images provided by designer/architect.

Main Level Floor Plan

Upper Level Floor Plan

Copyright by designer/architect.

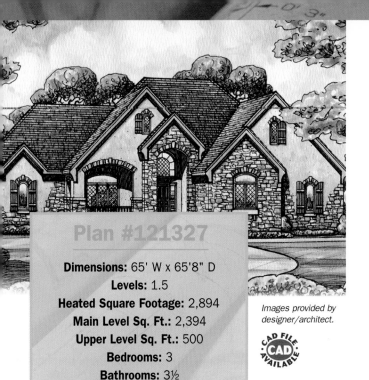

Main Level
Floor Plan

Images provided by
designer/architect.

Plan #121327

Dimensions: 65' W x 65'8" D
Levels: 1.5
Heated Square Footage: 2,894
Main Level Sq. Ft.: 2,394
Upper Level Sq. Ft.: 500
Bedrooms: 3
Bathrooms: 3½
Foundation: Basement
Materials List Available: Yes
Price Category: F

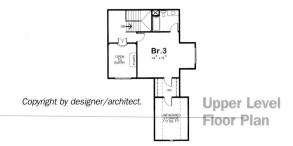

Copyright by designer/architect.

Upper Level
Floor Plan

Plan #121082

Dimensions: 68'8" W x 60' D
Levels: 2
Heated Square Footage: 2,932
Main Level Sq. Ft.: 2,084
Upper Level Sq. Ft.: 848
Bedrooms: 4
Bathrooms: 3½
Foundation: Basement
Materials List Available: Yes
Price Category: F

Images provided by
designer/architect.

Main Level Floor Plan

Copyright by designer/architect.

Upper Level
Floor Plan

Plan #291015

Dimensions: 88'6" W x 58'3" D
Levels: 1.5
Heated Square Footage: 2,901
Main Level Sq. Ft.: 2,078
Upper Level Sq. Ft.: 823
Bedrooms: 3
Bathrooms: 2½
Foundation: Basement
Materials List Available: No
Price Category: F

Upon entering this home, a cathedral-like timber-framed interior fills the eye.

Features:

- Great Room: This large gathering area's ceiling rises up two stories and is open to the kitchen. The beautiful fireplace is the focal point of this room.

- Kitchen: This island kitchen is open to the great room and the breakfast nook. Warm woods of all species enhance the great room and this space.

- Master Suite: This suite has a sloped ceiling and adjoins a luxurious master bath with twin walk-in closets that open to a sunroom with a private balcony.

- Upper Level: This upper level has an open lounge that leads to two bedrooms with vaulted ceilings and a generous second bath.

Images provided by designer/architect.

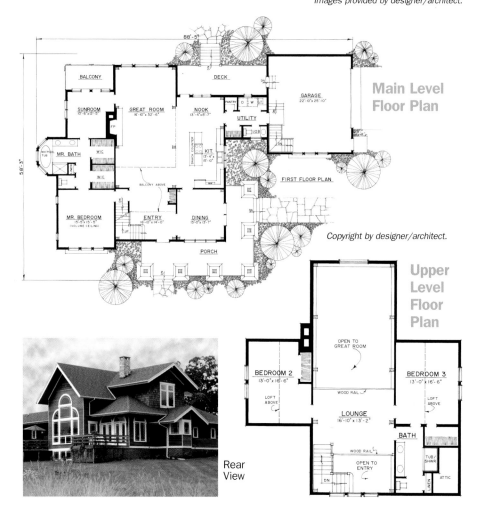

Copyright by designer/architect.

Main Level Floor Plan

Upper Level Floor Plan

Rear View

Master Bath

Kitchen

Dining Room

Rear Porch

Plan #141022

Dimensions: 90' W x 93' D

Levels: 1

Heated Square Footage: 2,911

Bedrooms: 3

Bathrooms: 2½

Foundation: Basement, or walkout

Materials List Available: No

Price Category: F

Images provided by designer/architect.

Rear View

Second-floor dormers accent this charming country ranch, which features a gracious porch that spans its entire front. A detached garage, connected by a covered extension, creates an impressive, expansive effect.

Features:

- Living Room: As you enter the foyer, you are immediately drawn to this dramatic, bayed living room.

- Study: Flanking the foyer, this cozy study features built-in shelving and a direct-vent fireplace.

- Kitchen: From a massive, partially covered deck, a wall of glass floods this spacious kitchen, breakfast bay, and keeping room with light.

- Master Suite: Enjoy the complete privacy provided by this strategically located master suite.

- Guest Quarters: You can convert the bonus room, above the garage, into a guest apartment.

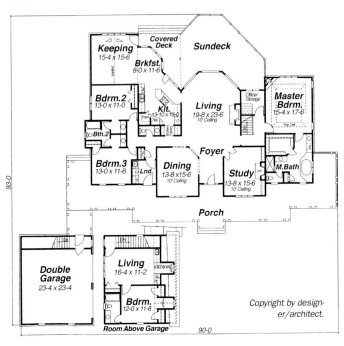

Copyright by designer/architect.

Plan #271099

Dimensions: 71' W x 74'2" D

Levels: 2

Heated Square Footage: 2,949

Main Level Sq. Ft.: 2,000

Upper Level Sq. Ft.: 949

Bedrooms: 3

Bathrooms: 2½

Foundation: Crawl space

Materials List Available: No

Price Category: F

Images provided by designer/architect.

Gracious symmetry highlights the lovely facade of this traditional two-story home.

Features:

- Foyer: With a high ceiling and a curved staircase, this foyer gives a warm welcome to arriving guests.

- Family Room: At the center of the home, this room will host gatherings of all kinds. A fireplace adds just the right touch.

- Kitchen: An expansive island with a cooktop anchors this space, which easily serves the adjoining nook and the nearby dining room.

- Master Suite: A cozy sitting room with a fireplace is certainly the highlight here. The private bath is also amazing, with its whirlpool tub, separate shower, dual vanities, and walk-in closet.

- Bonus Room: This generous space above the garage could serve as an art studio or as a place for your teenagers to play their electric guitars.

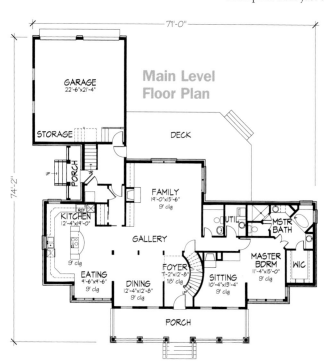

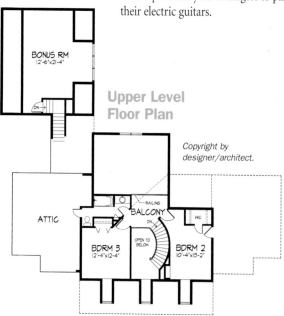

Copyright by designer/architect.

Plan #151057

Dimensions: 73'6" W x 80'6" D
Levels: 1
Heated Square Footage: 2,951
Bedrooms: 4
Bathrooms: 3
Foundation: Crawl space, slab, or basement
CompleteCost List Available: Yes
Price Category: F

Images provided by designer/architect.

- Bedrooms: Three large bedrooms are located on the opposite side of the home to give the master suite privacy. Two bedrooms share a Jack-and-Jill bathroom. The third bedroom has access to a common bathroom.

The stucco exterior and large windows give this ranch an elegant look.

CAD FILE AVAILABLE

Features:

- Foyer: Enter the covered porch, and walk through the beautiful front door to this large foyer with entry closet.

- Entertaining: The large great room has a cozy fireplace and built-ins for casual get-togethers. The formal living room, also with a fireplace, is for special entertaining.

- Kitchen: This large U-shaped island kitchen has a raised bar and is open to the breakfast area and the great room. A short step though the door brings you onto the rear lanai.

- Master Suite: This private retreat has a fireplace and a sitting area with access to the rear lanai. The master bath features dual vanities, a whirlpool tub, a glass shower, and a separate toilet room.

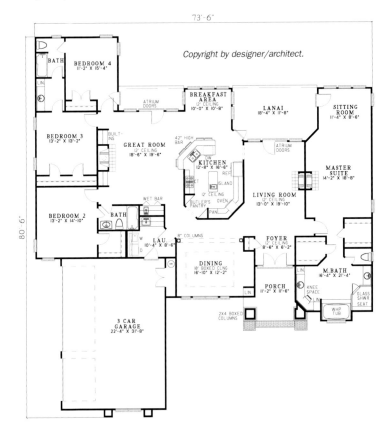

Plan #101019

Dimensions: 58'4" W x 55'2" D
Levels: 2
Heated Square Footage: 2,954
Main Level Sq. Ft. 2,093
Upper Level Sq. Ft. 861
Bedrooms: 4
Bathrooms: 3½
Foundation: Basement
Materials List Available: No
Price Category: F

Images provided by designer/architect.

This luxurious home features a spectacular open floor plan and a brick exterior.

Features:

- Ceiling Height: 9 ft. unless otherwise noted.

- Foyer: This inviting two-story foyer, which vaults to 18 ft., will greet guests with an impressive "welcome."

- Dining Room: To the right of the foyer is this spacious dining room surrounded by decorative columns.

- Family Room: There's plenty of room for all kinds of family activities in this enormous room, with its soaring two-story ceiling.

- Master Suite: This sumptuous retreat boasts a tray ceiling. Optional pocket doors provide direct access to the study. The master bath features his and her vanities and a large walk-in closet.

- Breakfast Area: Perfect for informal family meals, this bayed breakfast area has real flair.

- Secondary Bedrooms: Upstairs are three large bedrooms with 8-ft. ceilings. One has a private bath.

Main Level Floor Plan

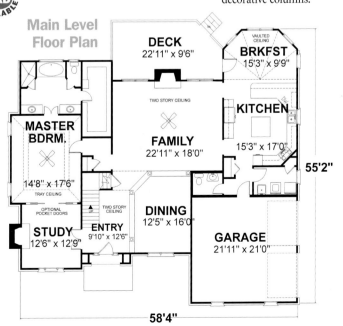

DECK
22'11" x 9'6"

BRKFST
15'3" x 9'9"
VAULTED CEILING

KITCHEN
15'3" x 17'0"

MASTER BDRM.
14'8" x 17'6"
TRAY CEILING

FAMILY
22'11" x 18'0"
TWO STORY CEILING

OPTIONAL POCKET DOORS

STUDY
12'6" x 12'9"

ENTRY
9'10" x 12'6"
TWO STORY CEILING

DINING
12'5" x 16'0"

GARAGE
21'11" x 21'0"

55'2"

58'4"

Upper Level Floor Plan

OPEN BELOW

BEDRM 4
13'0" x 11'6"

OPEN BELOW

BEDRM 2
12'5" x 12'5"

BEDRM 3
11'3" x 17'1"

PLANT SHELF

Copyright by designer/architect.

This article was reprinted from *Grand Master Baths* (Creative Homeowner 2008).

Choosing A Vanity

Because it is the major piece of furniture in the room, an attractive vanity is the obvious starting point in your master bath design. The vanity defines your space like nothing else can, so make sure that the piece you select reflects the overall feeling you are trying to achieve. Whether it's softly romantic, elegantly sophisticated, island casual, or Asian Zen, you'll want the vanity to be your first major purchasing decision when designing your master bath. Like other choices you will make, there are no hard-and-fast rules when it comes to the color and finish of your vanity. Keep in mind, however, that dark woods generally create a more formal feeling, while lighter tones and painted surfaces impart a more relaxed ambiance. You can also apply stain or glaze to add depth and character to the base and choose from a variety of vanity tops to create contrast and a sense of elegance. For a more daring look, dramatic backlit vanity tops make the ultimate design statement.

Of course, what's inside the vanity is every bit as important as its exterior design. A well-organized vanity with customizable storage options will help you create a peaceful sanctuary by streamlining your morning routine and keeping each person's stuff in its rightful place.

Furniture Style

Nothing personalizes the master bath like a freestanding, furniture-style vanity. Unlike boxy, built-in units that look as if they came right off the assembly line—and probably did—these unfitted pieces give the bath a unique elegance.

Surprisingly, these furniture styles do not have to be expensive. While freestanding vanities are now available in a range of prices, it's possible to reclaim a favorite armoire or antique desk from grandma's attic for a look that is truly one-of-a-kind. There is one caveat to this suggestion: the humid atmosphere in a bathroom can damage some furniture pieces that were not intended for use there. If you own a fragile antique, it might be more practical to use the piece in the master bedroom.

Fortunately, many cabinet manufacturers are now offering furniture-style pieces with high-grade finishes that are impervious to moisture. If you want something with a traditional look, there are many vanity options with accents such as turned legs, fluted moldings, rope columns, decorative bun feet, beaded detailing, toe cutouts, and unusual toe kicks. While beautiful detail work can add character, more is not always better. These days, manufacturers are paring down the fussy, ornate details of traditional vanities to make them easier to maintain. This "less is more" trend also allows the simple beauty of the wood to shine.

While scaled-down details work best, that doesn't mean your vanity can't be eye-catching. Distressed or glazed finishes can add textural interest without overwhelming the space.

When it comes to color choices, darker woods, such as walnut and cherry, add a fashionable, formal appeal to the bath. Some of the hottest new finishes include deep mahogany, exotic wenge wood, and waxed teak—all good choices for an upscale look, especially in shades such as rich cocoa, espresso, or plum-tone sable.

If your master bath is less than spacious, you can move to the lighter side. A golden maple or white painted finish can visually open up the room, lending an airy feeling to the space.

A freestanding armoire can provide additional storage for bath linens while adding a touch of polished appeal.

Clean and Contemporary

One of the hottest trends in bath design in recent years has been the movement toward open, clean-line spaces. This serene look is accomplished by paring down the distractions caused by too many ornate details.

As a result, there's been an increased demand for "floating" vanities that appear to hover above the floor, helping to open up the room's layout and make the space seem less cluttered. These European-inspired designs are often done in alluring wood choices, such as zebra or wenge wood, to add to the custom look.

Another major benefit of the floating vanity is that it's less likely to overpower a smaller space, even when you choose a dark wood finish. Decorative lighting can be installed below a floating vanity and, unlike a pedestal sink, this style provides both storage and counter space.

Vanities featuring curved shapes or modular cabinetry are another option for adding a contemporary touch to your master bath. Some even house refrigerated cabinets for holding chilled beverages as well as perfumes and cosmetics.

Another way to create a clean, uncluttered feeling is by choosing a vanity that provides closed storage, minimal hardware, and no glazes or embellishments. While simple is hot, super high-gloss is not. Very shiny surfaces are difficult to maintain, which defeats the idea of the clean-line look. What's more, shiny surfaces can create a glare that distracts from the space's user-friendly appeal.

Keep in mind that you needn't commit to either a traditional or a contemporary choice for your vanity. Today's most popular styles are transitional, which combines the best elements of both. What's more, experts expect this trend to continue well into the next decade. So, go ahead and mix turned feet with a bold splash of color, or choose a sleek, modular unit embossed with a demure leaf pattern. Just don't fall in love with beauty and ignore function. Open shelving can look wonderful, but unless you're committed to keeping it neat, this option may not be a practical choice for your lifestyle.

Bigger isn't always better when it comes to vanities. Instead of filling up this large space, the clean lines of this modern piece create an open, airy feeling.

Custom Spaces

To function at its peak, a master bath should have private space for each user. One of the best ways to create a truly comfortable and luxurious bath is to devise individual zones so that each user can get ready at the same time. Separate grooming areas prevent disagreements over who is taking too long at the sink, which partner's clutter is engulfing the vanity, who spends too much time preening in front of the mirror, or which party is responsible for the missing hair gel.

Ideally, you'll want to customize each person's space to meet his or her specific storage needs. This might mean deep drawers or multitier drawers with lots of little dividers; compartmentalized cabinets; shallow, rollout shelves; jewelry niches; or an appliance garage for hair dryers and other electronics.

Different grooming stations also allow for installing sinks and countertops at heights that are most efficient for each user, even if one person is over six feet tall and the other barely reaches five feet.

Separate spaces can make everyone's morning routine less stressful, but both parties must play fair. That means an

equal area for each user. Don't assume that just because he's a guy, he doesn't need as much space. Planning an equal division of space from the start also ensures that one party doesn't feel inclined to "borrow" a drawer or shelf later.

Rich, warm woods, left, with furniture detailing create a formal-looking bath environment.

Cherry and maple aren't the only wood choices in town; here, pecan adds pizzazz to this unit, right.

SMARTtip

Get Organized

Design your vanity space to minimize clutter and maximize organization. Drawer dividers provide a place for everything, from make up to safety pins, while pullout or rollout shelves make all your grooming products more accessible. An appliance garage—a clever idea borrowed from the kitchen—can also provide hidden storage for hair dryers and hot rollers.

Topping It Off

Whether your tastes run to richly veined marble, rough-hewn granite, confetti-pattern solid surfacing, textured terrazzo, or sparkling glass, a vanity top should be a striking complement to the vanity base and add sizzle to the entire bathroom.

Marble and granite provide a fine contrast to wood vanities and, like most natural materials, are likely to remain stylish for years to come. Natural stone is also a great way to personalize your space because no two slabs are exactly alike. Remember that part of natural stone's charm is its imperfections——there's no guarantee that a granite top won't have the odd streak or color whirl, or a less-than-symmetrical pattern.

While stone remains a leading option, some people prefer experimenting with other surfaces. Quartz blends—a composite of approximately 90 percent natural quartz mixed with a polymer to seal the material and ensure stain resistance have been growing in popularity in recent years. They offer the look and feel of natural stone, but with more color choices and pattern consistency and less maintenance.

Glass is also gaining ground in the bath. Its reflective properties help to distribute light and enhance the sense of openness in the room. Lighting can also be installed under a glass vanity top to create a stunning focal point.

Solid-surfacing material has long been a popular choice, particularly among those who want to keep maintenance to a minimum. It can be fabricated into a vanity that incorporates a sink of the same material, offering a streamlined look and equally effortless cleaning. As a bonus, it is available in a nearly endless array of colors and patterns. What's more, its solid color is consistent throughout—unlike genuine stone, there are no "natural variations" that can sometimes look like mistakes.

Finally, for those who seek something totally unique, there are hand-poured concrete countertops. These can be inlaid or stained in a variety of colors and formed in waves, curves, or imperfect angles to fit almost any installation.

Elegant legs and a curved front give this vanity, opposite top, a more delicate, stylish appearance.

This master bath's giant arches, opposite bottom, call attention to the various bath zones, including this stunning vanity area.

A light wood vanity, right, offers a feeling of warmth, while a black top provides dramatic contrast.

The Right Light

Position the vanity to take maximum advantage of any light coming in from existing windows or skylights. Not only will this provide more light for makeup application and grooming, but the mirror over the vanity will multiply the light effects by reflecting it through the space.

A multitiered grooming station, top, is ergonomically efficient and a good choice for users of different heights.

Drawer storage, bottom, is becoming increasingly common in bath vanities because it provides greater accessiblity.

Designer Insights

The focus of the vanity area should be its comfort, style, luxury, and functionality, says designer Julie Howes of Cherry Hill, New Jersey-based Strober Building Supply. Following are her suggestions for creating a vanity area for your master bath:

• Consider how your space will be used. For example, if you and your partner are busy professionals, your vanity could be a no-nonsense spot for getting your grooming routine done quickly. For those who are able to spend more time getting ready in the morning, it might make sense to create an area for a coffee maker, a refrigerator, or even a TV to watch the news.

• Because the master bathroom is the most private space in the home, it's important for the vanity to address the owner's comfort needs, taking into account the height of each user.

• For an elegant look, furniture-style pieces can add beauty and refinement to the room.

• In two-person baths, separate his and her areas are critical. There's a perception that having a private area in the bath is more important to women, but women aren't the only ones who want luxury. His and her spaces should be equalized, which means that personalized storage should be incorporated into both and geared for the specific needs of each user.

• For women, plenty of counter space and a makeup area with excellent lighting are essential. Dividers can help to organize makeup, hair-care products, and grooming items. Deep drawers are excellent for storage, while drawers lined with black velvet can be used for holding jewelry.

• Cabinetry in the makeup area should include enough built-in electrical outlets so that appliances can remain plugged into an outlet. Check your local building codes first, however.

• For a good visual flow when the bath is part of a master suite, consider the furniture in the master bedroom when choosing a bath vanity.

• If the bath is small, consider moving the grooming area into a walk-in closet. This can significantly open up the space.

• A splash of color can enliven the bath, but avoid trendy combinations on the vanity that can detract from your home's resale value.

• Think of the vanity area in conjunction with the entire space; remember, you want a harmonious look in which everything works together.

• When choosing cabinetry, let your own personality come forth. If you're romantic, let your vanity reflect that; if you prefer an uncluttered appearance, choose cabinetry that fits into the design.

Contemporary curves, echoed in the walls as well as the vanity, make a dynamic statement in this eye-catching bath.

Plan #111004

Dimensions: 76' W x 85' D
Levels: 1
Heated Square Footage: 2,968
Bedrooms: 4
Full Bathrooms: 3½
Foundation: Crawl space or slab
Materials List Available: No
Price Category: G

Images provided by designer/architect. Living Room

If you've been looking for a home that includes a special master suite, this one could be the answer to your dreams.

Features:

- **Living Room:** Make a sitting area around the fireplace here so that the whole family can enjoy the warmth on chilly days and winter evenings. A door from this room leads to the rear covered porch, making this room the heart of your home.

- **Kitchen:** An island with a cooktop makes cooking a pleasure in this well-designed kitchen, and the breakfast bar invites visitors at all times of day.

- **Utility Room:** A sink and a built-in ironing board make this room totally practical.

- **Master Suite:** A private fireplace in the corner sets a romantic tone for this bedroom, and the door to the covered porch allows you to sit outside on warm summer nights. The bath has two vanities, a divided walk-in closet, a standing shower, and a deluxe corner bathtub.

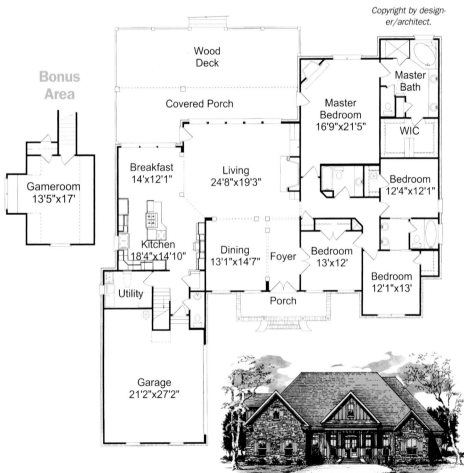

Kitchen

Dining Room

How to Quit Smoking — Lighting Your Fireplace

Before attempting to light a wood fire, make certain that the damper is open all the way. This allows a good draft (flow of air up the chimney) to prevent smoke from blowing back into the room. To ensure a good draft—particularly if your home is well insulated—open a window a bit when lighting a fire.

The opposite of draft is downdraft, which occurs when cold air flows down the chimney and into the room. If the fireplace is properly designed and maintained, the smoke shelf will prevent backpuffing from downdraft most of the time by redirecting cold air currents back up the chimney. The open damper also helps prevent backpuffing.

Also, build a fire slowly to let the chimney liner heat up, which will create a good draft and minimize the chances of downdraft.

Don't wait until fall to inspect the chimney. Do this job, or call a chimney sweep, when the weather is mild. Because some repairs take a while to make, it's best to have them done when the fireplace is not normally in use. If you do the inspection yourself, wear old clothes, eye goggles, and a mask.

Master Bath

Master Bath

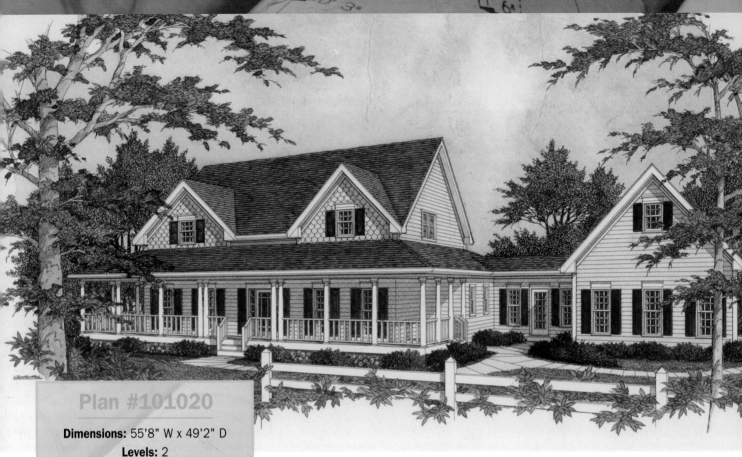

Plan #101020

Dimensions: 55'8" W x 49'2" D

Levels: 2

Heated Square Footage: 2,972

Main Level Sq. Ft.: 1,986

Upper Level Sq. Ft.: 986

Bedrooms: 4

Bathrooms: 3½

Foundation: Basement, or walkout

Materials List Available: No

Price Category: F

CAD FILE CAD AVAILABLE

Images provided by designer/architect.

This luxurious country home has an open-design main level that maximizes the use of space.

Features:

- Ceiling Height: 9 ft. unless otherwise noted.

- Foyer: Guests will be greeted by this grand two-story entry, with its graceful angled staircase.

- Dining Room: At nearly 12 ft. x 15 ft., this elegant dining room has plenty of room for large parties.

- Family Room: Everyone will be drawn to

this 17-ft. x 19-ft. room, with its dramatic two-story ceiling and its handsome fireplace.

- Kitchen: This spacious kitchen is open to the family room and features a breakfast bar and built-in table in the cooktop island.

- Master Suite: This elegant retreat includes a bayed 18-ft.-5-in. x 14-ft.-9-in. bedroom and a beautiful corner his and her bath/closet arrangement.

- Secondary Bedrooms: Upstairs you'll find three spacious bathrooms, one with a private bath and two with access to a shared bath.

Main Level Floor Plan

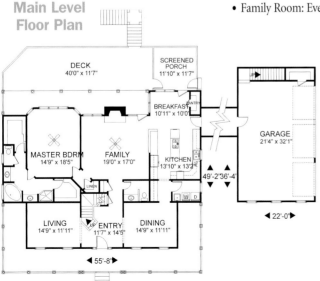

Upper Level Floor Plan

Copyright by designer/architect.

Plan #121122

Dimensions: 64' W x 65'4" D
Levels: 1.5
Heated Square Footage: 2,979
Main Level Sq. Ft.: 2,158
Upper Level Sq. Ft.: 821
Bedrooms: 4
Bathrooms: 3½
Foundation: Basement; crawl space for fee
Material List Available: Yes
Price Category: F

This classically designed home is the perfect place to raise your family.

Features:

- Great Room: This area was designed for formal entertaining and features an open two-story space. The large group of windows on the back wall will allow an abundance of natural light to fill the room.

- Master Suite: A 10-ft.-high stepped ceiling adds a touch of elegance to the sleeping area of this elegant master suite. The master bath boasts dual vanities and a whirlpool tub.

- Secondary Bedrooms: Three bedrooms are located on the upper level, away from the master suite. Bedroom 2 boasts a private bathroom, while bedrooms 3 and 4 share a Jack-and-Jill bathroom.

- Garage: This side-load three-car garage has room for both cars and storage. Located off of the laundry area close to the kitchen, unloading groceries is a easy and efficient.

Main Level Floor Plan

Upper Level Floor Plan

Copyright by designer/architect.

Plan #661191

Dimensions: 58'8" W x 68' D
Levels: 2
Heated Square Footage: 2,998
Main Level Sq. Ft.: 2,227
Upper Level Sq. Ft.: 771
Bedrooms: 4
Bathrooms: 4
Foundation: Slab
Material List Available: No
Price Category: F

This home, as shown in the photograph, may differ from the actual blueprints. For more detailed information, please check the floor plans carefully.

Images provided by designer/architect.

A soaring, two-story ceiling and dramatic staircase help create the "wow factor" in the grand entryway of this home.

Features:

• Family Room: This open, airy space is wonderful for entertaining guests or enjoying a movie with the family. Close proximity to the kitchen makes getting a quick snack even easier.

• Kitchen: This gourmet kitchen offers easy access to everything the family cook requires. A large pantry and plentiful counter space are just two of the special amenities.

• Rear Patio: This versatile covered patio at the back of the house is great for entertaining guests or watching the kids play in the backyard. It is conveniently accessed through the family room and kitchen, creating a wonderful flow during large get-togethers.

• Master Suite: You'll love to escape to this luxurious master suite, made complete with his and her sinks, walk-in closet, and large tub.

Main Level Floor Plan

Copyright by designer/architect.

Upper Level Floor Plan

Plan #121308

Dimensions: 60' W x 60' D
Levels: 1.5
Heated Square Footage: 2,999
Main Level Sq. Ft.: 1,872
Upper Level Sq. Ft.: 1,127
Bedrooms: 4
Bathrooms: 3½
Foundation: Basement
Materials List Available: Yes
Price Category: F

CAD FILE AVAILABLE

Images provided by designer/architect.

This spectacular home has beautiful architecture both inside and out.

Features:

• Family Room: This uniquely shaped family room is two-stories tall, with large windows on both levels to maximize views.

• Kitchen: This beautiful kitchen is a home cook's dream. Plentiful work and storage space, along with a center island bridging to the dining room, provide an efficient and attractive layout.

• Master Suite: Once you step into this luxurious master suite, you will never want to leave. An 11-ft.-high trayed ceiling tops the large bedroom area. There is also a walk-in closet with a sloped ceiling, a separate toilet room, a tub, and his and her sinks.

• Secondary Bedrooms: Up the stairs are three extra bedrooms, perfect for siblings or houseguests.

Main Level Floor Plan

Upper Level Floor Plan

Copyright by designer/architect.

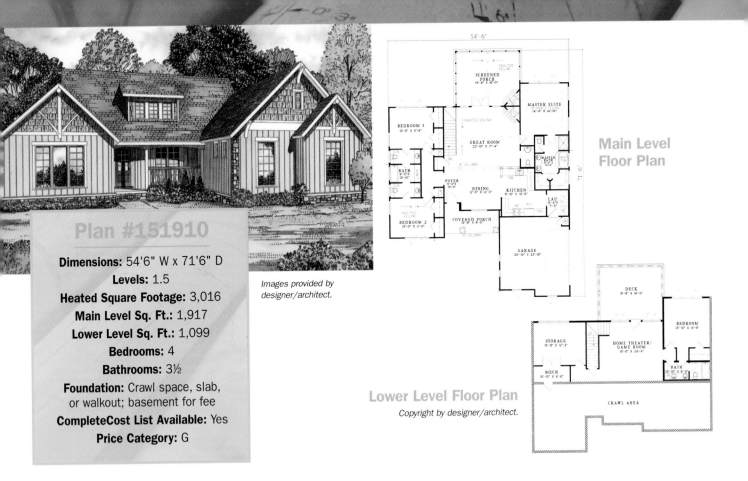

Plan #151910

Dimensions: 54'6" W x 71'6" D

Levels: 1.5

Heated Square Footage: 3,016

Main Level Sq. Ft.: 1,917

Lower Level Sq. Ft.: 1,099

Bedrooms: 4

Bathrooms: 3½

Foundation: Crawl space, slab, or walkout; basement for fee

CompleteCost List Available: Yes

Price Category: G

Images provided by designer/architect.

Main Level Floor Plan

Lower Level Floor Plan

Copyright by designer/architect.

Plan #121130

Dimensions: 66' W x 66' D

Levels: 1.5

Heated Square Footage: 3,040

Main Level Sq. Ft.: 2,215

Upper Level Sq. Ft.: 825

Bedrooms: 4

Bathrooms: 3½

Foundation: Basement; crawl space for fee

Material List Available: Yes

Price Category: G

Images provided by designer/architect.

CAD FILE AVAILABLE

Upper Level Floor Plan

Copyright by designer/architect.

Main Level Floor Plan

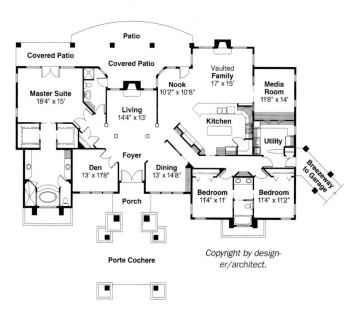

Patio

Covered Patio

Covered Patio

Master Suite
18'4" x 15'

Living
14'4" x 13'

Nook
10'2" x 10'8"

Vaulted
Family
17' x 15'

Media
Room
11'8" x 14'

Kitchen

Utility

Foyer

Den
13' x 11'8"

Dining
13' x 14'8"

Breezeway
to Garage

Bedroom
11'4" x 11'

Bedroom
11'4" x 11'2"

Porch

Porte Cochere

Copyright by designer/architect.

Images provided by designer/architect.

Plan #361001

Dimensions: 80' W x 68'11" D
Levels: 1
Heated Square Footage: 3,055
Bedrooms: 3
Bathrooms: 3
Foundation: Crawl space, basement
Material List Available: No
Price Category: G

Optional Garage

FAMILY
ROOM
18'-0" x 16'-0"
18' CH

PORCH

T.V.
ABOVE
F.P.

BREAKFAST
9' CH

LIVING
ROOM
13'-6" x 13'-6"
13' - 18' CH

MASTER
BEDROOM
17'-0" x 13'-0"
11'-13' CH

KITCHEN
9' CH

HIS
CLO.

F.P.

UTILITY

ENTRY
18' CH

PWDR

MASTER
BATH

COAT
CLO.

DINING
ROOM
12'-0" x 15'-0"
9' CH

PORCH

STUDY
11'-0" x 13'-0"
9' CH

HER CLO.

3-CAR
GARAGE
9' CH

**Main Level
Floor Plan**

LEDGE

2-STORY
FAMILY ROOM

W.I.C.

BEDROOM 2
12'-2" x 14'-0"
8'-3'-6" CH

OPEN TO
LIVING ROOM
BELOW
13' - 18' CH

W.I.C.

BATH

BATH 2

W.I.C.

BALCONY
8' CH

BEDROOM 3
12'-0" x 15'-0"
8'-9'-6" CH

PORCH

BEDROOM 4
11'-0" x 14'-4"
8'-9'-6" CH

**Upper Level
Floor Plan**

Copyright by designer/architect.

Plan #121152

Dimensions: 67'1" W x 65'10⅛" D
Levels: 1.5
Heated Square Footage: 3,094
Main Level Sq. Ft.: 2,112
Upper Level Sq. Ft.: 982
Bedrooms: 4
Bathrooms: 3½
Foundation: Slab; basement for fee
Material List Available: Yes
Price Category: G

Images provided by designer/architect.

This home, as shown in the photograph, may differ from the actual blueprints. For more detailed information, please check the floor plans carefully.

CAD FILE AVAILABLE
CAD

Plan #121076

Dimensions: 64' W x 60'8" D

Levels: 2

Heated Square Footage: 3,067

Main Level Sq. Ft.: 2,169

Upper Level Sq. Ft.: 898

Bedrooms: 4

Bathrooms: 3½

Foundation: Basement

Materials List Available: Yes

Price Category: G

Images provided by designer/architect.

You'll love the combination of formal features and casual, family-friendly areas in this spacious home with an elegant exterior.

Features:

- Entry: The elegant windows in this two-story area are complemented by the unusual staircase.

- Family Room: This family room features an 11-ft. ceiling, wet bar, fireplace, and trio of windows that look out to the covered porch.

- Living Room: Columns set off both this room and the dining room. Decorate to accentuate their formality, or make them blend into a more casual atmosphere.

- Master Suite: Columns in this suite highlight a bayed sitting room where you'll be happy to relax at the end of the day or on weekend mornings.

- Bedrooms: Bedroom 2 has a private bath, making it an ideal guest room, and you'll find private vanities in bedrooms 3 and 4.

Main Level Floor Plan

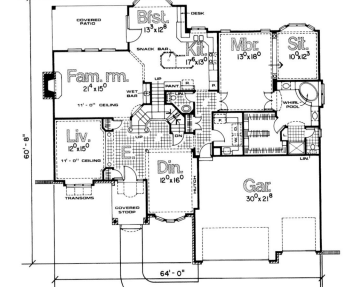

Upper Level Floor Plan

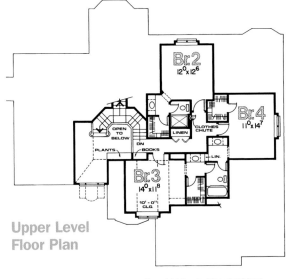

Copyright by designer/architect.

Plan #121047

Dimensions: 67'8" W x 57' D

Levels: 1.5

Heated Square Footage: 3,072

Main Level Sq. Ft.: 2,116

Upper Level Sq. Ft.: 956

Bedrooms: 4

Bathrooms: 3½

Foundation: Slab; basement for fee

Materials List Available: Yes

Price Category: G

Images provided by designer/architect.

A long porch and a trio of roof dormers give this gracious home a sophisticated country look.

Features:

- Ceiling Height: 8 ft. unless otherwise noted.

- Balcony: This balcony overlooks the entry and the staircase hall.

- Dining Room: Columns and a cased opening lend elegance, making this the perfect venue for stylish dinner parties.

- Family Room: A cathedral ceiling gives this room a light and airy feel. The handsome fireplace framed by windows is sure to become a favorite family gathering place.

- Master Suite: This architecturally distinctive bedroom features a bayed sitting area and a tray ceiling.

- Bedrooms: One of the bedrooms enjoys a private bath, making it a perfect guest room. Other bedrooms feature walk-in closets.

Main Level Floor Plan

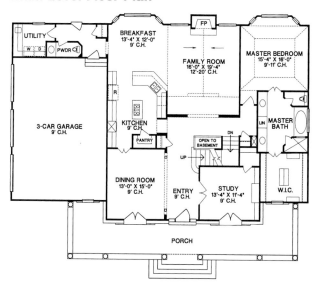

Upper Level Floor Plan

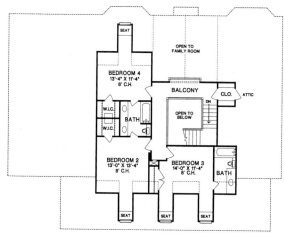

Copyright by designer/architect.

Plan #151001

Dimensions: 70' W x 88'2" D
Levels: 1
Heated Square Footage: 3,124
Bedrooms: 4
Bathrooms: 3½
Foundation: Crawl space, slab
CompleteCost List Available: Yes
Price Category: G

From the double front doors to sleek arches, columns, and a gallery with arched openings to the bedrooms, you'll love this elegant home.

Features:

- **Grand Room:** With a 13-ft. pan ceiling and column entry, this room opens to the rear covered porch as well as through French doors to the bay-windowed morning room that, in turn, leads to the gathering room.

- **Gathering Room:** A majestic fireplace, built-in entertainment center, and book shelves give comfort and ease.

- **Kitchen:** A double oven, built-in desk, and a work island add up to a design for efficiency.

- **Master Suite:** Enjoy the practicality of walk-in closets, the comfort of a private sitting area, and the convenience of an adjacent study or nursery. The bath features a step-up whirlpool tub and separate shower.

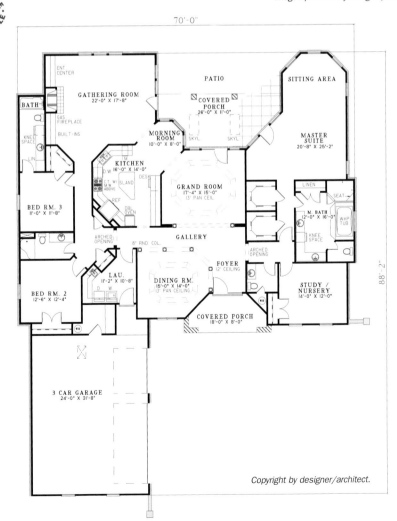

Plan #321062

Dimensions: 54' W x 57'4" D

Levels: 2

Heatd Square Footage: 3,138

Main Level Sq. Ft.: 1,958

Upper Level Sq. Ft.: 1,180

Bedrooms: 4

Bathrooms: 3½

Foundation: Basement

Materials List Available: Yes

Price Category: G

Images provided by designer/architect.

This home, as shown in the photograph, may differ from the actual blueprints. For more detailed information, please check the floor plans carefully.

This elegant home is spacious enough for an active family and lovely enough for entertaining.

Features:

- Family Room: Host a crowd in this enormous room, or enjoy a cozy chat beside the fireplace.

- Breakfast Room: Open to the family room, this breakfast room leads to the outdoor patio.

- Study: Situated for privacy and quiet, this study has large windows and handsome double doors.

- Dining Room: This large, private room is equally suitable for formal parties and family dinners.

- Master Suite: The vaulted ceiling and bay window make the bedroom elegant, while the two walk-in closets, linen closet, double vanity, tub, and separate shower make the suite luxurious.

- Loft: Use this spacious area as a playroom when the children are small and a media area later on.

Main Level Floor Plan

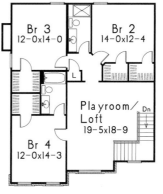

Upper Level Floor Plan

Copyright by designer/architect.

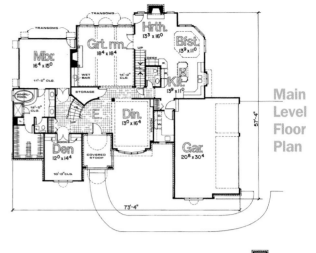

Main Level Floor Plan

Plan #121113

Dimensions: 73'4" W x 57'4" D
Levels: 1.5
Heated Square Footage: 3,172
Main Level Sq. Ft.: 2,252
Upper Level Sq. Ft.: 920
Bedrooms: 4
Bathrooms: 3½
Foundation: Basement; crawl space for fee
Material List Available: Yes
Price Category: G

Images provided by designer/architect.

Front View

Upper Level Floor Plan

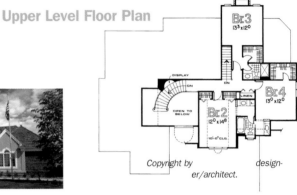

Copyright by   designer/architect.

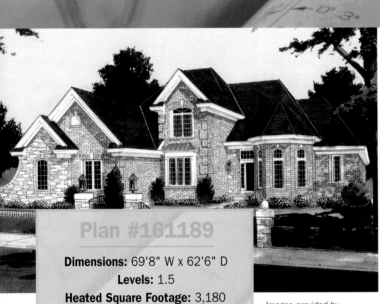

Main Level Floor Plan

Plan #161189

Dimensions: 69'8" W x 62'6" D
Levels: 1.5
Heated Square Footage: 3,180
Main Level Sq. Ft.: 2,270
Upper Level Sq. Ft.: 910
Bedrooms: 4
Bathrooms: 3½
Foundation: Basement; crawl space, slab, or walkout for fee
Materials List Available: Yes
Price Category: G

Images provided by designer/architect.

Upper Level Floor Plan

Copyright by designer/architect.

Plan #121331

Dimensions: 62' W x 48' D

Levels: 1

Heated Square Footage: 1,763

Bedrooms: 3

Bathrooms: 2½

Foundation: Basement

Materials List Available: Yes

Price Category: G

CAD FILE AVAILABLE

Images provided by designer/architect.

Copyright by designer/architect.

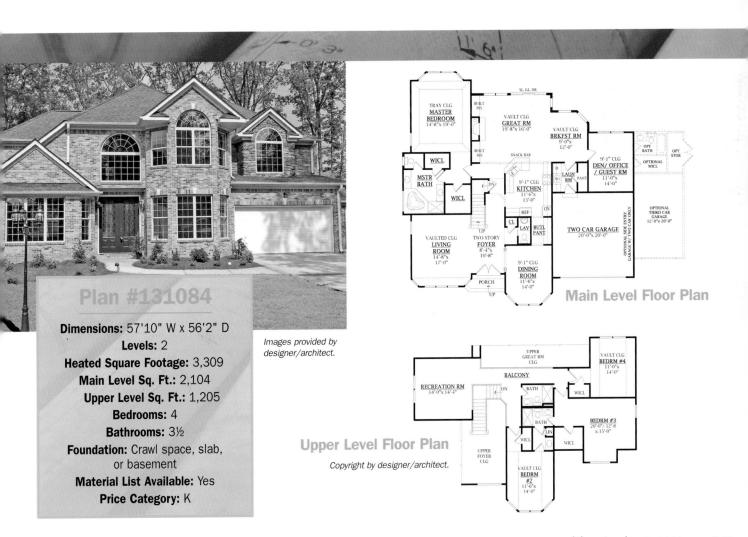

Plan #131084

Dimensions: 57'10" W x 56'2" D

Levels: 2

Heated Square Footage: 3,309

Main Level Sq. Ft.: 2,104

Upper Level Sq. Ft.: 1,205

Bedrooms: 4

Bathrooms: 3½

Foundation: Crawl space, slab, or basement

Material List Available: Yes

Price Category: K

Images provided by designer/architect.

Main Level Floor Plan

Upper Level Floor Plan

Copyright by designer/architect.

Plan #121275

Dimensions: 90'11" W x 81'3" D
Levels: 1
Heated Square Footage: 3,312
Bedrooms: 3
Bathrooms: 3
Foundation: Basement
Materials List Available: Yes
Price Category: G

Images provided by designer/architect.

Copyright by designer/architect.

Plan #121049

Dimensions: 82' W x 60'8" D
Levels: 2
Heated Square Footage: 3,335
Main Level Sq. Ft.: 2,054
Upper Level Sq. Ft.: 1,281
Bedrooms: 4
Bathrooms: 3½
Foundation: Slab; basement for fee
Materials List Available: Yes
Price Category: G

This home, as shown in the photograph, may differ from the actual blueprints. For more detailed information, please check the floor plans carefully.

Images provided by designer/architect.

Main Level Floor Plan

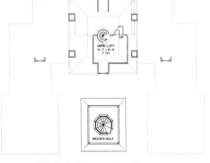

Third Floor Bedroom Floor Plan

Upper Level Floor Plan

Copyright by designer/ architect.

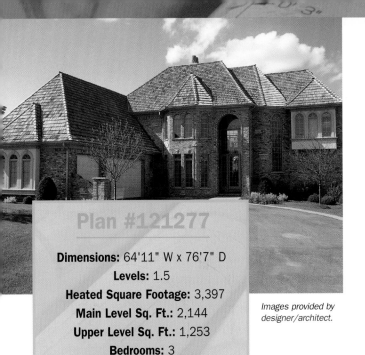

Main Level Floor Plan

Upper Level Floor Plan

Copyright by designer/architect.

Images provided by designer/architect.

Plan #121277

Dimensions: 64'11" W x 76'7" D
Levels: 1.5
Heated Square Footage: 3,397
Main Level Sq. Ft.: 2,144
Upper Level Sq. Ft.: 1,253
Bedrooms: 3
Bathrooms: 3½
Foundation: Basement
Materials List Available: Yes
Price Category: G

Main Level Floor Plan

Images provided by designer/architect.

CAD FILE AVAILABLE

Plan #661235

Dimensions: 68' W x 83'4" D
Levels: 1
Heated Square Footage: 3,446
Main Level Sq. Ft.: 2,837
Upper Level Sq. Ft.: 609
Bedrooms: 4
Bathrooms: 4
Foundation: Slab
Materials List Available: No
Price Category: G

Copyright by designer/architect.

Rear View

Plan #131025

Dimensions: 62'4" W x 65'10" D
Levels: 1.5
Heated Square Footage: 3,204
Main Level Sq. Ft.: 2,196
Upper Level Sq. Ft.: 1,008
Bedrooms: 4
Bathrooms: 4
Foundation: Crawl space, slab, or basement
Materials List Available: Yes
Price Category: H

Images provided by designer/architect.

You'll appreciate the flowing layout that's designed for entertaining but also suits an active family.

Features:

• Ceiling Height: 8 ft.

• Great Room: Decorative columns serve as the entryway to the great room that's made for entertaining. A fireplace makes it warm in winter; built-in shelves give a classic appearance; and the serving counter it shares with the kitchen is both practical and attractive.

• Kitchen: A door into the backyard makes outdoor entertaining easy, and the full bathroom near the door adds convenience.

• Master Suite: Enjoy the sunny sitting area that's a feature of this suite. A tray ceiling adds character to the room, and a huge walk-in closet is easy to organize. The bathroom features a corner spa tub.

• Bedrooms: Each of the additional 3 bedrooms is bright and cheery.

Main Level Floor Plan

Upper Level Floor Plan

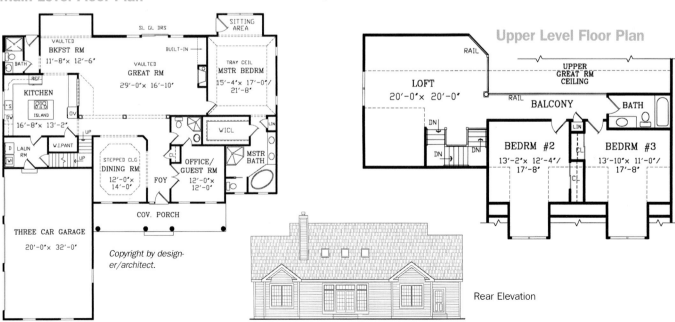

Copyright by designer/architect.

Rear Elevation

Plan #121062

Dimensions: 70' W x 62' D

Levels: 1.5

Heated Square Footage: 3,448

Main Level Sq. Ft.: 2,375

Upper Level Sq. Ft.: 1,073

Bedrooms: 4

Bathrooms: 3½

Foundation: Basement

Materials List Available: Yes

Price Category: G

Images provided by designer/architect.

You'll love this design if you're looking for a comfortable home with dimensions and details that create a sense of grandeur.

Features:

• Entry: A soaring ceiling, curved staircase, and balcony that overlooks a tall plant shelf combine to create your first impression of grandeur in this home.

• Great Room: A transom-topped bowed window highlights this room, with its 11-ft., beamed ceiling, built-in wet bar, and see-through fireplace.

• Kitchen: Designed for the gourmet cook, this kitchen has every amenity you could desire.

• Breakfast Room: Adjacent to the great room and the kitchen, this gazebo-shaped breakfast area lights both the kitchen and hearth room.

Main Level Floor Plan

Upper Level Floor Plan

Copyright by designer/architect.

Plan #121022

Dimensions: 76' W x 58'8" D
Levels: 2
Heated Square Footage: 3,556
Main Level Sq. Ft.: 2,555
Upper Level Sq. Ft.: 1,001
Bedrooms: 4
Bathrooms: 3 full, 2 half
Foundation: Basement
Materials List Available: Yes
Price Category: H

Images provided by designer/architect.

Dramatic soaring ceilings are the hallmark of this large and luxurious home.

Features:

• Ceiling Height: 8 ft. except as noted.

• Gathering Room: Guests and family will be drawn to this room with its cathedral ceiling and its fireplace flanked by built-ins.

• Den: To the right of the entry, French doors lead to a handsome den with a tall, spider-beamed ceiling.

• Great Room: This room will be flooded with sunlight thanks to stacked windows that take advantage of its 18-ft. ceiling.

• Formal Dining Room: Upon entering the 13-ft. entry, your guests will see this elegant room with its arched windows and decorative ceiling.

• Master Suite: Unwind at day's end in this luxurious suite featuring two walk-in closets, a sky-lit whirlpool and his and her vanities.

Main Level Floor Plan

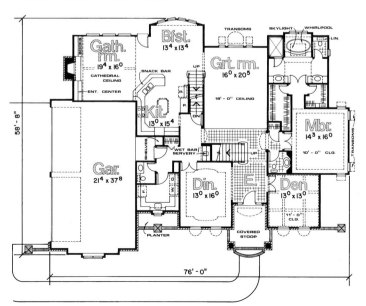

Upper Level Floor Plan

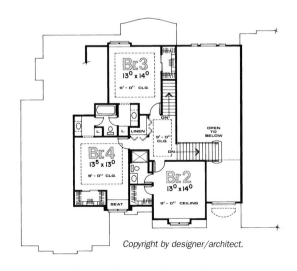

Copyright by designer/architect.

Plan #211075

Dimensions: 80' W x 84' D
Levels: 2
Heated Square Footage: 3,568
Main Level Sq. Ft.: 2,330
Upper Level Sq. Ft.: 1,238
Bedrooms: 4
Bathrooms: 3½
Foundation: Crawl space
Materials List Available: Yes
Price Category: H

The porte-cochere—or covered passage over a driveway—announces the quality and beauty of this spacious country home.

Features:

- Front Porch: Spot groups of potted plants on this 779-sq.-ft. porch, and add a glider and some rocking chairs to take advantage of its comfort.

- Family Room: Let this family room become the heart of the home. With a fireplace to make it cozy and a wet bar for easy serving, it's a natural for entertaining.

- Game Room: Expect a crowd in this room, no matter what the weather.

- Kitchen: A cooktop island and a pantry are just two features of this fully appointed kitchen.

- Master Suite: The bedroom is as luxurious as you'd expect, but the quarter-circle raised tub in the master bath might surprise you. Two walk-in closets and two vanities add a practical touch.

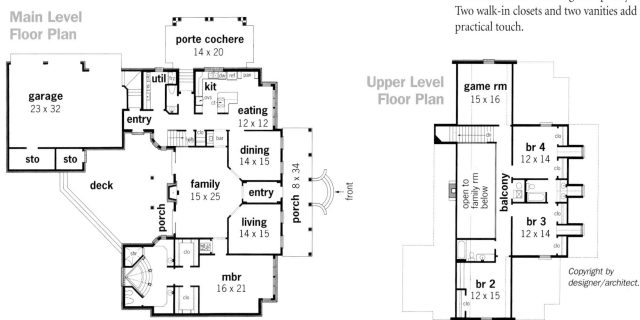

Main Level Floor Plan

Upper Level Floor Plan

Copyright by designer/architect.

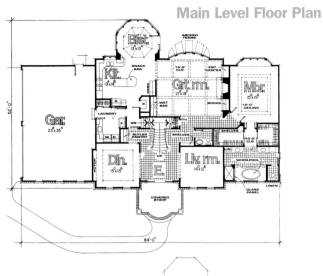

Main Level Floor Plan

Plan #121063

Dimensions: 84' W x 52' D
Levels: 1.5
Heated Square Footage: 3,473
Main Level Sq. Ft.: 2,500
Upper Level Sq. Ft.: 973
Bedrooms: 4
Bathrooms: 3½
Foundation: Basement;
crawl space or slab for fee
Materials List Available: Yes
Price Category: G

*Images provided by
designer/architect.*

Upper Level Floor Plan

Copyright by designer/architect.

Main Level Floor Plan

Plan #651149

Dimensions: 83' W x 87' D
Levels: 1.5
Heated Square Footage: 3,618
Main Level Sq. Ft.: 2,775
Upper Level Sq. Ft.: 843
Bedrooms: 3
Bathrooms: 2½
Foundation: Slab
Materials List Available: No
Price Category: H

*Images provided by
designer/architect.*

CAD FILE AVAILABLE

Upper Level Floor Plan

*Copyright by
designer/architect.*

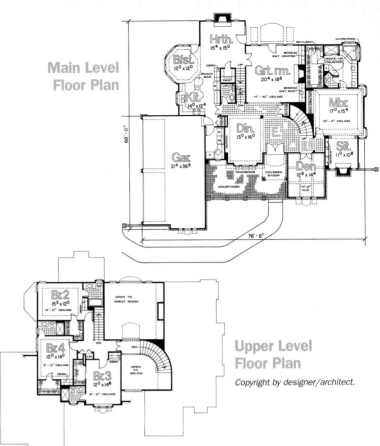

Main Level Floor Plan

Upper Level Floor Plan

Copyright by designer/architect.

Images provided by designer/architect.

This home, as shown in the photograph, may differ from the actual blueprints. For more detailed information, please check the floor plans carefully.

Plan #121081

Dimensions: 76'8" W x 68' D
Levels: 1.5
Heated Square Footage: 3,623
Main Level Sq. Ft.: 2,603
Upper Level Sq. Ft.: 1,020
Bedrooms: 4
Bathrooms: 4½
Foundation: Basement
Materials List Available: Yes
Price Category: H

Main Level Floor Plan

Upper Level Floor Plan

Copyright by designer/architect.

Images provided by designer/architect.

CAD FILE AVAILABLE

Plan #321214

Dimensions: 89' W x 42' D
Levels: 2
Heated Square Footage: 3,670
Main Level Sq. Ft.: 2,323
Upper Level Sq. Ft.: 1,347
Bedrooms: 4
Bathrooms: 3½
Foundation: Basement
Materials List Available: Yes
Price Category: H

Plan #161035

Dimensions: 75' W x 64'11" D
Levels: 1.5
Heated Square Footage: 3,688
Main Level Sq. Ft.: 2,702
Upper Level Sq. Ft.: 986
Bedrooms: 4
Bathrooms: 3½
Foundation: Basement
Materials List Available: No
Price Category: H

Images provided by designer/architect.

You'll appreciate the style of the stone, brick, and cedar shake exterior of this contemporary home.

Features:

- **Hearth Room:** Positioned for an easy flow for guests and family, this hearth room features a bank of windows that integrate it with the yard.

- **Breakfast Room:** Move through the sliding doors here to the rear porch on sunny days.

- **Kitchen:** Outfitted for a gourmet cook, this kitchen is also ideal for friends and family who can perch at the island or serve themselves at the bar.

- **Master Suite:** A stepped ceiling, crown moldings, and boxed window make the bedroom easy to decorate, while the two walk-in closets, lavish dressing area, and tub in the bath make this area comfortable and luxurious.

Main Level Floor Plan

Upper Level Floor Plan

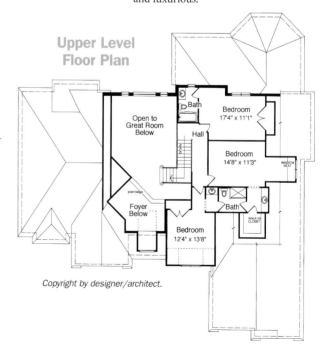

Copyright by designer/architect.

Left Elevation

Right Elevation

SMARTtip

How to Arrange Seating Around Your Fireplace

When the TV is near or on the same wall as the fireplace, you can arrange seating that places you at the best advantage to enjoy both. Position sofas and chairs in front of the fire, and remember that the distance between you and the TV should be at least three times the size of the screen.

Kitchen

Dining Room

Living Room

Master Bathroom

Main Level Floor Plan

Plan #661255

Dimensions: 76' W x 65'8" D

Levels: 2

Heated Square Footage: 3,719

Main Level Sq. Ft.: 2,677

Upper Level Sq. Ft.: 1,042

Bedrooms: 4

Bathrooms: 3½

Foundation: Slab

Materials List Available: No

Price Category: H

Images provided by designer/architect.

Upper Level Floor Plan

Copyright by designer/architect.

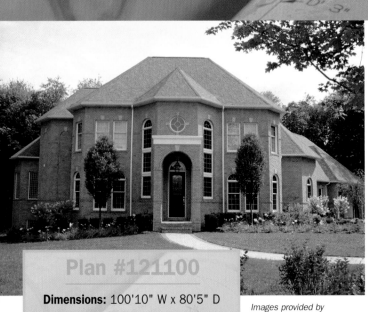

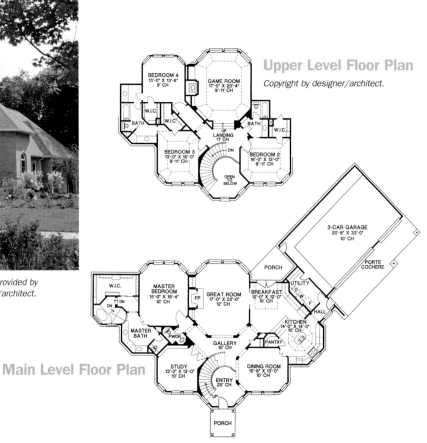

Upper Level Floor Plan

Copyright by designer/architect.

Main Level Floor Plan

Plan #121100

Dimensions: 100'10" W x 80'5" D

Levels: 2

Heated Square Footage: 3,750

Main Level Sq. Ft.: 2,274

Upper Level Sq. Ft.: 1,476

Bedrooms: 4

Bathrooms: 3½

Foundation: Slab

Materials List Available: No

Price Category: H

Images provided by designer/architect.

Plan #651147

Dimensions: 70' W x 83' D
Levels: 2
Heated Square Footage: 3,818
Main Level Sq. Ft.: 2,519
Upper Level Sq. Ft.: 1,299
Bedrooms: 3
Bathrooms: 4½
Foundation: Slab
Materials List Available: No
Price Category: H

Images provided by designer/architect.

CAD FILE AVAILABLE

Upper Level Floor Plan

Copyright by designer/architect.

Plan #661265

Dimensions: 75'4" W x 80'8" D
Levels: 2
Heated Square Footage: 3,892
Main Level Sq. Ft.: 3,079
Upper Level Sq. Ft.: 813
Bedrooms: 5
Bathrooms: 3½
Foundation: Slab
Materials List Available: No
Price Category: H

Images provided by designer/architect.

CAD FILE AVAILABLE

Upper Level Floor Plan

Copyright by designer/architect.

Plan #161061

Dimensions: 90' W x 69'10" D
Levels: 2
Heated Square Footage: 3,816
Main Level Sq. Ft.: 2,725
Upper Level Sq. Ft.: 1,091
Bedrooms: 4
Bathrooms: 3½
Foundation: Basement, walkout basement
Materials List Available: No
Price Category: H

Images provided by designer/architect.

Luxurious amenities make living in this spacious home a true pleasure for the whole family.

Features:

- **Great Room:** A fireplace, flanking built-in shelves, a balcony above, and three lovely windows create a luxurious room that's always comfortable.

- **Hearth Room:** Another fireplace with surrounding built-ins and double doors to the outside deck (with its own fireplace) highlight this room.

- **Kitchen:** A butler's pantry, laundry room, and mudroom with a window seat and two walk-in closets complement this large kitchen.

- **Library:** Situated for privacy and quiet, this spacious room with a large window area may be reached from the master bedroom as well as the foyer.

- **Master Suite:** A sloped ceiling and windows on three walls create a lovely bedroom, and the huge walk-in closet, dressing room, and luxurious bath add up to total comfort.

Main Level Floor Plan

Upper Level Floor Plan

Copyright by designer/architect.

Rear Elevation

Right Side Elevation

Left Side Elevation

Great Room

Hearth Room

Kitchen

Dining Room   Library

Plan #121023

Dimensions: 85'5" W x 74'8" D

Levels: 2

Heated Square Footage: 3,904

Main Level Sq. Ft.: 2,813

Upper Level Sq. Ft.: 1,091

Bedrooms: 4

Bathrooms: 3½

Foundation: Basement

Materials List Available: Yes

Price Category: H

CAD FILE AVAILABLE • CAD

Spacious and gracious, here are all the amenities you expect in a fine home.

Features:

- Ceiling Height: 8 ft. except as noted.

- Foyer: This magnificent entry features a graceful curved staircase with balcony above.

- Sunken Living Room: This sunken room is filled with light from a row of bowed windows. It's the perfect place for social gatherings both large and small.

- Den: French doors open into this truly distinctive den with its 11-ft. ceiling and built-in bookcases.

- Formal Dining Room: Entertain guests with style and grace in this dining room with corner column.

- Master Suite: Another set of French doors leads to this suite that features two walk-in closets, a tub flanked by vanities, and a private sitting room with built-in bookcases.

Main Level Floor Plan

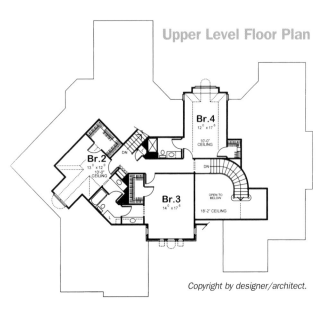

Upper Level Floor Plan

Plan #121026

Dimensions: 66'8" W x 76' D

Levels: 2

Heated Square Footage: 3,926

Main Level Sq. Ft.: 2,351

Upper Level Sq. Ft.: 1,575

Bedrooms: 4

Bathrooms: 3 full, 2 half

Foundation: Basement

Materials List Available: Yes

Price Category: H

Images provided by designer/architect.

Plenty of space and architectural detail make this a comfortable and gracious home.

Features:

- Ceiling Height: 8 ft. unless otherwise noted.

- Family Room: A soaring cathedral ceiling makes this family room seem even more spacious than it is, while the fireplace framed by windows lends warmth and comfort.

- Eating Area: There's a dining room for more formal entertaining, but this informal eating area to the left of the great room will get plenty of daily use. It features a built-in desk for compiling shopping lists and recipes and access to the backyard.

- Kitchen: Next door to the eating area, this kitchen is designed to make food preparation a pleasure. It features a center cooktop, a recycling area, and a corner pantry.

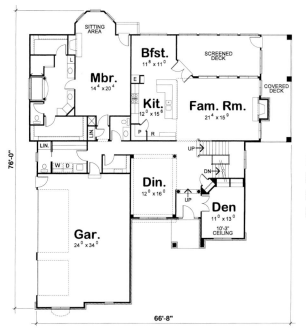

Main Level Floor Plan

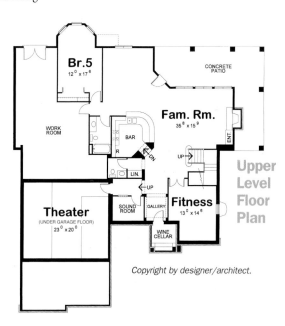

Upper Level Floor Plan

Copyright by designer/architect.

Plan #121018

Dimensions: 95'9" W x 70'2" D
Levels: 2
Heated Square Footage: 3,950
Main Level Sq. Ft.: 2,839
Upper Level Sq. Ft.: 1,111
Bedrooms: 4
Bathrooms: 4 full, 2 half
Foundation: Basement
Materials List Available: Yes
Price Category: H

Images provided by designer/architect.

A spectacular two-story entry with a floating curved staircase welcomes you home.

Features:

• Ceiling Height: 8 ft. except as noted.

• Den: To the left of the entry, French doors lead to a spacious and stylish den featuring a spider-beamed ceiling.

• Living Room: The volume ceiling, transom windows, and large fireplace evoke a gracious traditional style.

• Gathering Rooms: There is plenty of space for large-group entertaining in the gathering rooms that also feature fireplaces and transom windows.

• Master Suite: Here is the height of luxurious living. The suite features an oversized walk-in closet, tiered ceilings, and a sitting room with fireplace. The pampering bath has a corner whirlpool and shower.

• Garage: An angle minimizes the appearance of the four-car garage.

CAD FILE AVAILABLE

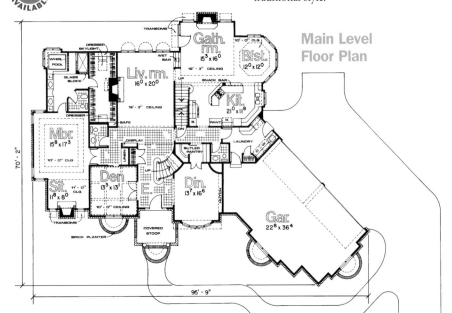

Main Level Floor Plan

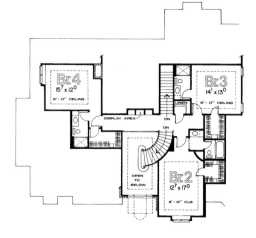

Upper Level Floor Plan

Copyright by designer/architect.

Plan #481028

Dimensions: 86'8" W x 53' D
Levels: 1
Heated Square Footage: 3,980
Main Level Sq. Ft.: 2,290
Lower Level Sq. Ft.: 1,690
Bedrooms: 3
Bathrooms: 2½
Foundation: Walkout basement
Material List Available: No
Price Category: H

Images provided by designer/architect.

• Lower Level: For fun times, this lower level is finished to provide a wet bar and a recreation room. Two bedrooms, which share a full bathroom, are also on this level. Future expansion can include an additional bedroom.

Rear View

This home, with its Southwestern flair, invites friends and family in for some down-home hospitality.

Features:

• Foyer: A 12-ft-high ceiling extends an open welcome to all. With a view through the great room, the open floor plan makes the home feel large and open.

• Kitchen: This spacious gourmet kitchen opens generously to the hearth room, which features an angled fireplace. A two-level island, which contains a two-bowl sink, provides casual seating and additional storage.

• Master Suite: This romantic space features a 10-ft.-high stepped ceiling and a compartmentalized full bath that includes his and her sinks and a whirlpool tub.

Copyright by designer/architect.

Lower Level Floor Plan

Main Level Floor Plan

Patio

Brk fst
13-5x9-0

Great Room
20-8x21-0
vaulted

Laundry

Pantry

Freezer

W D

Mud Rm.

Kitchen
13-5x16-10

Garage
23-4x29-4

76'-4"

48'-0"

MBr
14-4x21-0

Entry

Living Rm
13-7x17-7

Dining
12-8x15-0

Porch

Up

Dn

R

dw

Images provided by
designer/architect.

CAD FILE AVAILABLE

Plan #321215

Dimensions: 76'4" W x 48' D

Levels: 2

Heated Square Footage: 3,978

Main Level Sq. Ft.: 2,437

Upper Level Sq. Ft.: 1,541

Bedrooms: 4

Bathrooms: 3 full, 2 half

Foundation: Basement

Materials List Available: Yes

Price Category: H

Attic

Attic

Vaulted
Great Room Below

Bonus Rm
19-10x17-4

Sloped Ceiling

Dn

Dn

Br 2
13-0x17-3

Br 3
13-0x13-7

Br 4
13-5x13-3

Upper Level Floor Plan

Copyright by designer/architect.

Plan #551202

Dimensions: 94' W x 81' D

Levels: 2

Heated Square Footage: 4,000

Main Level Sq. Ft.: 3,496

Upper Level Sq. Ft.: 504

Bedrooms: 3

Bathrooms: 2½

Foundation: Crawl space; slab
or basement for fee

Materials List Available: No

Price Category: I

Images provided by
designer/architect.

Main Level Floor Plan

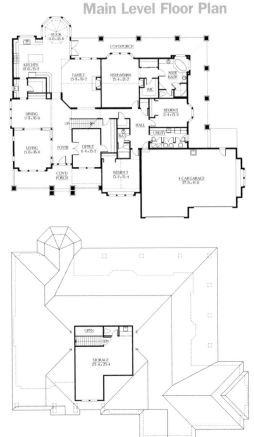

NOOK
11-0 x 15-6

KITCHEN
12-0 x 15-2

COV'D PORCH

FAMILY
15-8 x 19-2

MSTR BEDRM
15-4 x 21-2

MSTR
BATH

W.I.C.

DINING
11-8 x 15-0

BEDRM 2
11-4 x 15-2

LIVING
15-0 x 16-0

FOYER

OFFICE
11-4 x 15-2

HALL

UTILITY

BEDRM 3
13-2 x 15-0

4-CAR GARAGE
27-0 x 41-0

COV'D
PORCH

OPEN

STORAGE
23-4 x 25-4

DN

**Upper Level
Floor Plan**

*Copyright by
designer/architect.*

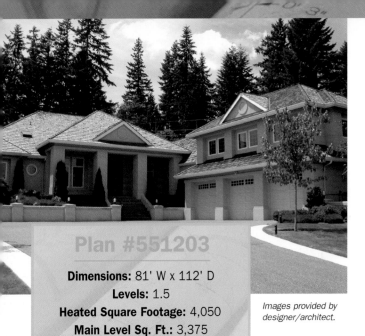

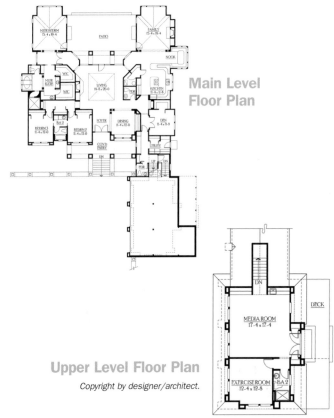

Main Level Floor Plan

Images provided by designer/architect.

Plan #551203

Dimensions: 81' W x 112' D

Levels: 1.5

Heated Square Footage: 4,050

Main Level Sq. Ft.: 3,375

Upper Level Sq. Ft.: 675

Bedrooms: 3

Bathrooms: 3½

Foundation: Crawl space; slab, basement, or walkout for fee

Materials List Available: No

Price Category: I

Upper Level Floor Plan

Copyright by designer/architect.

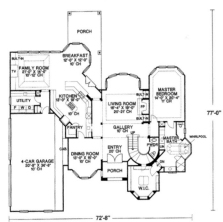

Main Level Floor Plan

77'-0"

72'-8"

Plan #121227

Dimensions: 72'8" W x 77' D

Levels: 1.5

Heated Square Footage: 4,139

Main Level Sq. Ft.: 2,489

Upper Level Sq. Ft.: 1,650

Bedrooms: 4

Bathrooms: 3½

Foundation: Slab

Material List Available: Yes

Price Category: I

Images provided by designer/architect.

Upper Level Floor Plan

Copyright by designer/architect.

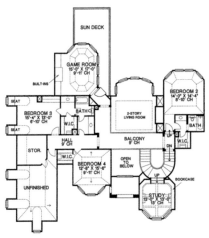

Plan #211076

Dimensions: 95' W x 90' D
Levels: 2
Heated Square Footage: 4,242
Main Level Sq. Ft.: 3,439
Upper Level Sq. Ft.: 803
Bedrooms: 4
Bathrooms: 4 full, 3 half
Foundation: Raised slab
Materials List Available: Yes
Price Category: I

Images provided by designer/architect.

Build this country manor home on a large lot with a breathtaking view to complement its beauty.

Features:

- Foyer: You'll love the two-story ceiling here.

- Living Room: A sunken floor, two-story ceiling, large fireplace, and generous balcony above combine to create an unusually beautiful room.

- Kitchen: Use the breakfast bar at any time of the day. The layout guarantees ample working space, and the pantry gives room for extra storage.

- Master Suite: A sunken floor, wood-burning fireplace, and 200-sq.-ft. sitting area work in concert to create a restful space.

- Bedrooms: The guest room is on the main floor, and bedrooms 2 and 3, both with built-in desks in special study areas, are on the upper level.

- Outdoor Grilling Area: Fitted with a bar, this area makes it a pleasure to host a large group.

Kitchen

Kitchen

Plan #321194

Dimensions: 81'8" W x 72'6" D
Levels: 2
Heated Square Footage: 4,370
Main Level Sq. Ft.: 3,299
Upper Level Sq. Ft.: 1,071
Bedrooms: 4
Bathrooms: 3½
Foundation: Basement
Materials List Available: Yes
Price Category: I

Images provided by designer/architect.

This home, as shown in the photograph, may differ from actual blueprints. For more detailed information, please check the floor plans carefully.

CAD FILE AVAILABLE

Main Level Floor Plan

Upper Level Floor Plan

Copyright by designer/architect.

Plan #611192

Dimensions: 54'9" W x 105'9" D
Levels: 2
Heated Square Footage: 4,370
Main Level Sq. Ft.: 3,608
Upper Level Sq. Ft.: 762
Bedrooms: 4
Bathrooms: 3 full, 2 half
Foundation: Slab
Materials List Available: No
Price Category: I

Images provided by designer/architect.

CAD FILE AVAILABLE

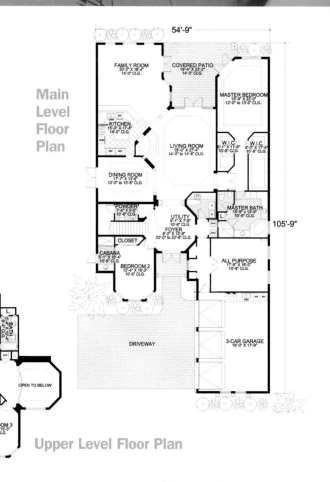

Main Level Floor Plan

Upper Level Floor Plan

Copyright by designer/architect.

Plan #151524

Dimensions: 79'10" W x 60'6" D
Levels: 2
Heated Square Footage: 4,461
Main Level Sq. Ft.: 2,861
Upper Level Sq. Ft.: 1,600
Bedrooms: 5
Bathrooms: 4½
Foundation: Crawl space or slab; basement or walkout available for fee
CompleteCost List Available: Yes
Price Category: I

Features:

- Great Room: This gathering area features a vaulted ceiling and a built-in media center. Step through the French doors to the rear porch.

- Kitchen: An island kitchen is the most desirable layout in today's home. The raised bar in this kitchen is open to the breakfast room.

- Master Suite: The tray ceiling in this room adds a unique look to the sleeping area. The master bath features a large walk-in closet, vaulted ceiling, and whirlpool tub.

- Secondary Bedrooms: Four bedrooms and three bathrooms are located on the upper level.

This home is the culmination of classic French design and ambiance.

CAD FILE AVAILABLE

Upper Level Floor Plan

Main Level Floor Plan

Plan #121167

Dimensions: 84'10" W x 102'3" D

Levels: 1.5

Heated Square Footage: 4,629

Main Level Sq. Ft.: 3,337

Upper Level Sq. Ft.: 1,292

Bedrooms: 4

Bathrooms: 4½

Foundation: Slab; basement for fee

Material List Available: No

Price Category: I

Images provided by designer/architect.

Front View

The exquisite exterior of this stunning design offers hints of the stylish features waiting inside.

Features:

- **Family Room:** This large entertaining area features a coffered ceiling and a beautiful fireplace. French doors allow access to the rear yard.

- **Kitchen:** This island workspace has everything the chef in the family could want. The breakfast room merges with the main kitchen, allowing conversation during cleanup.

- **Master Suite:** This ground-level suite features a cathedral ceiling and access to the rear yard. The master bath has a marvelous whirlpool tub, dual vanities, and a separate toilet room.

- **Upper Level:** A large game room, with an overhead view of the family room, and bedrooms 3 and 4 occupy this level. Each bedroom has a private bathroom.

Main Level Floor Plan

Upper Level Floor Plan

Copyright by designer/architect.

Main Level Floor Plan

Images provided by designer/architect.

Plan #321245

Dimensions: 77'6" W x 68'4" D

Levels: 2

Heated Square Footage: 4,465

Main Level Sq. Ft.: 2,817

Upper Level Sq. Ft.: 1,648

Bedrooms: 4

Bathrooms: 3½

Foundation: Walkout

Materials List Available: Yes

Price Category: I

Upper Level Floor Plan

Copyright by designer/architect.

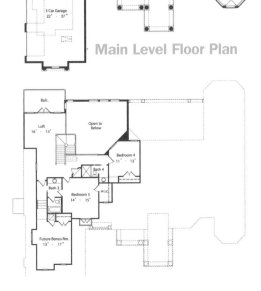

Main Level Floor Plan

Plan #661277

Dimensions: 86'8" W x 84'4" D

Levels: 2

Heated Square Footage: 4,515

Main Level Sq. Ft.: 3,478

Upper Level Sq. Ft.: 1,037

Bedrooms: 4

Bathrooms: 4½

Foundation: Slab

Materials List Available: No

Price Category: I

Images provided by designer/architect.

Upper Level Floor Plan

Copyright by designer/architect.

**Main Level
Floor Plan**

*Images provided by
designer/architect.*

Upper Level Floor Plan

Copyright by designer/architect.

Plan #551194

Dimensions: 82' W x 86' D

Levels: 2

Heated Square Footage: 4,684

Main Level Sq. Ft.: 2,661

Upper Level Sq. Ft.: 1,648

Bedrooms: 4

Bathrooms: 3½

Foundation: Crawl space; slab, basement, or walkout for fee

Materials List Available: No

Price Category: I

Main Level Floor Plan

*Images provided by
designer/architect.*

Plan #551205

Dimensions: 97' W x 70' D

Levels: 2

Heated Square Footage: 5,300

Main Level Sq. Ft.: 2,850

Lower Level Sq. Ft.: 2,450

Bedrooms: 5

Bathrooms: 4

Foundation: Crawl space; slab, basement, or walkout for fee

Materials List Available: No

Price Category: J

Lower Level Floor Plan

Copyright by designer/architect.

Plan #441015

Dimensions: 130'3" W x 79'3" D
Levels: 1
Heated Square Footage: 4,732
Main Level Sq. Ft.: 2,902
Lower Level Sq. Ft.: 1,830
Bedrooms: 4
Bathrooms: 3 full, 2 half
Foundation: Walkout basement
Materials List Available: No
Price Category: I

An artful use of stone was employed on the exterior of this rustic hillside home to complement other architectural elements, such as the angled, oversize four-car garage and the substantial roofline.

CAD FILE AVAILABLE

Features:

• **Great Room:** This massive vaulted room features a large stone fireplace at one end and a formal dining area at the other. A built-in media center and double doors separate the great room from a home office with its own hearth and built-ins.

• **Kitchen:** This kitchen features a walk-in pantry and snack counter and opens to a skylighted outdoor kitchen. Its appointments include a cooktop and a corner fireplace.

• **Home Theatre:** This space has a built-in viewing screen, a fireplace, and double terrace access.

• **Master Suite:** This private space is found at the other side of the home. Look closely for expansive his and her walk-in closets, a spa tub, a skylighted double vanity area, and a corner fireplace in the salon.

• **Bedrooms:** Three family bedrooms are on the lower level; bedroom 4 has a private bathroom and walk-in closet.

• **Garage:** This large garage has room for four cars; don't miss the dog shower and grooming station just off the garage.

Entry

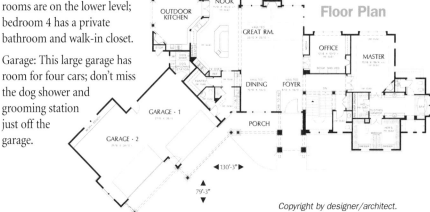

Main Level Floor Plan

Copyright by designer/architect.

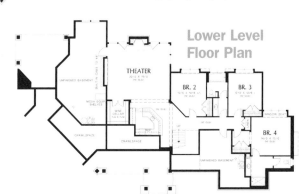

Lower Level Floor Plan

Master Bath

Rear View

Foyer

Dining Room

Great Room

Main Level Floor Plan

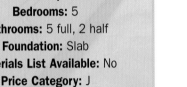

Plan #661229

Dimensions: 105'6" W x 100'4" D
Levels: 1
Heated Square Footage: 5,420
Main Level Sq. Ft.: 4,431
Upper Level Sq. Ft.: 939
Bedrooms: 5
Bathrooms: 5 full, 2 half
Foundation: Slab
Materials List Available: No
Price Category: J

Images provided by designer/architect.

CAD FILE **CAD** AVAILABLE

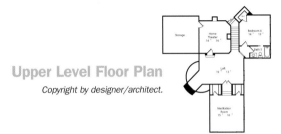

Upper Level Floor Plan

Copyright by designer/architect.

Main Level Floor Plan

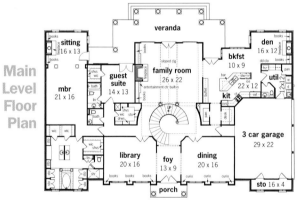

Plan #211077

Dimensions: 94' W x 68' D
Levels: 2
Heated Square Footage: 5,560
Main Level Sq. Ft.: 4,208
Upper Level Sq. Ft.: 1,352
Bedrooms: 4
Bathrooms: 4 full, 2 half
Foundation: Slab; crawl space for fee
Materials List Available: Yes
Price Category: J

Images provided by designer/architect.

Upper Level Floor Plan

Copyright by designer/architect.

Let Us Help You
Plan Your Dream Home

Whether you've always dreamed of building your own home or you can't find the right house from among the dozens you've toured, our collection of Baby Boomer plans can help you achieve the home of your dreams. You could have an architect create a one-of-a-kind home for you, but the design services alone could end up costing up to 15 percent of the cost of construction—a hefty premium for any building project. Isn't it a better idea to select from among the hundreds of unique designs shown in our collection for a fraction of the cost?

What does Creative Homeowner Offer?

In this book, Creative Homeowner provides hundreds of home plans from the country's best architects and designers. Our designs are among the most popular available. Whether your taste runs from traditional to contemporary, Victorian to early American, you are sure to find the best house design for you and your family. Our plans packages include detailed drawings to help you or your builder construct your dream house. **(See page 278.)**

Can I Make Changes to the Plans?

Creative Homeowner offers three ways to help you achieve a truly unique home design. Our customizing service allows for extensive changes to our designs. **(See page 279.)** We also provide reverse images of our plans, or we can give you and your builder the tools for making minor changes on your own. **(See page 282.)**

Can You Help Me Manage My Costs?

To help you stay within your budget, Creative Homeowner has teamed up with the leading estimating company to provide one of the most accurate, complete, and reliable building material take-offs in the industry. **(See page 280.)** If that is too much detail for you, we can provide you with general construction costs based on your zip code. **(See page 282.)** Also, many of our plans come with the option of buying detailed materials lists to help you price out construction costs.

How Can I Begin the Building Process?

To get started building your dream home, fill out the order form on page 283, call our order department at 1-800-523-6789, or visit ultimateplans.com. If you plan on doing all or part of the work yourself, or want to keep tabs on your builder, we offer best-selling building and design books available at www.creativehomeowner.com.

Our Plans Packages Offer:

"Square footage" refers to the total "heated square feet" of this plan. This number does not include the garage, porches, or unfinished areas. All of our home plans are the result of many hours of work by leading architects and professional designers. Most of our home plans include each of the following:

Frontal Sheet

This artist's rendering of the front of the house gives you an idea of how the house will look once it is completed and the property landscaped.

Detailed Floor Plans

These plans show the size and layout of the rooms. They also provide the locations of doors, windows, fireplaces, closets, stairs, and electrical outlets and switches.

Foundation Plan

A foundation plan gives the dimensions of basements, walk-out basements, crawl spaces, pier foundations, and slab construction. Each house design lists the type of foundation included. If the plan you choose does not have the foundation type you require, our customer service department can help you customize the plan to meet your needs.

Roof Plan

In addition to providing the pitch of the roof, these plans also show the locations of dormers, skylights, and other elements.

Exterior Elevations

These drawings show the front, rear, and sides of the house as if you were looking at it head on. Elevations also provide information about architectural features and finish materials.

Interior Elevations and Details

Interior elevations show specific details of such elements as fireplaces, kitchen and bathroom cabinets, built-ins, and other unique features of the design.

Cross Sections

These show the structure as if it were sliced to reveal construction requirements, such as insulation, flooring, and roofing details.

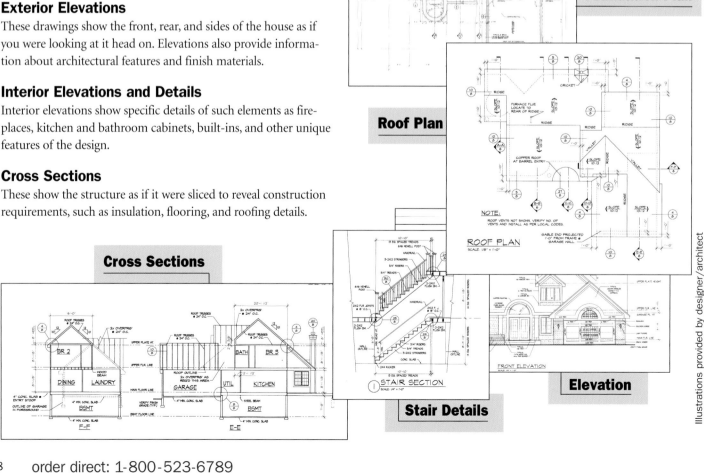

Frontal Sheet

Floor Plan

Foundation Plan

Roof Plan

Cross Sections

Stair Details

Elevation

Illustrations provided by designer/architect

Customize Your Plans in 4 Easy Steps

1 **Select the home plan** that most closely meets your needs. Purchase of a reproducible master is necessary in order to make changes to a plan.

2 **Call 1-800-523-6789 to place your order.** Tell our sales representative you are interested in customizing your plan. To receive your customization cost estimate, our modification company will contact you (via fax or email) requesting a list or sketch of the changes requested to one of our plans. There is a $50 nonrefundable consultation fee for this service. If you decide to continue with the custom changes, the $50 fee is credited to the total amount charged.

3 **Fax or email your request** to our modification company. Within three business days of receipt of your request, a detailed cost estimate will be provided to you.

4 **Once you approve the estimate,** a 75% retainer fee is collected and customization work begins. Preliminary drawings typically take 10 to 15 business days. After approval of the design, the balance of your customization fee is due before modified plans can be shipped. You will receive five sets of blueprints, a reproducible master, or CAD files, depending on which package was purchase.

Modification Pricing Guide

Categories	Average Cost For Modification
Add or remove living space	Quote required
Bathroom layout redesign	Starting at $150
Kitchen layout redesign	Starting at $120
Garage: add or remove	Starting at $600
Garage: front entry to side load or vice versa	Starting at $300
Foundation changes	Starting at $220
Exterior building materials change	Starting at $200
Exterior openings: add, move, or remove	$75 per opening
Roof line changes	Starting at $600
Ceiling height adjustments	Starting at $280
Fireplace: add or remove	Starting at $90
Screened porch: add	Starting at $300
Wall framing change from 2x4 to 2x6	Starting at $250
Bearing and/or exterior walls changes	Quote required
Non-bearing wall or room changes	$65 per room
Metric conversion of home plan	Starting at $495
Adjust plan for handicapped accessibility	Quote required
Adapt plans for local building code requirements	Quote required
Engineering stamping only	Quote required
Any other engineering services	Quote required
Interactive illustrations (choices of exterior materials)	Quote required

Note: *Any home plan can be customized to accommodate your desired changes. The average prices above are provided only as examples of the most commonly requested changes, and are subject to change without notice. Prices for changes will vary according to the number of modifications requested, plan size, style, and method of design used by the original designer. To obtain a detailed cost estimate, please contact us.*

Before Customization

After

Turn your dream home into reality with

UltimateEstimate

When purchasing a home plan with Creative Homeowner, we recommend you order one of the most complete materials lists in the industry.

1 What comes with an Ultimate Estimate?

Quote

- Basis of the entire estimate.

- Detailed list of all the framing materials needed to build your project, listed from the bottom up, in the order that each one will actually be used.

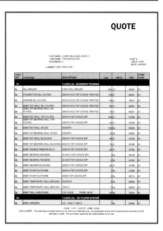

Comments

- Details pertinent information beyond the cost of materials.

- Includes any notes from our estimator.

Express List

- A version of the Quote with space for SKU numbers listed for purchasing the items at your local lumberyard.

- Your local lumberyard can then price out the materials list.

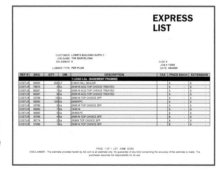

Construction-Ready Framing Diagrams

- Your "map" to exact roof and floor framing.

Millwork Report

- A complete count of the windows, doors, molding, and trim.

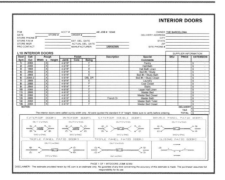

Man-Hour Report

- Calculates labor on a line-by-line basis for all items quoted and presented in man-hours.

2 Why an Ultimate Estimate?

Accurate. Professional estimators break down each individual item from the blueprints using advanced software, techniques, and equipment.

Timely. You will be able to start your home-building project quickly — knowing the exact framing materials you need to order from your local lumberyard.

Detailed. Work with your local lumberyard associate to complete your quote with the remaining products needed for your new home.

3 So how much does it cost?

Pricing is determined by the total square feet of the home plan — including living area, garages, decks, porches, finished basements, and finished attics.

Square Feet Range	UE Tier*	Price
Up to 5,000 total square feet	XB	$345.00
5,001 to 10,000 total square feet	XC	$545.00

*Please see the Plan Index to determine your plan's Ultimate Estimate Tier (UE Tier).
Note: All prices subject to change.

Call our toll-free number (800-523-6789), or visit ultimateplans.com to order your Ultimate Estimate.

4 What else do I need to know?

Call our toll-free number (800-523-6789), or visit **ultimateplans.com** to order your Ultimate Estimate.

Turn your dream home into reality.

Decide What Type of Plan Package You Need

How many Plans Should You Order?

Standard 8-Set Package. We've found that our 8-set package is the best value for someone who is ready to start building. The 8-set package provides plans for you, your builder, the subcontractors, mortgage lender, and the building department.

Minimum 5-Set Package. If you are in the bidding process, you may want to order only five sets for the bidding round and reorder additional sets as needed.

1-Set Study Package. The 1-set package allows you to review your home plan in detail. The plan will be marked as a study print, and it is illegal to build a house from a study print alone. It is a violation of copyright law to reproduce a blueprint without permission.

Buying Additional Sets

If you require additional copies of blueprints for your home construction, you can order additional sets within 60 days of the original order date at a reduced price. The cost is $45.00 for each additional set. For more information, contact customer service.

Reproducible Masters

If you plan to make minor changes to one of our home plans, you can purchase reproducible masters. These plans are printed on bond or vellum paper that is easy to alter. They clearly indicate your right to modify, copy, or reproduce the plans. Reproducible masters allow an architect, designer, or builder to alter our plans to give you a customized home design. This package also allows you to print as many copies of the modified plans as you need for the construction of one home.

CAD (Computer Aided Design) Files

CAD files are the complete set of home plans in an electronic file format. Choose this option if there are multiple changes you wish made to the home plans and you have a local design professional able to make the changes. Not available for all plans. Please contact our order department or visit our Web site to check the availability of CAD files for your plan.

Mirror-Reverse Sets/Right-Reading Reverse

Plans can be printed in mirror-reverse—we can "flip" plans to create a mirror image of the design. This is useful when the house would fit your site or personal preferences if all the rooms were on the opposite side than shown. As the image is reversed, the lettering and dimensions will also be reversed, meaning they will read backwards. Therefore, when ordering mirror-reverse drawings, you must order at least one set of the original plan unreversed. A $50.00 fee per plan order will be charged for mirror-reverse (regardless of the number of mirror-reverse sets ordered). Some plans are available in right-reading reverse, this feature will show the plan in reverse, but the writing on the plan will be readable. A $150.00 fee per plan order will be charged for right-reading reverse (regardless of the number of right-reading reverse sets ordered). Please contact our order department or visit our website to check the availibility of this feature for your chosen plan.

EZ Quote: Home Cost Estimator

EZ Quote is our response to one of the most frequently asked questions we hear from customers: "How much will the house cost me to build?" EZ Quote: Home Cost Estimator will enable you to obtain a calculated building cost to construct your home, based on labor rates and building material costs within your zip code area. This summary is useful for those who want to get an idea of the total construction costs before purchasing sets of home plans. It will also provide a level of comfort when you begin soliciting bids. The cost is $29.95 for the first EZ Quote and $19.95 for each additional one. Available only in the U.S. and Canada.

Materials List

Available for most of our plans, the Materials List provides you an invaluable resource in planning and estimating the cost of your home. Each Materials List outlines the quantity, dimensions, and type of materials needed to build your home (with the exception of mechanical systems). You will get faster, more-accurate bids from your contractors and building suppliers. A Materials List may only be ordered with the purchase of at least five sets of home plans.

CompleteCost Estimator

CompleteCost Estimator is a valuable tool for use in planning and constructing your new home. It provides more detail than a materials list and will act as a checklist for all items you will need to select or coordinate during your building process. CompleteCost Estimator is only available for certain plans (please see Plan Index) and may only be ordered with the purchase of at least five sets of home plans. The cost is $125.00 for CompleteCost Estimator.

Ultimate Estimate (See page 280.)

Order Toll Free by Phone
1-800-523-6789
By Fax: 201-760-2431

Orders received 3PM ET, will be processed and shipped within two business days.

Order Online
www.ultimateplans.com

Mail Your Order
Creative Homeowner
Attn: Home Plans
24 Park Way
Upper Saddle River, NJ 07458

Canadian Customers
Order Toll Free 1-800-393-1883

Mail Your Order (Canada)
Creative Homeowner Canada
Attn: Home Plans
113-437 Martin St., Ste. 215
Penticton, BC V2A 5L1

Before You Order

Our Exchange Policy

Blueprints are nonrefundable. However, should you find that the plan you have purchased does not fit your needs, you may exchange that plan for another plan in our collection within 60 days from the date of your original order. The entire content of your original order must be returned before an exchange will be processed. You will be charged a processing fee of 20% of the amount of the original order, the cost difference between the new plan set and the original plan set (if applicable), and all related shipping costs for the new plans. Contact our order department for more information. Please note: reproducible masters may only be exchanged if the package is unopened and CAD files cannot be exchanged and are nonrefundable.

Building Codes and Requirements

All plans offered for sale in this book and on our website (www.ultimateplans.com) are continually updated to meet the latest International Residential Code (IRC). Because building codes vary from area to area, some drawing modifications and/or the assistance of a professional designer or architect may be necessary to comply with your local codes or to accommodate specific building site conditions. We strongly advise you to consult with your local building official for information regarding codes governing your area.

Multiple Plan Discount

Purchase **3** different home plans in the **same order** and receive **5% off** the plan price.

Purchase **5** or more different home plans in the **same order** and receive **10% off** the plan price.

(Please Note: Study sets do not apply.)

Blueprint Price Schedule

Price Code	1 Set	5 Sets	8 Sets	Reproducible Masters	CAD	Materials List
A	$400	$440	$475	$575	$1,025	$85
B	$440	$525	$555	$685	$1,195	$85
C	$510	$575	$635	$740	$1,265	$85
D	$560	$605	$665	$800	$1,300	$95
E	$600	$675	$705	$845	$1,400	$95
F	$650	$725	$775	$890	$1,500	$95
G	$720	$790	$840	$950	$1,600	$95
H	$820	$860	$945	$1,095	$1,700	$95
I	$945	$975	$1,075	$1,195	$1,890	$105
J	$1,010	$1,080	$1,125	$1,250	$1,900	$105
K	$1,125	$1,210	$1,250	$1,380	$2,030	$105
L	$1,240	$1,335	$1,375	$1,535	$2,270	$105

Note: All prices subject to change

Ultimate Estimate Tier (UE Tier)

UE Tier*	Price
XB	$345
XC	$545

*Please see the Plan Index to determine your plan's Ultimate Estimate Tier (UE Tier).

Shipping & Handling

	1-4 Sets	5-7 Sets	8+ Sets or Reproducibles	CAD
US Regular (7–10 business days)	$18	$20	$25	$25
US Priority (3–5 business days)	$25	$30	$35	$35
US Express (1–2 business days)	$40	$45	$50	$50
Canada Express (3-5 business days)	$100	$100	$100	$100
Worldwide Express (3–5 business days)			** Call for price quote **	

Note: All delivery times are from date the blueprint package is shipped (typically within 1-2 days of placing order).

Order Form — Please send me the following:

Plan Number: _____ **Price Code:** _____ (See Plan Index.)

Indicate Foundation Type: (Select ONE. See plan page for availability.)
❏ Slab ❏ Crawl space ❏ Basement ❏ Walk-out basement
❏ Optional Foundation for Fee _____ $_____
(Please enter foundation here)

*Please call all our order department or visit our website for optional foundation fee

Basic Blueprint Package — Cost
❏ CAD Files — $_____
❏ Reproducible Masters — $_____
❏ 8-Set Plan Package — $_____
❏ 5-Set Plan Package — $_____
❏ 1-Set Study Package — $_____
❏ Additional plan sets:
___ sets at $45.00 per set — $_____
❏ Print in mirror-reverse: $50.00 per order — $_____
  *Please call all our order department or visit our website for availibility
❏ Print in right-reading reverse: $150.00 per order — $_____
  *Please call all our order department or visit our website for availibility

Important Extras
❏ Ultimate Estimate (See Price Tier above.) — $_____
❏ Materials List — $_____
❏ CompleteCost Materials Report at $125.00 — $_____
  Zip Code of Home/Building Site _____
❏ EZ Quote for Plan #_____ at $29.95 — $_____
❏ Additional EZ Quotes for Plan #s_____ at $19.95 each — $_____

Shipping (see chart above) — $_____
SUBTOTAL — $_____
Sales Tax (NJ residents only, add 7%) — $_____
TOTAL — $_____

Order Toll Free: 1-800-523-6789   By Fax: 201-760-2431
Creative Homeowner (Home Plans Order Dept.)
24 Park Way
Upper Saddle River, NJ 07458

Name _____
(Please print or type)

Street _____
(Please do not use a P.O. Box)

City _____ State _____

Country _____ Zip _____

Daytime telephone ( ) _____

Fax ( ) _____
(Required for reproducible orders)

E-Mail _____

Payment ❏ Bank check/money order. No personal checks.
Make checks payable to Creative Homeowner

❏ VISA   ❏ MasterCard   ❏ American Express Cards   ❏ Discover

Credit card number _____

Expiration date (mm/yy) _____

Signature _____

Please check the appropriate box:
❏ Building home for myself   ❏ Building home for someone else

SOURCE CODE **CA125**

Copyright Notice

Index

For pricing, see page 283.

Index *For pricing, see page 283.*

order direct: 1-800-523-6789

Index

For pricing, see page 283.

Ultimate**Estimate**

The **fastest** way to get started **building** your **dream home**